THE BEST OF

Inc.

GUIDE TO

BUSINESS STRATEGY

THE BEST OF

Inc.

GUIDE TO

BUSINESS
STRATEGY

BY

THE EDITORS OF
Inc. MAGAZINE

PRENTICE HALL PRESS
NEW YORK · LONDON · TORONTO · SYDNEY · TOKYO

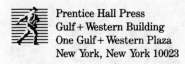 Prentice Hall Press
Gulf + Western Building
One Gulf + Western Plaza
New York, New York 10023

Published by the Prentice Hall Trade Division

PRENTICE HALL PRESS and colophon are registered
trademarks of Simon & Schuster, Inc.

Library of Congress Cataloging-in-Publication Data
Inc. guide to business strategy.
  (The Best of Inc.)
  ISBN 0-13-453978-8
  Includes index.
  1. Strategic planning. I. Inc. II. Title:
Incorporated guide to business strategy. III. Series.
HD30.28.I53   1988   658.4′012   87-43159

Designed by Stanley S. Drate/Folio Graphics Company, Inc.

Produced by Rapid Transcript, a division of March Tenth, Inc.

Manufactured in the United States of America

BOMC offers recordings and compact discs, cassettes
and records. For information and catalog write to
BOMR, Camp Hill, PA 17012.

CONTENTS

PART

III

PART

IV

PRACTICAL GUIDELINES

Defining long-term goals, establishing responsibilities and lines of authority, developing a smooth-running system of operations—that is the stuff of business planning. But many CEOs and senior managers either find they don't have the time, or worse, don't see the need to spell out plans and operational guidelines. A "strategy" to some people in the highest management circles turns out to be a narrowly defined set of plans for, say, marketing a product or increasing sales. While these short-range thinkers are adept at putting a particular tactic into effect, overall planning—the big picture—is often forgotten in the scramble for higher earnings.

But without a set of plans and a method of operations, unexpected growth can be a disaster. When the velocity of growth, rather than the balanced needs of an organization, begins to dictate what will happen and when, entire companies can go under in a matter of weeks. The *Inc.* articles in this *Guide to Business Strategy* have been compiled to illustrate the importance of laying down established methods of operation and defining various roles among the leadership of a company. Once a context for growth and development has been created, the uncertainty that is an integral part of growth—spurts of increased demand, followed by periods of decreased activity—won't rock the foundations of a company.

A good starting point for developing an effective management structure and a comprehensive system of operations is with the founder or CEO himself. When are his efforts essential, and when should he leave decisions up to other managers? Which operations should he monitor on a daily basis, and what can he evaluate on a monthly basis, or not at all? Our first story, "What to Monitor to Stay in Control," is written by a CEO who overhauled his method of management. Targeting his concentration on two things—where his company was at the moment and where he wanted it to be—helped Axel Grabowsky run his company more smoothly.

It's not just founders and CEOs who stand to benefit from a bit of soul searching. Anyone in a management position needs to maximize his effectiveness by examining proper roles for himself and his subordinates. In "Three Rules for Getting Good Results," Thomas K. Connellan outlines a strategy for effective management that involves identifying appropriate responsibilities, teaching and delegation, and targeting key problem areas.

Apart from determining lines of authority and assigning various responsibilities to senior managers, the prudent business planner will take a close look at how business is actually conducted in his company. "Five Tips for Making Plans Tick" offers a checklist of five elements that are essential in the development of a good business plan. Creating concise, clear guidelines for projects and tasks, we find out, is one of the key factors to consider.

Location can play a major role in how well a company operates, both financially and in terms of logistics. Local taxes, labor costs, property leasing, utilities, and a mass of local government restrictions and regulations can have a significant impact on any business. "Your Business: Right Ingredients, Wrong Location?" focuses on what costs businesses should consider before relocating, and it offers an easy method of evaluating your present business location.

Nuts and bolts issues that have a direct effect on the bottom line —inventory, cash flow, invoicing, credit checks, taxes—can be the trickiest issues to resolve, particularly for a founder who has watched his company grow from a small team of loyal enthusiasts to an organization with hundreds of employees in a dozen departments. What was easy in the days when you personally signed each and every paycheck suddenly seems out of control as you begin to realize that you can't maintain your company's high level of performance without some grass roots changes. "LIFO Saves," "Financial Expertise: What Level Should Your Company Have?" and "You and Your Accountant" address the crucial issues that can make your business profit in new ways or contribute to its eventual demise.

When a CEO finds that his company is in serious trouble, odds are he doesn't care what led him into trouble as much as he cares about how to get out. But all troubled companies tend to demonstrate similar symptoms. Management consultants Gary Goldstick and George Schreiber should know—they've spent years helping companies that suffer from problems ranging from cash flow to employee morale. What they have discovered is thirteen common problems that occur in all ailing companies regardless of industry. Though each of the identified problems may have different sources, all could be avoided, say the consultants, if senior management paid more attention. Read with care. "Thirteen Ways to Get a Company in Trouble" lists thirteen straightforward ways to stay *out* of trouble.

Once trouble does hit, it's very likely to snowball unless swift— and appropriate—action is taken. "Nine Steps to Save Troubled Companies" offers some sage advice from turnaround expert Red Scott, himself the veteran of a company whose losses mounted to $4.3 million before it was reprieved. Scott's central theme? "The single most important ingredient in achieving a turnaround is the building of an enthusiastic, cohesive team."

With a clearly defined set of goals—and a system of operations that is designed to support it—a company is properly armed to move into the market and cultivate growth. Without a system of support, unexpected growth quickly becomes overgrowth. Part I of *The Best of Inc. Guide to Business Strategy* addresses the important tactical questions that top management must consider in the interest of developing and strengthening a company.

WHAT TO MONITOR
TO STAY IN CONTROL

One wintry evening, early in my managerial career, I was slogging home through a foot of Boston snow with an overstuffed briefcase in one hand and two three-ring binders full of additional office reading under my other arm. I was trying to figure out how I would manage to go over all the paperwork I was lugging home when a snowball knocked my hat off. The missile was followed by several ill-aimed volleys that my fiancée, Mary, valiantly assisted by a girlfriend, hurled at me.

Most of them missed, but still I could not respond. Although it was possible to put down my briefcase, I couldn't just lay the three-ring binders in the snow. And I couldn't figure out how to make snowballs with one hand. That was the moment I realized I had to do something about the impossible amount of company operating information I was trying to absorb. My compulsion to monitor every detail had put me in the ridiculous position of not being able to defend myself in a snowball fight!

Every manager knows the problem of battling the daily, even hourly, barrage of operating data that assaults his mind. The realization that I could not track every detail of my business came as my days got longer, my nights got shorter, and my leaden briefcase seemed increasingly likely to unhinge my right shoulder.

Like most executives faced with this problem, I tried delegating. Yet I still monitored—or second-guessed—everything I delegated. That didn't save any time either.

Once, I delegated responsibility for export sales to Aruba to a young man in my department. He was to obtain $10,000 in sales per month with a 30 percent gross profit. After two weeks I was itching to look at the incoming orders and check the gross profit. After three weeks my curiosity got the best of me, and I plunged into the numbers. After four weeks I also started to track prices paid and purchases made per customer.

The young man soon realized that I had taken back his job. His enthusiasm understandably ebbed. I, in the meantime, sat at my desk until 10 P.M., or toted my bulging briefcase home, hoping to find the time to check our more important activities in Brazil and Argentina.

5

Since then, I've developed an internal monitoring system that's comprehensive and tailored to my needs. I compare a selected set of current figures with our projections. In this way, I don't get bogged down in the past with last year's or last month's figures. Instead, I concentrate on more important benchmarks—where we *are* (current figures) vis-à-vis where we want to be (projected).

Here are the major categories that I monitor:

• *Sales*. I check *total* sales daily. While it's nice to know how sales are doing every day in Chicago, El Paso, or Hartford, I've found that I don't really need that much detail. But once a week, I look at three or four major product divisions. And at the end of each month, I review our sales by geographical region and by our current twelve major product categories. I may also check sales to our top customers.

• *Ratio of gross profit to net sales*. You can sell yourself into bankruptcy if you look just at sales figures and neglect to examine costs. The difference between the selling price and what it costs to manufacture, assemble, or acquire, as well as to deliver your goods—expressed as a percentage of the selling price—is a good way to gauge your business's performance.

So once a week, I look at gross profit ratios for the total business, for our twelve major product categories, and for ten to fifteen major individual items. Only when a ratio is off do I dig deeper to find and correct the problem.

• *Direct expenses*. These I review monthly in all areas of the company. The larger and more discretionary the individual item, the more I scrutinize it—travel and entertainment expenses, for example. I have found that simply raising the question of how much gross profit we earn for every travel and entertainment dollar spent helps reduce T&E expenses.

I also check any expense item that exceeds $3,000 per month. Incidentally, I've found that accountants are fond of putting "other" at the end of the direct expense schedule, and that vague category is frequently larger than any other expense line. While "other" may make sense to accountants, I don't like flying blind. I therefore insist on a breakout of the "other" category that explains all items of $100 or more.

• *Other income and expenses*. I track this seemingly innocuous item at least monthly, preferably weekly. This is where we show interest payments, currency exchange gains and losses, and similar nonoperational factors. The importance of this income statement item was underscored during last year's 20 percent interest rates, when even modest bank loans required significant payments.

• *Net profit*. I check it monthly. It's always an exciting figure to look at, but by the time I've reached it, I already have a pretty clear picture of whether net profit is going to be higher or lower than planned, and why. If net profit isn't where I expect it to be, then I'll go over my other monitoring steps to discover why I was off track.

• *Cash flow*. A positive cash flow is vital. A profitable company can fail rapidly if it doesn't keep generating enough cash flow to pay its suppliers. Banks become reluctant to extend lines of credit if there isn't enough cash to keep the business going. And more bank credit reduces profitability because of increased interest payments. I monitor our cash flow every week to make sure we're staying ahead of the game.

• *Accounts receivable*. It is easy to let accounts receivable pile up. By extending extra credit, I tell myself, we can sell more; or this customer is a good credit risk and will certainly pay eventually; or it is too expensive to go after every tardy account.

I carefully examine an accounts receivable schedule every month. I want the total of accounts that are current to increase proportionally to the overdues, and I want our average days outstanding to stay in line.

• *Inventory*. It's easy to misjudge the market. I check inventory levels and composition every week and every month. This is done against a projection of how much inventory we will need to support average estimated sales. Our projections of inventory needs also depend in part on answers to questions such as: "How fast can we get material when we run out?" and "Are costs rising or falling?" We're also careful to ensure that as much of our inventory as possible is current and sellable.

• *Research and development*. To measure what R&D has contributed to our business, I can look at current sales and determine what percentage resulted from R&D over, say, the last five years. But this doesn't work for projects that are under way or recently completed. Only a constant, monthly review of current R&D gives me an effective monitoring handle. I measure the potential of each initiative by comparing its projected gross profit against its cost. I also review all continuing projects to make sure that they still fit our plans and are still based on reasonable assumptions.

In any of these areas, I can burrow much deeper—and the temptation to do so is always great. But I have realized, while working long weekends and during many a late night, that the return on scrutinizing such details diminishes faster than a snowball in the Sahara.

If the major indicators show no warning signals, I don't analyze further. Only by rigorously limiting myself to the daily, weekly, and monthly checks that I've listed do I find time to devote to the future of the business—to new product development, acquisitions, and to short- and long-range planning.

This selective pulse-taking not only gives me more time and opportunity to focus on the big picture, it also acts as a management tool by (1) in effect delegating responsibility, and (2) giving me clearer criteria on which to communicate goals and judge performance.

I tell the managers responsible for each area what I monitor. I also make clear that I expect detailed explanations from all important variances from objectives within twenty-four to forty-eight hours. I stress that everyone will be a decision maker and that I will not interfere with day-to-day operations as long as there aren't any serious problems. I emphasize, however, that I also have the obligation to step in when disturbing variances do occur, and will not hesitate to do so.

Not every executive will want to employ the identical monitoring factors that I find useful. Even the figures that I track can change with time and circumstance. Once each quarter I ask myself, "What operating data do I really need? Am I really keeping tabs on just the essentials?"

In sum, this system helps me do the job that I'm supposed to be doing—running the entire company. It saves me time, it contributes to the development of competent and confident managers, and it frees me to see the forest as well as the trees. Besides, I haven't lost a snowball fight in years.

KEEPING THE BUSINESS UNDER CONTROL

Below is a summary of the operating information that CEO Grabowsky tracks:

	Daily	Weekly	Monthly
Total company sales	●		
Sales by convenient product groupings		●	
Sales by major product category, territory, and major customer			●
Average sales prices of major products or product groups			●
Gross profit margin for company, large product groupings, and major products		●	
Production costs of major products			●
Direct expenses, with particular attention to large or discretionary items			●
Other income and expenses		●	●
Net profit			●
Cash flow		●	
Accounts receivable			●
Inventory		●	●
R&D status and expenses			●

And once every quarter Grabowsky monitors what he monitors by asking himself: "Am I limiting myself to just the essentials I need to keep track of our day-to-day business?"

—AXEL L. GRABOWSKY

THREE RULES FOR
GETTING GOOD RESULTS

Nicholas Murray Butler, former president of Columbia University, once described organizations as containing three kinds of people: those who make things happen, those who watch things happen, and those who don't know what has happened.

The difference between those in the first category and those in the other two is *management*. Managers make things happen. Why are some more successful at it than others? There are three basic reasons, each of which can be formulated as a rule for running a business successfully.

- *Rule 1. There's no point in doing well that which you should not be doing at all.*

Most managers of smaller businesses are "out of balance" in terms of where they apply their talents. The imbalance is a natural result of their rise through the ranks. They were good (i.e., made things happen) in finance, manufacturing, marketing, or merchandising. Because of their skill in a particular function, they eventually rose to the top. Having a specific skill in one area is important. But too often individuals spend too much time in the single area they know best. Managers who have come up through marketing, for example, are not only competent and confident, but also most comfortable, making marketing decisions. As a result, they tend to spend too much time on that function.

Because a top manager in a smaller company often can do many things as well as (or better than) other employees, he may hamper their growth. If the president with particular competence in finance regularly interferes with the accounting staff, he damages their potential by denying them experiences they could learn from.

Managers in smaller firms must keep informed about each operation and maintain central control. But control must be maintained in a way that does not impair development of subordinates. One of the keys to success is to have one-person control and multiperson operations—not one-person control and one-person operations.

9

Each time you take on a task, ask yourself, Is this something that I should be doing, or is it something someone else should be doing? Focus on *effective* use of time rather than *efficient* use of time. Efficiency is doing things right. Effectiveness is doing the right things. When you find yourself lamenting that there is never enough time in the day to do all the things you're doing, ask yourself a critical question: Should I be doing all the things that I'm doing?

To answer that, try this method. For a one-week period, keep track of how much time you spend in various activities and what those activities contribute to the productivity or profitability of the firm. At the end of that week, make one of three decisions about each task you have listed.

1. Is this a task I should keep doing?
2. Is this a task that should be delegated to someone else?
3. Is this a task that could be totally eliminated?

Research demonstrates that 70 to 80 percent of the tasks that you will list should be continued, 10 to 15 percent should be delegated, and 10 to 15 percent should be eliminated. The latter are usually tasks that were necessary at an earlier stage of the business but are now obsolete. Such an analysis should be conducted every six months, to keep unnecessary tasks from creeping into your daily routine.

• *Rule 2. When you find something that works for you, find out why so you can teach it to someone else.*

Consider people in terms of two scales. One is vertical, representing degrees of competence. The other is horizontal, representing "consciousness." That is, the individual is either aware of what he is doing or he does things unconsciously.

Combined, the two scales create a matrix that represents the four types of individuals in any organization: (1) conscious competent, (2) unconscious competent, (3) conscious incompetent, and (4) unconscious incompetent.

Consider how each of these types works. The unconscious incompetent (4) is barely able to perform. If questioned about his performance, he will quietly reply he didn't know what he was supposed to do. It's probably true. More important, however, he not only doesn't know what he's doing, but he also doesn't know what he doesn't know. His performance is relatively harmless, at least until he makes a serious mistake. But because his intentions are often good, management seldom catches that mistake until it's too late. The unconscious incompetent is distinguished by his helpful attitude, friendly demeanor—and totally ineffective performance.

The conscious incompetent (3) is an individual who deliberately sets out to be incompetent. He is tough to recognize because he does exactly as he is told. He does no more and no less and takes everything that is given him, interpreting it literally and moving ahead.

He's dangerous. If, by mistake, someone gives him the wrong task, the conscious incompetent will move ahead knowing full well the error of his ways but carrying out the job to completion. Sooner or later, he gives himself away. When caught doing things wrong, he righteously and indignantly states that he was "only doing what he was told."

The unconscious competent (2) is much like the natural athlete. He's a star performer. He's good and everyone knows it—including him. The problem is, the unconscious competent doesn't know *why* he's good. It's often due to a talent or instinct that comes naturally. But because of that, he can't teach his skill to anyone else. Result: While he is a good performer in a technical sense, the star often makes a very poor coach.

Many top managers are unconscious competents. They're good, and everyone recognizes it. However, caught up in the day-to-day pressures of running the business, they never sit down and analyze why they're good. As a result, they may have trouble teaching others the skills they have mastered.

If you're in this category, learn to take a few minutes as you perform tasks to analyze why something works, so that you can teach someone else that skill. When you can spend less time performing it, you'll have more time for building the business and learning new things yourself.

The most effective manager is the conscious competent (1). He knows he's good and other people know it, But he has to work at being good. He is aware of his strengths and limitations, and he is determined to maximize those strengths and improve his weaknesses. Most important, the conscious competent not only knows why he's successful, but he can teach that success to others.

If you want to build a team that works, take thirty minutes a week to analyze *why* what you did that week worked, and be prepared to teach some part of it to someone else during the following week. This will help you help others in your firm grow. And when people grow, companies grow.

• *Rule 3. Use a rifle approach to focus on high-priority areas.*

You have a choice in how you manage. You can use a shotgun or a rifle. A shotgun covers a wide area, but it has a lot less power than a rifle. Shotgun management, for the same reason, is usually a poor tactic.

The successful manager in smaller firms is a rifleman. He picks his targets carefully, aims, and fires. By focusing corporate resources on only a few key areas, he moves his company ahead farther and faster.

Why does the rifle approach work? It goes back to Pareto's Optimal Law of Maldistribution—the old 20/80 principle. Vilfredo Pareto observed that events are not distributed equally throughout the population. The successful manager recognizes this maldistribution and uses it to advantage.

The essence of the 20/80 rule is that a small percentage of events yields the majority of company results. The ratio is typically 20 to 80, and it applies to many business concerns: For example, 20 percent of the product line produces 80 percent of the profit; 20 percent of the customers are responsible for 80 percent of the past-due accounts; 20 percent of the inventory items account for 80 percent of the inventory dollars.

To use this maldistribution to your advantage, find out which 20 percent of your product line produces 80 percent of your profit, and focus efforts on that segment. When you've got a problem with receivables, find out which 20 percent are causing 80 percent of the past-due accounts. Once those accounts have been identified, direct all resources to eliminating them, and you will eliminate 80 percent of your past-due problems.

That's the rifle approach. It calls for focusing on problems, determining which one deserves attention first, drawing a bead on it, and targeting resources.

In sum, these are the three most important rules for running a business and getting results: Delegate responsibilities; teach subordinates; and take close aim in problem solving.

—THOMAS P. CONNELLAN

FIVE TIPS
FOR MAKING PLANS TICK

Every company that aspires to grow must have a business plan that defines corporate objectives and the steps for attaining them. Plans vary widely by type of company, size, market, and industry. However, all successful business plans have five elements in common. In order of importance, they are:

1. The president serves and is recognized as the top planning officer in the company. In many cases, top management mistakenly delegates the responsibility for planning to other officers. Too often, an executive vice-president or a planning assistant is charged with mapping out the company's business strategy, while the president remains oblivious to the process.

The chief executive's active participation in the planning process is required to impart credibility and to inspire dedication from the rank and file. When top management maintains a highly visible commitment to planning, line employees view the activity as a way of life rather than an intrusion.

2. The plan is prepared with input from all departments. For a business plan to be effective, it must be based on a consensus of the key personnel involved and must represent all who will play a role in its implementation. In a company heavily oriented toward marketing, for example, the marketing plan will trigger other functional and support plans. Therefore, to succeed, it must be developed with input from employees outside the marketing group who will be affected.

3. The primary goal is to create concise, easy-to-follow guidelines. Typically, business planning is characterized by a period of three to eight weeks of disassociated activity, resulting in complicated and forbidding reports. Yet the primary emphasis should be on making the planning process work, rather than on detail and adherence to cumbersome procedures.

A business plan should include one implementation schedule, rather than a multiplicity of forms that can bog down critical employees. The schedule—which can be set up in a simple four-column format—should identify the task in support of each major objective, the individuals responsible for performance of each task, and the start-up and completion date of each task. The entire plan should be outlined in less than thirty pages.

4. Resources are concentrated on achieving a limited number of major, quantified objectives rather than many insignificant ones. In his book *Management: Tasks, Responsibilities, Practices,* Peter Drucker cites management's common failure to concentrate human and other resources on the achievement of a handful of major objectives. As Drucker points out, "A small company needs the concentration decision more than a big one. Its resources are limited and will produce no results unless concentrated."

If planning analysis is performed properly, the plan's designers will identify as many as three dozen potential projects or opportunities. At the same time, the company's capabilities, strengths, and limitations will be defined, and alternative means of achieving objectives will be evaluated. The company's financial plan will then be used to establish priorities and determine which projects are beyond the firm's resources.

5. Objectives are tested for compatibility with each other. Development of a single quantified objective is relatively easy. Development of a *set* of objectives that are compatible with one another is more difficult, but it is essential. For example, plans that focus on increasing a company's market share while reducing marketing expenses obviously won't work, since these objectives are contradictory. Objectives that are incompatible must be identified and reconciled before the plan is implemented.

—IVAN C. SMITH

YOUR BUSINESS:
Right Ingredients, Wrong Location?

For managers, keeping an eye on the bottom line is a fact of business life. But, in a classic example of not seeing the forest for the trees, many overlook the impact of their company's location on operating costs. Although few factors are more important to a business, location is often the result of a historical accident.

Before you extend your current lease or expand your present facility, ask yourself if your business is being cheated by its location (see checklist 1). For instance, how much are you paying for freight shipping? And how much less could you be paying if your business were located closer to the market and shipping destinations?

Similarly, are your labor costs unnecessarily high? The Bureau of Labor Statistics publishes data that enable you to compare expenses in your location with approximate costs in the rest of the country. For example, average rates for unskilled manufacturing workers vary by as much as 20 percent within California alone.

Another useful cost indicator is a recent Department of Energy publication, "Typical Electric Bills," which shows that the monthly electric bill of a company with an average demand of 300 kilowatts and 60,000 kilowatt-hours could vary by almost $4,000, depending on location.

Stages in a product's life cycle should also help determine whether or not you can take advantage of geographic cost variations. A company with a product under development may require the engineering and technological resources available in such areas as Boston, southern California, and the San Francisco peninsula. However, a product ready for mass production can often be manufactured more cheaply in less technologically oriented communities, where labor, rent, and tax expenses tend to be lower.

It's important to assess operating conditions at your current location. Is there an adequate supply of skilled labor to meet your future needs? If not, it is doubtful that the situation will improve. The baby-boom children have all entered the workforce, and fewer individuals are now approaching working age. Since labor markets will continue to tighten, location will become increasingly important in recruiting.

15

Are transportation, government, and utility services adequate? Could you operate more efficiently in a building better suited to your needs? If your current location comes up short, perhaps you should be looking for a new one. And if you do decide to expand your current location, investigating the alternatives can satisfy you that you have not ignored an opportunity elsewhere.

1. ANALYZING YOUR PRESENT LOCATION

Here's a list of factors that should be evaluated in sizing up your current plant location. Rate each according to this scale: A (surpasses company needs/excellent); B (adequate); C (acceptable, but sometimes a problem); D (frequent problem/poor); or E (major threat to ability to operate and compete/unacceptable).

Cost Factors	A	B	C	D	E
A. Freight costs	☐	☐	☐	☐	☐
B. Labor costs	☐	☐	☐	☐	☐
C. Tax costs	☐	☐	☐	☐	☐
D. Utility costs	☐	☐	☐	☐	☐
E. Occupancy costs (rent or annualized construction)	☐	☐	☐	☐	☐

Other Operating Factors	A	B	C	D	E
A. Access to customers	☐	☐	☐	☐	☐
B. Transportation services					
1. Air	☐	☐	☐	☐	☐
2. Truck	☐	☐	☐	☐	☐
3. Rail	☐	☐	☐	☐	☐
4. Water	☐	☐	☐	☐	☐
C. Labor					
1. Supply and quality of unskilled workers	☐	☐	☐	☐	☐
2. Supply and quality of skilled workers	☐	☐	☐	☐	☐
3. Supply and quality of managerial and technical workers	☐	☐	☐	☐	☐
4. Labor-management relations	☐	☐	☐	☐	☐
D. Quality of utility service					
1. Power	☐	☐	☐	☐	☐
2. Fuel	☐	☐	☐	☐	☐
3. Water	☐	☐	☐	☐	☐
4. Sewer	☐	☐	☐	☐	☐
5. Telephone	☐	☐	☐	☐	☐
E. Government					
1. Quality of local government services	☐	☐	☐	☐	☐
2. Business climate (regulatory climate, red tape, etc.)	☐	☐	☐	☐	☐
F. Site and building					
1. Size of site	☐	☐	☐	☐	☐
2. Terrain and access	☐	☐	☐	☐	☐
3. Efficiency of building (maintenance/production flow; energy; traffic patterns, etc.)	☐	☐	☐	☐	☐
4. Expansion potential	☐	☐	☐	☐	☐
G. Living conditions in surrounding area	☐	☐	☐	☐	☐

If the decision is to relocate, carefully analyze what a new location should provide. Don't make the common mistake of focusing on remedying one issue that has been a particular problem at the current location at the expense of overall requirements.

Answers to the questions in checklist 2 will help determine the type of community you should consider. For instance, if you employ many professional or technical people or require frequent technical services, you would probably do best in a metropolitan area. If, on the other hand, you require few specialized skills and need to keep labor, occupancy, and tax costs at a minimum, and you rarely need services of a large airport, you would probably benefit from a rural area.

2. EVALUATING YOUR COMPANY IN A NEW LOCATION

Policy issues

How close do you need to be to customers, suppliers, and other company operations?
Why do you need a new location?
How soon do you need it?
How close to a competitor are you willing to locate?
How important are community incentives?
Do you prefer to lease or own your facility?

Transportation

A. Freight

What will you be shipping in, from where?
In what quantities?
Who will pay shipping costs?
What will you be shipping out and where will you ship it?
In what quantities?
What mode of transportation will be used?
Do you have any unusual service requirements?

B. Passenger

Where will company personnel be traveling? How often?
Where will visitors be coming from? How often?

Labor

A. Exempt (managerial and technical) staff

How many professional and technical workers will be required at the new facility?
What will their income levels be?
Where will they be coming from?

B. Nonexempt (hourly) workers

How many and what types of skilled, semiskilled, and unskilled workers will be required at the new facility?
What are you currently paying employees? What benefits do they receive? Do you hope to change this at the new location?

How much training are you willing to do?
How do you feel about unions?
Do you plan to use an incentive system?
How many shifts will you have?
Will your employment fluctuate seasonally or cylically?

Utilities requirements

A. Electric power
B. Fuel
C. Water
D. Sewer
E. Telephone

Environmental characteristics

A. Emissions
B. Effluent
C. Solid waste

Site and building

A. Acres required. Does this figure leave enough room for future expansion?
B. Building requirements

Size in square feet of plant, office, and warehouse space
Preferred shape
Minimum ceiling height
Floor load bearing capacity
How many truck bays will you require?
Do you require rail or barge service?

Investment

What will be your projected investment in real estate, machinery and equipment, and inventory? You will need these figures to calculate taxes at alternative communities.

Information about various cities can be obtained from state development agencies and local chambers of commerce. Follow your analysis of this information with on-site investigation of promising locations.

Take nothing for granted. Although most industrial developers will do their best to provide the information you request, few will point out local problems unless you specifically ask about them. After all, they are salesmen for their communities.

Companies inexperienced in selecting locations frequently overestimate the labor supply at a new location. Check with employers in the candidate communities to see what their recruiting experiences have been, and compare your proposed wage scale and working conditions with theirs. As a rule, the highest-paying employer in town is least likely to suffer from a labor shortage, while the lowest-paying is most likely to. Where would your company's wage structure fit in each local pay scale?

Cost miscalculations are another common error. Determine what fringe benefits are customary in the new location; they vary among areas just as wages do. Make sure that utility cost estimates include all applicable taxes and that site cost estimates include any necessary improvements, such as utility extensions, grading, or road improvements. And pin down exactly how real estate, machinery and equipment, and different types of inventory are treated for local property tax purposes. One company expected its expensive warehousing machinery to be exempt from property taxation at a new location, but because it was attached to the building's vertical roof supports, it was considered real property and was therefore taxable.

Anticipate growth requirements and select a site or building that will accommodate expansion. Don't forget such issues as easements, utility line location and capacity, road and rail access, protective covenants, soil conditions, and title and taxing jurisdictions. One machine tool manufacturer recalls that the site he had selected had a small water line across the middle that the industrial developer didn't know about. Realizing that the company might locate elsewhere, the town agreed to move the line at its own expense.

To evaluate your company's current location, begin with checklist 1. Delete any items that do not apply, and add any major items that are not included. Then rate each factor.

Review the list. Are any changes to the community anticipated that might alter your assessment of a specific item? The opening or closing of a large plant, for example, can radically alter labor supply. Adjust your ratings accordingly.

Evaluate your ratings. A majority of *A* and *B* responses indicates that you have a good location. If you list few *A*'s and *B*'s, you should at least consider a new site. And some *E*'s indicate that you could probably find a better location.

—CHARLES F. HARDING

LIFO SAVES

In times of inflation, what provisions, if any, can save the *Inc.* reader money?

To answer that question *Inc.* senior editor Bradford W. Ketchum, Jr., interviewed two of the nation's top tax authorities: Irving L. Blackman, C.P.A., senior tax partner of the Chicago accounting firm of Blackman Kallick Bartelstein; and John R. Klug, president and publisher, Continental Communications Group Inc., a business publications company based in Denver.

INC.: If you were to pick the single greatest tax savings opportunity for small business during inflation, what would you choose?

BLACKMAN: It's a real sleeper, but the answer is LIFO—a method for valuing inventory on a last-in-first-out basis.

INC.: Why LIFO? It's been around for more than forty years. Why the resurgence of interest?

BLACKMAN: There are two basic methods of valuing inventory, both of which actually account for the value of items sold. One is an assumption that says, first in first out (FIFO). This means that you value your inventory on the basis of the cost of the *last* item placed in stock. The other method is last in first out (LIFO). This means you value your inventory on the basis of the cost of the *first* item placed in stock. Under LIFO, the last items purchased—at presumably higher prices due to inflation—are assumed to be the first items sold. Thus, when you use LIFO, you remove the inflation rate from your inventory value. This eliminates phantom profits, reduces your taxable income, cuts your income tax, and therefore increases your cash flow.

KLUG: For example, let's say you're selling widgets at $1 each. Let's also say that your inventory consists partly of widgets that cost you 50¢ apiece five years ago and partly of widgets that cost you 75¢ last year. Under FIFO, you would have a 50¢ profit on each widget sold—and pay taxes accordingly. Under LIFO, you would show only 25¢ profit on each widget, with a consequent savings in taxes.

INC.: So LIFO can be used as a hedge against the steady rise in inventory replacement costs.

KLUG: Double-digit inflation rates make it a smart move. Double-digit interest rates make it a mandatory one. But there is another reason why LIFO is catching on. IRS regulations now permit a business to show the figures for both LIFO and FIFO in the same financial statement. In short, you can use LIFO for tax purposes and FIFO for reporting purposes. This eliminates one of the big objections to LIFO—that it reduces reported earnings and equity and therefore reduces credit capacity.

INC.: How can LIFO provide cash flow relief? Aren't those just buzz words?

BLACKMAN: If you pay less income tax, you improve your net cash flow. It's as simple as that. And under LIFO, you pay less tax because you show less income. LIFO reduces your year's income by the higher costs of inventory purchased to replace stock that has been used or sold. The price increases built into your replacement inventory don't become part of your inventory value.

KLUG: Improved cash flow also relates to a company's ability to compete. If you stick with a traditional inventory method like FIFO, you pay more income tax. Therefore you can't match your competitor's cash flow. And you don't have the cash to invest in new equipment, new people, new inventory, or whatever your company needs most. You literally have to go to the bank to borrow money and pay 14 percent to 18 percent to finance what your competition is saving from LIFO. You're at a distinct disadvantage.

INC.: Okay, so there are benefits in switching to LIFO. But it's a very complex procedure. Where does the decision to switch to LIFO start?

BLACKMAN: LIFO essentially starts with Section 472 of the Internal Revenue Code.

INC.: But that's a major point—if small businesses have to switch to LIFO based on information found in the Internal Revenue Code, very few will ever do it. Doesn't it take a highly experienced accountant to decipher the regulations and make LIFO work?

KLUG: True, the Internal Revenue Code itself is quite confusing. In fact, there's nothing in the Code or the regulations that tells you exactly how to institute the different methods or make the various elections that the IRS will accept. It's done on a taxpayer-by-taxpayer basis, and it does require a professional.

BLACKMAN: I think there are only two companies in the *Fortune* 500 that aren't on LIFO, and that has given the mistaken impression that LIFO is an election for the giants—that it's too complex, too involved for the mid-size or smaller company. But that myth has been perpetuated only because the expertise that was necessary to implement it was transferred from one very sophisticated tax person to another. Now the secret is out. The little guy can take advantage of LIFO under exactly the same rules as the giant.

INC.: Who are you calling the "little guy"? What's the cutoff point?

KLUG: Opinions vary. Some experts suggest that a business shouldn't consider LIFO unless it has at least $2 million in sales.

Others believe that a business with $500,000 in sales can elect LIFO.

To get to the bottom end figure, let's just run some numbers. The savings formula is the rate of inflation times your ending inventory times your tax bracket. So if you have $1 million in inventory at 10 percent inflation, you're talking profits that are overstated by $100,000. If you're in a 46 percent tax bracket, you've spent $46,000 in income taxes that you didn't need to pay. That makes LIFO worth electing.

INC.: When can a company make the switch?

BLACKMAN: You can't adopt LIFO for a previous year once you've filed a tax return for that year. If you've already filed your return for last year, for example, you can't amend it for LIFO and you'll have to wait until next year. But if you haven't filed yet, it's not too late.

INC.: How does a company file for LIFO?

BLACKMAN: You simply attach a Form 970 to your corporate tax return.

KLUG: In effect, you can file retroactively for one year.

BLACKMAN: Let's use an example. You're a corporate taxpayer on calendar year. Your initial tax return is due on March 15. You get an automatic extension for ninety days, which brings you to June 15. You can get another extension with Uncle Sam's permission, which is usually granted; that will take you to September 15. As long as you attach the 970 to that return, Uncle Sam must grant you your election to adopt LIFO.

INC.: Why does that amount to filing retroactively?

KLUG: In the sense that you're adopting LIFO for the previous tax year. On September 15, you can look back to the previous year and adopt LIFO for that year.

BLACKMAN: It's the only election I know of in the tax law where you can look backward after the year is over and save dollars.

INC.: Is it possible to create a tax refund?

BLACKMAN: Yes. If a company has paid estimated taxes anticipating a large profit, and it then elects LIFO and reduces its profits, it can go back and reclaim the estimated tax by adjusting future payments.

KLUG: Furthermore, if the company not only reduces its profits but creates a loss, it can then get a loss carryback. The loss can be carried back to a prior year, reducing the prior year's income and creating a tax refund. LIFO will help a company that is in the black reduce its profits for tax purposes. It also will help a company in a loss position increase its loss carryback and thus its refund.

INC.: Once a company elects LIFO, is the decision irreversible?

BLACKMAN: No, you can drop LIFO if it's not working to your advantage for some reason. All you have to do is file a Form 3115 requesting permission from Uncle Sam, and permission will be granted. However, when you terminate your LIFO election, you must increase your income by the amount of tax savings—the difference between LIFO and FIFO—that you accumulated while on LIFO. Call

HOW HIGH ARE THE STAKES?
(Table assumes 46% tax rate and 10% inflation.)

Year-end inventory level	Annual increased cash flow from LIFO election	10-year compound increase in cash flow (20% return)
$ 100,000	$ 4,600	$ 119,410
200,000	9,200	238,820
500,000	23,000	597,050
1,000,000	46,000	1,194,100
5,000,000	230,000	5,970,500
10,000,000	460,000	11,941,000

it "savings repayments." Uncle Sam allows you to report this income over an extended period of up to twenty years, depending on how long you've been on LIFO.

INC.: Once a company has terminated LIFO, can that company get back into it if things change and LIFO would work to its advantage?

BLACKMAN: Yes. However, if you want to get back into LIFO and you're in the process of making savings repayments, you must get the IRS's permission to reelect LIFO. If you have finished that extended repayment period, then you can go back into LIFO without permission. Just refile Form 970 with your return.

INC.: What if permission is refused?

LIFO vs. FIFO: What's the Tax Impact?

The table below shows how LIFO can cut business taxes. The example assumes an inventory of 100,000 units that cost 45¢ each at the beginning of the year and 55¢ apiece by year end. Under LIFO, it's assumed that the most recently purchased (last in) inventory was the first to be sold (first out). Therefore, the cost of goods sold is higher, resulting in lower profits and a smaller tax bite. In contrast FIFO assumes that the beginning inventory (first in) was the first sold (first out), resulting in lower cost of goods sold, higher profits, and higher taxes.

	FIFO Income	LIFO Income
Selling price	$56,000	$56,000
Cost of goods sold	45,000	55,000
Profit on sales	11,000	1,000
Income tax (46%)	5,060	460
Real tax savings ($5,060–$460)		$ 4,600

BLACKMAN: It won't be. The IRS can't turn you down as long as you have cleaned up the repayment period and taken the difference between LIFO and FIFO back into income. Electing LIFO originally, or subsequently, is a taxpayer's right. The government cannot deny it to you. The only thing Uncle Sam will do is make sure the taxpayer is following the rules once the taxpayer exercises the right to use LIFO.

KLUG: To put it another way, any company has the right to adopt LIFO to eliminate the insidious effects of inflation and phantom profits. The federal government cannot hassle you on this choice.

INC.: Let's go back to the repayment question. Does a company ever have to pay back what it saves if it sticks with LIFO?

KLUG: No company has to pay back what it saves by using LIFO. It's a perpetual deferral as long as you stay in business and maintain your LIFO inventory level. The typical American business is passed from generation to generation, so as a practical matter, the business may never pay back what it saves by using LIFO.

INC.: Must LIFO be applied to all inventories across the board?

BLACKMAN: No. If you're a manufacturer, for example, you have three basic costs: material, labor, and overhead. You can use LIFO for material only, including your raw material, work in process, and finished goods. But the labor and overhead cost components in your work in process and finished goods can stay on your old method.

INC.: The "pooling" requirements of the LIFO regulations are generally regarded as a nightmare. What about inventory pools?

BLACKMAN: Pooling is a concept that allows the taxpayer to take similar items and combine them all in one pool. For example, if you make 7,249 different styles of widgets, you can identify them all as the "widget pool." Instead of making 7,249-plus computations to determine their value, you have to make relatively few because you're working with one pool.

KLUG: Pooling took LIFO from the horse-and-buggy stage and brought it into the Space Age. A lot of people are under the mistaken notion that they literally have to go out and count every widget and determine which was the last in and which was the first out and what the price of each widget was. But that is not necessary because pooling greatly simplifies the computations. A hardware store that has 5,000 inventory items, for example, might reduce its inventory to three or four pools of items.

INC.: How does the IRS feel about LIFO?

BLACKMAN: The IRS recognized that the inability of companies to report FIFO on their financial statements was causing some of them to lose borrowing power. So the IRS, on its own, changed the regulations to meet the financial needs of business by allowing companies to report both FIFO and LIFO on the same year-end statement.

INC.: So LIFO is here to stay?

KLUG: Absolutely. It's one of the greatest weapons in the artillery of the business taxpayer. When a company, regardless of size, analyzes

LIFO's benefits, it will find that it can't afford *not* to adopt the last-in-first-out method of inventory valuation.

Editor's Note: Irving Blackman and John Klug collaborated on a manual that offers step-by-step LIFO implementation instructions for manufacturers, wholesalers, and retailers. The *LIFO-$AVE Implementation Manual* explains the specific methods for adopting LIFO, inventory pooling, reporting requirements, and pertinent IRS Code sections and regulations. For information write to Blackman Kallick Bartelstein, 300 South Riverside Plaza, Chicago, IL 60606.

FINANCIAL EXPERTISE:
What Level Should Your Company Have?

That good financial management is crucial to any company's success is obvious. What isn't as clear, however, are the expertise and responsibilities demanded at different times in a company's growth. No garage-shop operation needs a Ph.D. in finance to manage its books. But neither can a multiproduct manufacturing firm with $20 million in sales expect to survive with just a part-time bookkeeper.

As a company grows and changes, so must the financial expertise of its people. At first, a CEO with some financial smarts needs only in-house bookkeeping assistance for internal records and an outside accountant for regular statements and a little advice. Soon, however, there's a need for a broader base of financial understanding. An accountant, and later a controller, can begin to fulfill the added responsibilities of systems design, control mechanisms, and relations with the outside financial community. Finally, as the company becomes more complex and the CEO becomes increasingly engaged in general management, the growth will require a financial vice-president or treasurer.

But when is one level of expertise not enough? When is it time to make the change to more sophisticated financial management? What are the danger signs? What are the guideposts?

The need for something beyond bookkeeping—with the CEO overseeing financial matters—usually doesn't arise until after the company passes the $1-million sales mark. Then, according to Caleb Loring III, vice-president of the First National Bank of Boston, two considerations come into play—the type of industry and the financial acumen of the CEO. A wholesale supplier, for example, won't experience drastic changes in its accounting needs whether its sales are $1 million or $25 million. But a manufacturer with an increasing number of divisions requires added sophistication as its sales grow.

Further, if the CEO has financial expertise, he may function as the company controller for a much longer time than a CEO with a marketing or production background. With his financial expertise, he is likely to want to oversee the development and implementation of new reporting and control systems. In this case, he primarily needs bookkeeping and accounting support. His experience determines the general policies of the company.

But before long, even he'll have to divest himself of his financial role. "When questions are being asked that the CEO can't answer, when things he used to do aren't being done anymore, that's when the firm needs to develop more internal accounting expertise," says James Stam, director of consulting at Arthur Young & Company's Boston office.

For Jay Kamen, partner at Coopers & Lybrand, one clear indication of the need for upgrading the financial function is the number of adjustments that the auditors have to make. "This is a reflection of the quality of accounting," he says. "Too many adjustments, and there's need for better financial management."

That means a greater level of accounting proficiency. But that's not to say that an outside firm should be asked to handle internal financial management. "Outside accountants should not be used as substitutes for an inside accounting staff," says Kamen, "because they have no feel for day-to-day procedures. You need someone who's there full-time." It's simply not cost-effective to have an outside firm—one that would prefer to review, audit, and advise anyway—to handle the bookkeeping and accounting basics for your firm.

FNBB's Loring cites several other signals that indicate a need for upgrading the accounting expertise. "Trouble usually starts in cash, accounts receivable, and accounts payable," he says. Stretched receivables, frequent customer inquiries, lagging order processing, and arbitrary inventory levels are sure signs that better financial management is necessary.

Going beyond bookkeeping involves an accountant. He will eliminate bottlenecks and will streamline existing reporting systems. Credit checks, invoicing, and collections should be part of his responsibilities. He will see that payrolls are handled correctly, that proper inventory levels are maintained, and that receivables and payables are properly controlled. He will advise the CEO on cash management options and controls and, in conjunction with the CEO and department heads, will help prepare forecasts, budgets, and loan proposals. Nevertheless, his critical function is to provide accurate financial statements produced on a timely basis so that management knows where it stands.

That's also the primary task of a controller. The controller, however, must have a more organizational, conceptual nature than the accountant. "The controller should be able to wear more hats," says F. Grant Waite, partner with Peat, Marwick, Mitchell & Company. He usually has to deal more with suppliers and customers and is much more involved in planning and policy implementation. A controller is more likely to be responsible for tax matters and should have a thorough understanding of the tax consequences of management options. In short, the controller must not only be able to manage accounting well, he must also be able to work in finance.

Increasingly, company controllers are being relied on to handle regulatory compliance with federal, as well as state and local, agencies. Also, they are expected to have a working understanding of electronic data processing to be able to advise management and oversee at least the accounting aspects of EDP.

At what point should a treasurer or vice-president of finance be brought into the organization? When the organizational complexity demands it—for an average manufacturer that's probably between $15 million and $20 million in sales. For Kamen of Coopers & Lybrand, the right time occurs when the controller is working seven days a week—"assuming he's not simply inefficient"—or when he's spending 25 percent of his time on matters that would normally be handled by a vice-president for finance.

The differences between a controller and a financial vice-president are primarily qualitative. A partial distinction can be made between advising on and implementing policy on the one hand and setting and implementing policy on the other. The financial vice-president is less involved in the day-to-day accounting matters and deals more with financial planning—cash management, capital acquisition, and the financial structure of the company. While a controller is likely to have established solid bank lines for short-term financing, he probably hasn't fully explored sources of long-term capital. The financial vice-president is probably more familiar with various options for structuring the company's balance sheet. He should also be sensitive to the condition of the public market should a capital offering be in order.

In a public company, the financial vice-president has the added responsibility of ensuring compliance with the Securities and Exchange Commission. He must also be able to deal directly with industry analysts and stockholders.

Although there is an obvious danger of not having enough financial expertise while the company grows, there's also the danger of having too much too early. In 1974, the Pulley-Kellam Company Inc. of Huntington, Indiana, was projecting a sales increase from $750,000 to $1.5 million. The president of the fabricated metal products company had been running things by the seat of his pants and knew he'd need help soon. "I hired a hotshot," he says, "to set up administrative systems and financial controls. Well, the sales never materialized, but general and administrative expenses rose out of the ballpark, and profits were clobbered. We had to let him go."

—HARRISON L. MOORE

YOU AND YOUR ACCOUNTANT:
An *Inc.* Survey

The public accountant is a powerful force. The quality of his advice directly affects a company's taxes, its balance sheets, and even its management decisions. Yet many small business executives find it difficult to work with accountants, since their own backgrounds are more likely to be in sales, engineering, or research. More than two out of three (69 percent) of the chief executives surveyed by *Inc.*, for example, have no finance or accounting background.

As a result, many small businesses find public accountants somewhat intimidating, regarding them as outsiders who serve as buffers against an even more intimidating Internal Revenue Service. At best, the public accountant is considered an impartial paper-pusher who comes in periodically to wrestle with the company's books at a borrowed desk.

But an increasing number of small businesses view their outside accountants in a different role. Asked to identify their number one advisers, for example, more than half of the respondents to *Inc.*'s study cited their public accountants. Many of these companies have established a working relationship in which the accountant is an indispensable sounding board and business counselor. In short, their accountants not only review the books and compute taxes, but also provide crucial advice on such matters as cash flow, credit, cost control, and systems management.

To help small companies evaluate and improve their rapport with accounting professionals, *Inc.* surveyed more than 5,000 small business executives and over 2,000 public accountants. The results of the study are summarized in the following eight-point checklist and accompanying tables.

1. How big should your own staff be?

Most small companies have limited in-house accounting staffs. The majority of those with sales of less than $1 million employ only one person in a bookkeeping or accounting function. Those with sales of up to $5 million generally employ only two or three in accounting,

29

THE INSIDE STORY

How in-house staff size relates to annual sales, fees paid, and type of accounting firm used.

Annual company sales	No. on internal accounting staff								
	0	1	2	3	4	5	6	7–10	11+
	Percent of respondents								
Under $1 million	13	55	22	5	2	1	—	1	1
$1 million–2.9 million	3	27	40	17	8	3	—	1	1
$3 million–4.9 million	6	14	32	23	13	5	2	5	—
$5 million–24.9 million	4	7	13	17	11	13	13	11	11
$25 million or more	8	—	3	—	6	8	9	23	43
Percent of all respondents	8	32	25	13	7	4	3	4	4

Annual fee paid to outside firm	No. on internal accounting staff								
	0	1	2	3	4	5	6	7–10	11+
	Percent of respondents								
Under $1,000	15	56	22	7	—	—	—	—	—
$1,000–5,000	8	42	31	10	6	1	1	1	—
$5,000+	5	17	21	18	9	8	6	8	8

Type of accounting firm used	No. on internal accounting staff								
	0	1	2	3	4	5	6	7–10	11+
	Percent of respondents								
Sole practitioner	9	43	27	8	7	3	1	1	1
Local	8	34	25	14	8	3	2	4	2
Regional	6	30	29	16	5	4	4	3	3
National	2	19	29	16	6	6	6	8	8
Big Eight	5	9	17	11	7	12	7	10	22

Most small companies with annual sales of less than $5 million employ internal accounting staffs of three or less, while larger company staffs range from six to sixteen. Companies with smaller accounting staffs also spend less for outside services and are more likely to employ sole practitioners or local firms than regional or national accounting firms.

and the number jumps to five or six as company size grows toward $25 million. Only in companies with sales of more than $25 million is the in-house accounting staff likely to exceed half a dozen employees. Furthermore, in two out of three companies surveyed by *Inc.*, the chief executive also doubles as the chief financial officer. Only among companies with sales of more than $5 million does the majority have full-time chief financial officers. In these cases, the top financial manager is generally a vice-president, treasurer, or controller heading an accounting staff.

Whether it consists of one person or half a dozen people, your internal staff is a vital link between your business and its outside accountants. While any decision about your accounting firm is up to top management, it is one that should not be made without consulting your staff, which may have different insights into the technical competence and personal chemistry necessary for a productive relationship. Does your staff feel free to call the company accountant with questions? Do they receive a ready response, and does the advice work? How often has your outside accountant shown your staff how to streamline its paperwork? Does the accountant take the time to make sure your staff understands the finer points in a company statement? Answers to such questions represent the first step in evaluating your outside accounting firm.

2. What should your public accountant be telling you?

Some 51 percent of the respondents to *Inc.*'s survey regard their public accountants as their chief outside advisers (followed by their attorneys and bankers). Preparation of tax returns and financial statements may be your accountant's primary responsibility, but it should not be his only duty. The documents he prepares should satisfy Uncle Sam's requirements, but they should also be treated as financial tools that meet management's needs.

Besides combing your books, your accountant should monitor your business and suggest alternatives for controlling costs and improving profits. In short, he should serve not as a part-time manager but as a full-time adviser to mangement.

The recent changes in the tax law provide a good test of your accountant's technical competence and ability to keep you advised. Understandably, the impact of the new tax law was the chief topic of discussion between small business executives and their public accountants. Close to half (49 percent) of the respondents to *Inc.*'s 1981 survey cited that year's tax act as a matter on which they had recently received accounting advice. Other key concerns included state and local tax laws, reporting rules, employee retirement programs, estate planning, and inventory valuation.

Top management apparently keeps business and personal matters separate, however. Less than 1 percent of the respondents noted that they rely on the company's public accountant for personal needs.

3. How often should you talk with your accountant?

You should talk with your accountant whenever the need arises. And for most small businesses that's no more than once a month. While one out of three small companies is in touch with its accounting firm on a weekly basis, most of them talk with their public accountants about every four to six weeks. Among respondents to the *Inc.* survey, 57 percent report thirty days or more between contacts, with the average frequency running thirty-nine days.

Although lack of communication is a source of dissatisfaction among small businesses, less than 1 percent of the survey participants cited availability of the accountant as a problem. The more important question, therefore, is how often your accountant should talk with you. If the communication is always a one-way street, it's time to reevaluate the entire relationship.

4. What type of accounting firm do you need?

The accounting profession suffers from what can only be described as "Big Eight Syndrome," a disorder that suggests bigger means better. Fortunately, it's not necessarily contagious. While the prestige of a multinational public accountant may impress your banker and attorney, the horsepower and expense that such services represent may be impossible to justify. Size is important only to the extent that it represents sufficient staff to meet your needs.

If your sales have topped $25 million, if your accounting needs are highly complex, or if you're moving toward public ownership, a na-

HOW ACCOUNTANTS LOOK AT SMALL BUSINESS

Typical client (annual sales)	Type of accounting firm				
	Sole practitioner	Local	Regional	National	Big Eight
	Percent of respondents				
Under $100,000	4	1	0	0	0
$100,000–499,999	22	16	14	0	0
$500,000–999,000	34	29	14	0	0
$1 million–1.9 million	17	21	21	30	6
$2 million–4.9 million	18	20	15	20	18
$5 million or more	5	13	36	50	76
Average ($ million)	$1.3	3.1	5.4	6.0	13.8

To most local accounting firms, *small business* means a company whose sales are less than $5 million. By contrast, most national and Big Eight firms define small companies as those with sales of less than $20 million. The local accountants' small business clients average $3.1 million in sales; the Big Eight, $13.8 million.

tional or Big Eight accounting firm may be the best bet. Otherwise, smaller companies generally stick with smaller accounting firms.

The majority (56 percent) of the respondents to *Inc.*'s study deal with sole practitioners or local accountants. Another 26 percent rely on regional accounting firms. Only 18 percent indicate use of a national or Big Eight organization. Not surprisingly, the last group of respondents includes 80 percent of the companies with sales of $25 million or more. But it also represents a sprinkling of companies with sales of less than $5 million and even a few whose sales are under $1 million. Such figures testify to the inroads being made by accounting's giants.

All of the Big Eight now boast separate small-business staffs. Overall, half of the national firms responding indicated that they offer discrete small-business advisory services. Among the national accountants, the average small-business client is a company with sales of $6 million, while among the Big Eight, the smaller client is more typically a company with sales of about $14 million.

Few local or regional accounting firms seem to have separate small-business staffs within their organizations. Most of these firms consider themselves small-business specialists to begin with. Four out

HOW OUTSIDE ACCOUNTANTS ARE USED

Accounting services used (ranked by total mentions)	Annual company sales				
	Under $1 mil.	$1 mil.– 2.9 mil.	$3 mil.– 4.9 mil.	$5 mil.– 24.9 mil.	$25 mil. or more
	Percent of respondents				
Preparation of tax returns	93	91	90	84	52
Preparation of financial statements	77	73	72	51	27
Audits of financial statements	32	46	48	71	88
Tax planning	42	51	55	49	39
Review of tax returns	44	46	42	46	49
Preparation of government reports	38	40	37	19	15
Accounting systems design	32	30	25	17	15
Help with employee benefits plans	21	23	27	22	12
Accounting systems implementation	17	20	13	4	3
Forecasting & long-range planning	12	14	17	11	9
Help with loan application	12	15	15	8	6
Evaluation of data processing	5	10	16	15	21
Capital investment analysis	9	10	10	10	3
Design of financial analysis systems	8	9	8	7	3
Evaluation of compensation practices	6	9	7	7	3
Other (bookkeeping; payroll; personal)	3	2	0	3	6

Preparation of tax returns and financial statements tops the list of accounting services used by smaller businesses. While the figures show a direct relationship between company size and audit activity, they also reveal that size has little to do with the limited use of accounting services tied to long-range planning, data processing, and compensation practices.

of five of their clients are small companies, typically ranging in size from $1.3 million for sole practitioners to $5.4 million for regional accountants.

Boding well for small business and reflecting the intensified competition for small-company clients, 94 percent of the accountants responding to *Inc.*'s survey plan to expand their small-business services.

5. What services should you be using?

For nine out of ten small companies, outside preparation of tax returns and financial statements is standard. Beyond that, close to half of the small businesses responding to *Inc.*'s survey also rely on their public accountants for tax planning and auditing services.

Not surprisingly, the use of auditors is directly related to company size. Only one out of three firms with sales of less than $1 million has its statements audited, while close to half (48 percent) of those in the $3-million-to-$5-million category obtain audits. The number rises to seven out of ten companies in the $5-million-to-$25-million sales range, and for those with sales of more than that, independent audits are a standard procedure.

PICKING AN OUTSIDE ACCOUNTANT

Types of firms used, and how they're chosen

Type of accounting firm used	Percent of respondents
Sole practitioner	16
Local	40
Regional	26
National (other than Big Eight)	8
Big Eight	10
Top 10 factors*	
1. Personal contact	41
2. Reputation	36
3. Prior relationship	25
4. Recommended by banker or attorney	21
5. Recommended by other clients	16
6. Location	13
7. Range of services	12
8. Industry expertise	9
9. Fee	7
10. Small business's parent company	3
*Total exceeds 100% due to multiple responses	

Although 18 percent of smaller companies surveyed retain national or Big Eight accounting firms, the majority (56 percent) rely on either sole practitioners or local firms. The two biggest influences on small business's choice of public accountants are personal contact and reputation of the firm.

The rest of the services used by small business range from help in designing internal accounting systems to capital investment analysis and evaluation of compensation programs.

In weighing your needs for accounting services, consider the five basic benefits any accounting firm, regardless of size, should provide your company: (1) competent tax assistance; (2) better cost control; (3) order in your accounting system; (4) credibility in your statements; and (5) compliance with the law. Those are the basic payoffs that should govern not only your choice of services but the determination of their value.

6. What should you be paying your accountant?

Among companies with sales of less than $1 million, the average annual accounting fee is about $3,000. The tab jumps to $5,300 for companies in the $1-million-to-$3-million sales category, and to $10,600 for those in the $3-million-to-$5-million group. Above that size, the annual fees average anywhere from $16,600 to $42,600.

Accountants responding to the *Inc.* survey indicated that the average annual fee paid by their small-business clients is $4,373. The figures range from $2,590 billed by sole practitioners to $13,058 among the Big Eight accountants.

Overall, the *Inc.* study shows that fees are not a major factor in the relationship between small companies and their accountants. While accounting charges could be lower and fee structures could be clearer, very few of the respondents indicated that fees influence the selection or retention of their public accounting firm. Almost two out of three small companies compensate their accountants on an hourly basis; the rest rely on a flat-fee arrangement.

Taking a cue from the banking industry, perhaps, 19 percent of the public accountants report that they offer preferential rates for small companies. Such rates take the form of reduced fees for start-ups and initial clients, special "introductory" rates, and, in some cases, small-business discounts.

In the final analysis, your accounting costs should reflect the quality of services performed. If the fee seems high, weigh it in terms of the "product" you're getting. If you're getting better financial statements and improved tax work, chances are the higher tab can easily be justified.

7. When should you change accountants?

Unlike some larger corporations, small business does not make a practice of rotating accountants. Some 39 percent of the respondents to *Inc.*'s survey report that their present accounting firm is the only accounting firm they have ever had. Among the 61 percent who have had more than one accountant, seven out of ten have changed firms only once or twice. On average, the survey participants have retained

HOW—AND HOW MUCH—ACCOUNTANTS ARE PAID

How Accountants Are Paid

Annual company sales	Hourly	Flat fee	Retainer	Negotiated fee	Other
			Percent of respondents		
Under $1 million	63	30	7	2	2
$1 million–$2.9 million	58	35	7	2	2
$3 million–$4.9 million	63	29	11	3	4
$5 million–$24.9 million	64	25	10	7	2
$25 million +	52	18	12	21	—
Percent of all respondents	61	30	9	4	2

How Much Accountants Are Paid

Annual company sales	Under $1,000	$1,000–$2,999	$3,000–$4,999	$5,000–$9,999	$10,000–$19,999	Over $20,000	Average annual fee
			Percent of respondents				
Under $1 million	22	44	16	12	5	1	$ 3,000
$1 million–$2.9 million	6	23	25	25	14	2	$ 5,300
$3 million–$4.9 million	1	13	28	29	19	14	$10,600
$5 million–$24.9 million	1	7	7	19	33	33	$16,600
$25 million +	—	—	—	7	11	82	$42,600

Regardless of company size, the majority of smaller businesses pay their public accountants by the hour. The larger the business, the bigger the tab. Among the smallest companies, the annual accounting bill averages $3,000, while the largest firms incur accounting fees that top $42,000.

their present accountants for more than eight years. Among the larger companies, where one might expect changes in accountants due to company age and growth, the average period of service is more than ten years.

The lack of turnover is testimony to the value of retaining an accounting firm that knows your business. It also suggests that the real question is not *when* you should change accounting firms, but *why*. Many companies rotate accountants as a matter of policy, to generate new ideas and keep the professional on his toes. If all you're getting out of your accountant is tax returns and financial statements, if your accountant thinks only as an auditor and not as an adviser, then a switch probably makes sense. Change for the sake of change, however, is neither productive nor profitable.

Small companies should evaluate their accountants at least once a year to identify anything that may justify a change. The business may simply have outgrown the accountant's capabilities. Is your accountant, for example, keeping pace with your company's needs for more sophisticated advice on matters such as data processing, inflation management, new cost controls, and benefit packages? If your accountant has a thorough knowledge of your business and continues to serve as a sounding board for top management, then there is little merit in making a change.

8. How should you choose an accountant?

Suppose a switch is recommended: What guidelines should you use to select a new accounting firm? Small-business executives and public accountants agree that the three most important criteria are personal attention, reputation, and experience. Each of these factors, in turn, translates to several critical considerations.

Personal attention, for example, should be synonymous with commitment, compatibility, and responsiveness. Will the principal of the accounting firm be directly involved in your business? Will you and your staff be comfortable with the individuals who will actually be doing the accounting work? Responsiveness should be measured not only in terms of how long it takes the accountant to return phone calls

HOW ACCOUNTANTS WOULD CHOOSE AN ACCOUNTANT

Criteria ranked most important	Percent of accountants
Personal attention	30
Reputation	17
Experience	16
Range of services	13
Knowledge of industry	5
Professional competence	5
Quality of service	4
Ability to communicate	3
Accessibility/availability	2
Adequacy of trained personnel	2
Integrity/confidentiality	1
Creativity in planning	1
Timely completion of work	1

Accountants stress personal service, reputation, and experience as the keys to selecting an outside firm. Ironically, timely service—the factor that concerns small businesses most—ranks as the professionals' least important consideration.

but what it takes to get him out of his office. If you plan a special year-end tax meeting, for example, how much notice will you have to give the accountant to assure that he'll be there to sit in on the session?

Reputation—the second most important criterion—has little to do with prestige. It's a matter of how bankers, attorneys, and other businesses in your community regard the accounting firm. And don't forget to get a reading on how the accountant stands within his own profession.

Finally, experience counts. What does the accountant know about your industry—specifically, small business in your industry? A current client list will help answer that question, but it is also one that should be addressed personally by those who will be working with your company. Assume that the professional is fluent in accounting and finance; the important question is whether or not he can speak your business's language.

Your accountant should be someone you can trust, someone who understands how your business operates, and someone who is willing to listen and respond with ideas. When you find a public accountant who fits that description, chances are you've found your best professional adviser.

THE TEN BIGGEST GRIPES ABOUT ACCOUNTANTS

Source of dissatisfaction	Percent of respondents*
1. Timely service	35
2. Reasonable and clear fee structure	22
3. Turnover of professional staff	20
4. Services beyond standard reports	19
5. Knowledge of client business/industry	18
6. Communication and rapport	18
7. Technical knowledge/expertise	18
8. Limited staff	15
9. Orientation toward larger corporations	10
10. Ability to provide clear/concise reports	8

*Total exceeds 100% due to multiple response.

Small businesses cite slow service, confusing fees, and high turnover as the biggest problems in dealing with their outside accountants. Among smaller complaints: ability to keep up with changing regulations and the tendency to be too conservative.

The Facts Behind the Figures

This article summarizes a national study of smaller companies and their public accountants. The primary research for the report was conducted in November and December 1981. It included two mail surveys supplemented by dozens of telephone interviews with a cross section of small business executives and public accountants.

A four-page questionnaire was mailed to a random sampling of 4,995 *Inc.* subscribers, followed by a two-page questionnaire sent to a random sampling of 2,058 public accountants. Excluding undeliverable and incomplete returns, the net response rates were 20.4 percent and 21.8 percent, respectively. Some 993 subscriber returns and 440 accountant returns were then delivered to an independent computer facility for tabulating and forty-six cross-reference summaries.

The subscriber respondents represent all fifty states and the District of Columbia, 24 percent of them with headquarters in the Northeast, 13 percent in the Southeast, 40 percent in the Central region, and 23 percent in the Mountain/Pacific states. Separated into seven industry categories, the majority of respondents are in manufacturing (32 percent) or wholesale/retail businesses (25 percent). Other major groups include business services (17 percent), professional services (13 percent), and construction/real estate (7 percent).

The accountant respondents represent forty-seven states and the District of Columbia; 32 percent of them have headquarters in the Northeast, 13 percent in the Southeast, 36 percent in the Central region, and 19 percent in the Mountain/Pacific states. While more than 90 percent of the respondents are certified public accountants, about three out of four represent small accounting firms with one office and no more than three partners.

Vital statistics of the two respondent groups in this study include the following:

Subscribers (993)		Accountants (440)	
Avg. annual sales ($ mil.)	$5.1	Sole practitioner	34%
Avg. number of employees	62	Local	46%
Privately held corporation	84%	Regional	8%
Publicly held corporation	6%	National	3%
Proprietorship	7%	Big Eight	9%
Partnership	3%	Under 50 employees	83%
Use public accounting firm	89%	Median no. of clients	269

COMING TO TERMS WITH ACCOUNTANTS

Like most specialists, accountants have their own set of acronyms and terms. Here is a glossary of the accounting profession's most common ones.

Big Eight: The eight major multinational public accounting firms. Listed alphabetically, with number of U.S. offices in parentheses, the Big Eight includes Arthur Andersen (65); Arthur Young (84); Coopers & Lybrand (85); Deloitte Haskins & Sells (105); Ernst & Whinney (116); Peat, Marwick, Mitchell & Company (100); Price Waterhouse (69); and Touche Ross (77).

CMA: Certificate in Management Accounting. The CMA is granted by the NAA's Institute of Management Accounting to management accountants who meet certain educational standards, pass a five-part exam, and have at least two years of related professional experience.

CPA: Certified public accountant. A CPA is an accountant who has passed certain state requirements, including education, work experience, and an examination prepared by the AICPA and administered by the state.

FASB: Financial Accounting Standards Board. The FASB is an independent body maintained by the Financial Accounting Foundation in Stamford, Connecticut. Founded in 1972, its purpose is to define, improve, and promote accounting and reporting standards. The board is currently studying the need to develop different standards of financial reporting for small companies.

GAAP: Generally accepted accounting principles. These are the conventions and rules that define accepted practice in preparing general-purpose financial statements.

MAS: Management advisory services. This is the term CPAs commonly use to describe their consulting services.

PA: Public accountant. A PA is an accountant who may meet certain state requirements, is usually registered in the state, but is not certified—i.e., has not passed the Uniform CPA exam.

Major Professional Groups

AAA: American Accounting Association. This is an organization for promoting research and education in accounting. Based in Sarasota, Florida, the AAA has 12,000 members, most of whom are academics.

AICPA: American Institute of Certified Public Accountants. A national society for CPAs, this group prepares and grades the CPA exam for state licensing bodies. With headquarters in New York and 175,000 members, the AICPA is the oldest and largest group in the accounting profession.

NAA: National Association of Accountants. Composed of management accountants, this New York–based group has 100,000 members.

NCCPAP: National Conference of CPA Practitioners. This is a new organization for local and medium-size accounting firms. Founded in 1979 and based in New York, the group now has about 1,000 members.

NSPA: National Society of Public Accountants. Based in Alexandria, Virginia, the NSPA is a professional society of 16,000 public accountants.

All five groups above are represented among the 440 respondents to *Inc.*'s survey of accountants. The largest number of respondents belong to AICPA (90 percent), followed by NCCPAP (27 percent), NAA (25 percent), NSPA (4 percent), and AAA (2 percent). The total exceeds 100 percent because some accountants belong to more than one organization. More than seven out of ten accountants who responded to the survey also indicated membership in state societies. The participation in state professional groups ranged from 77 percent of the local accountants to 28 percent of those representing Big Eight accounting firms.

—BRADFORD W. KETCHUM, JR.

THIRTEEN WAYS TO GET A COMPANY
IN TROUBLE

Management consultants Gary Goldstick and George Schreiber specialize in rescuing companies on the brink of disaster, and they insist they've seen just about every fiasco under the sun. Goldstick and Schreiber are likely to show up when problems have peaked, with management under siege from creditors, emotional employees, and worried customers. Their job: to spot the fundamental problems and figure out a quick, practical solution.

After years of this kind of corporate troubleshooting, Goldstick and Schreiber have concluded that there are thirteen common reasons why companies need to be rescued. Like a recurrent nightmare, the same scenes reappeared wherever they went. And all too often, management ignored the warning signs until it was too late for simple solutions.

In fact, says Goldstick, the vast majority of the problems he and Schreiber have to solve could have been avoided if their clients had done a better job of listening and communicating—with other managers, with employees, with customers, with investors and bankers. That's why the first task the two partners undertake is to reopen channels of communication across the board. In the process, they say, they often feel "like priests in a confessional."

"When managers start talking about the company's problems," says Goldstick, "everything else seems to tumble out—personal problems, internal conflicts, expectations that have never been met. When top management gets an opportunity to talk to someone not directly involved in day-to-day operations, they sometimes come up with the answers themselves," he adds.

Good communication, Goldstick and Schreiber insist, is the key to both curing and preventing a crisis. This fact is underscored by their list of ways companies get into trouble.

Of their thirteen prime troublemakers, six involve external problems, four internal, and three financial. But in all three categories, the majority of problems could be avoided if senior management *listened* harder.

"A lot of problems are caused by not being sensitive to the marketplace and taking precautionary measures," says Goldstick. "Better planning is another critical factor. It's the only way to avoid some problems before they crop up." And good planning, of course, must be based on good input, a clear-eyed perception of what's going on where.

Here are the Goldstick-Schreiber "terrible thirteen"—the recurring reasons companies find themselves in trouble:

1. Changes in the marketplace

If management is out of touch, change can come with breathtaking speed, leaving a company on the defensive and in financial trouble when it's forced to catch up. American automakers learned this principle the hard way when consumers began to switch to smaller, more fuel-efficient foreign cars after the Arab oil embargo.

The solution? Goldstick and Schreiber suggest management planning that consciously looks ahead and is sensitive to the volatility of the marketplace. Don't be afraid to rely on independent advisers who are not directly involved in the day-to-day operations of your company. Says Schreiber, "An outside observer could provide a more detached view that will serve as a safeguard against getting caught in a marketing shift."

2. Changes in technology

Not keeping current with changes in technology, Goldstick and Schreiber point out, can often cause trouble for a company by making its products suddenly obsolete or less competitive. Even if the new technology offers no real advantage, they add, technological changes can be dangerous, because consumers often base their purchase on perceived, not real, value. While your product may stand up to your competition, a new technological twist could persuade buyers that the newer item is better.

Again, better planning and more sensitivity to change is essential. "More important, though, is adequate financing for a research and development effort to explore and develop their technology," says Goldstick.

3. Increased cost of debt

Learning to live with chronic inflation has become a problem for consumers and businesses alike. One of the most difficult aspects of this late twentieth-century phenomenon is the erratic, usually accelerating prime lending rate. For small businesses, trouble can come quickly when cost of debt increases are built into their capital structure. For example, today many mortgages involve variable rates tied to the cost of living or the prime, and routine working capital loans, tied to a floating prime rate, can change borrowing costs dramatically from quarter to quarter.

To deal with uncertainties in the cost of debt, Goldstick and Schreiber have several suggestions. "Keep your eye on the money market," says Schreiber. That's important—and not too difficult since financial news has become front-page stuff. Seek long-term financing during periods of peak interest rates. Plan for equity infusion to replace debt when your company's debt-to-net-worth ratio becomes out of balance. Finally, attempt to remain flexible in your inventory levels and labor structure so you can strategically "shrink" your business if necessary.

4. The Peter Principle syndrome

This famous theory (which says that people are promoted to their level of incompetency), as applied by Goldstick and Schreiber, suggests that businesses also can succeed to a point where they grow beyond the skills or expertise of their management. Recently, for example, the consultants were called on for help when an air freight company with annual revenues of $40 million began posting a series of losses after several years of rapid growth and high profitability. Goldstick and Schreiber finally reported to the president—who was also the firm's founder—that his insistence on being a part of every decision was hurting the company's performance. He had two choices: delegate or reduce company size. "He chose to reduce the size of the firm so he could retain total control. He enjoyed working like that," Schreiber remembers.

Schreiber admits this problem can be "very difficult to deal with in an owner-operated, wholly owned business." He advises senior management not to confuse hard work and enthusiasm with managerial skills, however. Understandably, homemade remedies are of little help in such cases; objective outside evaluations are needed. Goldstick recommends bringing in behavioral consultants periodically to audit all company managers, seeing whether their performance keeps pace with expanding job requirements and the desired organizational climate of the firm.

5. Development of a location disadvantage

Sometimes, says Goldstick, as a result of changes in a local economy, an element of the production cost (raw materials, transportation, or labor) suddenly becomes more critical and, consequently, creates an economic disadvantage for a company.

A good example, says Goldstick, was the rising cost of unionized labor in the northern states, which forced companies either to absorb these costs to remain competitive or else relocate to the South, where labor costs are lower.

Schreiber offers this advice: "Diversify, plan ahead to finance plant locations, and don't be afraid to shut down one operation to concentrate investment in another more cost-effective location."

6. Management short of guts

When management sees but is unwilling or unable to effect the streamlining that has become necessary for the survival of the company, there can be a slow, ongoing decline just from carrying too much weight. Example: Certain expenses become what Schreiber terms "institutionalized," and certain employees become sacred cows—to the detriment of the company.

Schreiber recommends a periodic review of all personnel and expenses, using the techniques of zero-base budgeting. This means going back to square one and fully justifying every dollar spent, every staff position on the payroll. He believes this is another case where an audit by independent consultants can be particularly effective. Among other things, "it will put everyone on notice that you mean business."

7. Company becomes hostage to others

Goldstick says he has seen a surprising number of companies lose control of their own affairs and become "hostage to groups or individuals who place pressure on the business, both legal and illegal, in order to pursue their own selfish ends." A typical example, he says, is the banker who puts payment of his loans ahead of the purchase of goods or services the firm needs to survive.

Safeguards? Be continuously aware of how anyone with whom you are dealing could adversely affect your business. If, for business reasons, you have to tolerate this kind of risky relationship, be sure you prepare alternative plans for action if what Goldstick calls "negative leverage" is applied.

8. Limited financial resources for the market

For various reasons, companies don't always have the ready cash to remain competitive. As a result, they get in trouble because their competitors do have the resources to invest in engineering, manufacturing, tooling, and marketing.

Schreiber's recommendation: "Be realistic. If you can't afford to market the product, consider selling it or the entire company and use the added cash to exploit another product line or service."

9. Precipitous changes in distribution system

Trouble may arise from rapid changes in the economic demands, market prices, or legal constraints that affect a product, the consultants say. For example, arbitrary increases in world oil prices have dramatically increased the cost to produce such oil by-products as plastics and fertilizers. Goldstick says, "Diversification of product lines and markets is the best protection against such changes."

10. Internal conflicts

Bad blood among board members or senior managers can threaten a firm's stability if allowed to go unchecked. A typical example, reports Goldstick, is the chief executive who pursues a conservative growth program to conserve assets and develop a strong balance sheet. But then some board members become unhappy over the poor performance of their stock. They challenge him as well as his supportive board members over this policy, demanding a whole new direction for the company. Regardless of who is right or wrong, the conflict dissipates company vigor. What is needed, says Goldstick, is preventive communication at an early stage. The chief executive must be his firm's primary salesman, not only before the outside world but also to those he asks to accept his leadership. And this selling job never ends; the "buyer" can never be taken for granted. If matters reach an impasse, he's bound to lose control. Says Schreiber, "At the risk of sounding like I believe consultants are the cure for every ill, this case is a classic example of when it's best to call in an independent third party. He can audit, review, and recommend objective decisions."

11. Business grows beyond sources of working capital

Since it involves success, this may sound like a dream problem, but it can be devastating, says Schreiber, and it happens all too often. When a thinly capitalized company overmarkets a high-demand product and can't borrow or attract investment capital sufficient to manufacture and deliver on schedule, goodwill evaporates and the entire organization is put in jeopardy.

"Planned growth is absolutely essential for any business," states Schreiber. If it's too late and management already finds itself in such a predicament, he would recommend they consider raising prices strategically to curtail demand. The resulting drop in unit volume will be balanced by the fact that sales will be at a higher profit margin.

12. Inadequate control systems

There are several ways this kind of problem can occur. A company, for example, plans and designs a product, organizes a manufacturing facility, staffs it with competent personnel, but doesn't install adequate quality control procedures.

The result? Poor quality merchandise—and financial trouble for the company. Likewise, failure to modernize on a timely basis can result in control problems.

Schreiber recommends, "In a small business, the proprietor must protect himself by controlling invoice numbers, check numbers, receiving documents, et cetera."

The same holds true for the larger company, only it will involve more people. Accounting and other control personnel should be dedicated and assigned to separate functions to produce a coordinated control system.

13. Depending on a single customer

Many companies start out this way, but they'd better not remain so indefinitely. It's an example of putting all your eggs in one basket, and it's most risky. If a major buyer who represents 40 percent or 50 percent of your business suddenly goes elsewhere or changes into a competitor, your company can be destroyed, warns Schreiber.

"Expanding into new product lines or developing a range of customers," he says, "is the only real protection against such a problem."

A DOUBLE-BARRELED APPROACH TO CRISIS MANAGEMENT

Like the companies they work for Goldstick and Schreiber have an advantage in being a small, two-man outfit. This keeps them organizationally lean, flexible, able to move as needed and with little ceremony. They also enjoy the advantage of being almost complete opposites—sort of an "odd couple" of the business administration world.

Goldstick, a gregarious individual, explodes with phrases like "stereo view of things" and "cash is king."

Schreiber comes across as his perfect counterpart, the buttoned-down financial whiz with horn-rimmed glasses and a style of commentary as even and measured as a heartbeat.

In this case, opposites not only attract, they click. The friendship goes back fifteen years.

Goldstick founded Information Control Corporation, a Los Angeles–based manufacturer of minicomputers and computer peripherals, in 1965. ("Before then I was a technocrat," he says.) Today he remains chairman of the board. At one point his chief financial officer was George Schreiber. But in 1976 Schreiber went off to establish his own consulting firm, concentrating in the areas of debt reorganization, operational analysis, and financial profiles.

Last year they were brought together again professionally by a friend who asked them to join forces in finding and defusing an imminent crisis at his computer company. Thus was born Goldstick & Schreiber Inc., with offices in Englewood, California, a suburb of Los Angeles.

Their clients range from high-tech companies to agricultural businesses, most with annual revenues of under $50 million. So far, they've worked with firms only as far afield as Oregon and Texas. But both men take it as a matter of course that they'll be serving clients across the nation within the next three years—and they intend to see that their own growth doesn't make them a victim of any of their thirteen problems.

—JOHN BANASZEWSKI

NINE STEPS TO SAVE
TROUBLED COMPANIES

A company in trouble is like an army fighting a losing battle," says Charles "Red" Scott. "The grandest plans of its generals have been abandoned, bravery turns to panic, and the organization crumbles as the casualties mount."

Scott should know. As president of Intermark Inc., a $125-million miniconglomerate based in La Jolla, California, Scott has become something of an expert at turning around small companies that were dangerously close to becoming casualties. It's a role he's played since 1971, when he stepped in to salvage his $2.9-million investment in Intermark. Scott doesn't bail out companies just because it's a nice thing to do. "At Intermark," he says, "I wanted to save my bacon. That's the best reason I know of to turn a company around."

Along the way, Scott has saved a good deal more than his own bacon. When he assumed the presidency of Intermark ten years ago, the company reported a $4.3-million loss. Four hard years later, the red ink had been erased. Last year Intermark reported net earnings of $7.9 million on revenues of $107.5 million. Bank borrowing has dropped from $14 million to zero, working capital is up from $1.3 million to $32.2 million, and the company now has about $10 million in cash and short-term investments ready to put to work.

The experience of turning Intermark around gave Scott a chance to develop a nine-step plan he has followed ever since with the firms that Intermark has acquired, rehabilitated, and eventually taken public. Intermark's current crop of small companies includes two printing businesses, two electronics firms, a retail garden center chain, and a furniture manufacturer. Its flagship company is Anthem Electronics, a semiconductor distributor that last year turned a $5-million pretax profit on sales of $34.5 million. Anthem is a classic turnaround: In 1976, the company had only $5.4 million in sales and lost $389,000.

Scott now has a checklist of what he terms "the more obvious symptoms" of a company in need of help:

- It is losing money. The company shows regular, perhaps worsening, operational losses.

- It is short of cash. Bills from vendors and suppliers are stretched to 90 or 120 days. The company is borrowing against fresh receivables and barely making its payroll.
- It is losing market share.
- Key, quality employees are deserting in a steady stream.
- Physically, the company is deteriorating. Paint is peeling. Plants and parking lots are dirty. Only breakdown maintenance is being done. Machinery is repaired by cannibalizing other machinery.
- Emotionally, it is reeling. Pride is gone. Employees are sullen, dispirited, pessimistic.

When a company reaches this point, says Scott, it's probably time for a new manager to take charge and start the nine-step turnaround process.

1. Take control of the cash.

When a company is hurting, Scott says, cash is its lifeblood. Go to the treasurer's office immediately and take personal responsibility for all disbursements. Keep an up-to-the-minute awareness of all incoming funds. Keep your hands on the cash and dispense it sparingly. Pay only those items that will literally keep the doors open, and in this order: payroll, utilities, key suppliers, withholding taxes.

When the cash is firmly under your control, Scott says, you have a tenuous foothold, a place from which to rebuild. "This isn't the way they teach at business school," Scott admits, "and it isn't the way they talk at banks. But as a guy whose belly has been black and blue and whose feet are blistered, I'll tell you it's the way to stay alive when you take over a sick company."

2. Listen.

It's still far too early to start giving orders. Instead, gather as much data as possible, as quickly as possible. Pay visits immediately to your first-level managers and supervisors, Scott says. When you get there, ask dozens of questions—for example, What's wrong with this company? Who are the key people? The good suppliers? The best customers? What would you do if you were me?

"Listen carefully and write it all down," he says. "Take notes until you have writer's cramp."

After hearing out your own people, Scott says, go to the banks, to key suppliers, and to good customers and ask the same questions, listening just as carefully to their answers.

Chances are, he says, many of these people will have correct ideas of what is right and wrong. Chances also are good that your predecessor either never asked their opinion or ignored them. Your coming on the scene and listening will be seen as a positive sign.

3. Stop the hemorrhaging.

Almost all sick companies have one division, one plant, or one product line that is losing money hand over fist, Scott says. Many times this loser is some executive's pet or ego trip. Everyone sees it and knows it, but the problem area goes on bleeding precious cash.

"You must stop this operating loss in its tracks," he says firmly. This can be done by selling it, disposing of its assets, or simply locking it up. Such a step has several positive results, he claims. It conserves cash. It puts everyone on notice that there will be no sacred cows. And it demonstrates that you are a leader who can make tough decisions.

4. Find the positives.

The time is fast approaching for you to make a move, and you want that first move to be from strength. You want to capitalize on a positive element. Usually the positives are people, but often they are products, facilities, even divisions or subsidiary companies.

Scott explains that when he became president of Intermark, he spotted an opportunity to enhance the company's public image and boost employee morale at low cost. Intermark approved construction of a new garden center connected with Nurseryland Garden Centers, one of its small but promising subsidiary companies. The move was noticed by Wall Street analysts, creditors, and even San Diego–area housewives, Scott says. The reaction was: "If Intermark is as sick as they say, why are they expanding instead of liquidating?"

To start the rebuilding process, Scott says, keep an eye out for what he calls "eagles." Eagles come in all shapes and sizes, but you will recognize them chiefly by their attitudes. With things crumbling around them, they still will have some optimism. They haven't given up. They have ideas, plans, and solutions to problems. Scott says he found only seven or eight such "eagles" at Intermark, but that was enough.

"Remember," Scott says, "eagles don't flock—you find them one at a time. And don't be afraid of a guy who has a chip on his shoulder. Some of the very best people we saved out of Intermark were the most difficult to deal with at first. They were mad. Their careers were in jeopardy. And they vented their spleen on me, even though I didn't cause the problems. I just happened to be the first guy to show up that they could jump on."

5. Make a plan.

Now that you have gathered your data, found your strengths, identified your eagles, and stopped the one big hemorrhage, pull back and think. Formulate a plan of action that takes advantage of strengths, neutralizes weaknesses, and that will win the support of at least your eagles. "Remember," Scott says, "people are looking for leadership. It's up to you to provide it."

With a clear-cut plan, you can now start giving directions. Most importantly, he says, show people *how* you will lead them. Establish a corporate definition, a corporate purpose, and a strategy. Set long-term and short-term goals, and make clear the principles by which you intend to run the company. Most of all, he says, make sure your people understand your plan and their role in it.

Here are just a few of what Scott calls his corporate "cardinals," the principles by which he operates Intermark:

- Don't run out of cash—no matter what.
- Create values—not earnings.
- Never get organized by a trade union.
- Never compromise quality for price.
- Don't promote a function manager to a chief executive officer.
- Beware of "quick-fix" managers.
- Creativity is great—but not in accounting.
- Hire smart and manage hard.

6. *Raise new cash.*

Don't forget, your corporate patient is still sick and still needs massive transfusions of cash to stay alive, Scott says. Get it—in the easiest ways first. When Scott became president of Intermark, he immediately sold off some of its subsidiaries to raise cash. But there are other techniques he also recommends:

- Collect receivables. Redouble your efforts with your debtors until they are current.
- Liquidate inventory, supplies, and materials, even if it means taking paper losses.
- Sell nonproductive assets, such as idle machinery, equipment, empty buildings, company cars.
- Sell successful product lines, patents, even entire businesses.
- Sell and lease back real estate.

With a stronger cash position, says Scott, you are now ready for what he terms the psychological part of the turnaround.

7. *Establish credibility.*

Any company that has been in trouble for a while probably has been breaking a lot of promises, Scott points out. New claims will be met with skepticism. Scott says there is only one way to counteract this situation: Make only promises you can keep, and keep comfortably.

Rebuilding your credibility begins with small things, he says, like appointments. When you say you'll meet someone at 11 A.M., be there at 10:45. When you promise a check on the thirtieth, send it on the twenty-eighth. In other words, he adds, whatever you agree to do, do a bit more. Start first with your employees, then extend it to everyone you deal with. News will soon get around that you are a person of your word.

Scott has advice for dealing with your bankers, too. Tell them the bad news first—all of it. No matter how black it sounds, let them have it. Then tell them the good news, however insignificant it may be. Scott believes this tactic will leave the banker with a good taste in his mouth, and he may be less reluctant to see you the next time.

8. Improve attitudes.

Scott considers this the key to the turnaround. And the process begins with you. The manager must have absolute faith in his own ability and the company's ability to carry out the plan. As soon as the leader loses faith, the plan is functionally dead.

"The manager who has faith is enthusiastic, determined, and committed," says Scott. "These emotions and attitudes are contagious and soon spread to other workers. Improved attitudes result in an improved bottom line.

"The real secret to making a profit is to increase human productivity. The key to increasing productivity is to improve employee attitudes. Therefore, the job of management is to continually improve attitudes.

"The single most important ingredient in achieving a turnaround is the building of an enthusiastic, cohesive team. The key to that is communication."

9. Show a profit.

Scott says this step is included not because it is essential to the turnaround, but because making a profit is the ultimate reason for a commercial business to stay in business.

It is important to show black ink on the bottom line, Scott says, but only after:

- Maintenance has been elevated from the breakdown to the preventive stage.
- Personnel has been given in-service training, exposure to new developments, and refresher courses.
- Investments have been made for the future—for example, in new machinery, real estate for expansion, and new research employees.

"A turnaround is a unique management process, completely different from operating a successful growth company or from building a new business from scratch," says Scott. "And it's tough. Unless you know the company intimately, it's virtually impossible for the smartest analyst to look at the surface and see what's really happening.

"Instead," he recommends, "I'd look at the people. Check out the person at the helm. If he or she is a winner, is honest, and has a deep personal commitment to the company, you've got a good bet on a turnaround. If any of those three elements is missing, don't touch it."

—JOHN BANASZEWSKI

PLANNING FOR GROWTH

Business folklore is rich with stories of companies that explode onto the commerce scene from obscurity, only to return to their roots after a brief period of heady success. We'd mention their names, but we've probably forgotten them. The companies that we do remember may not always have been instant successes, but most have managed to plan their success, to understand the connection between the ends and means. In this collection of *Inc.* articles we look at the many ways an articulated business strategy can save one ailing company, put others in the lead, and keep still others progressing at a healthy—if sometimes modest—pace.

Perhaps the greatest danger facing any successful entrepreneur is the possibility that he will begin to believe all of the stories and myths that surface as a result of his tremendous success. Overconfident management has been responsible for the demise of many an otherwise healthy venture. Our first piece, "Growing Steady," looks at three companies that have found a comfortable market position but have kept their success in control by slowing down, and in some cases halting their growth while they absorb the volume of business they presently incur and prepare themselves for more.

For some, the value of planning growth comes a little late. That was the case with David Wolfberg, a Miami architect whose firm grew 2,950 percent in a six-year period. It's tough to keep that kind of success at bay, and Wolfberg did what most any entrepreneur in his position would do—he fueled growth by spending more and more. First there was a series of new offices, then more and better trained personnel, and then a fancy computer. "During the period of conquest and glory, we were great guys, great leaders," says Wolfberg's partner, Julio Alvarez. "Then we hit the recession. We were no longer growing. Money wasn't flowing in." Ultimately, Wolfberg and Alvarez had to lay off some seventy-one employees in an environment that became increasingly hostile. "You'd Be Surprised How Easy It Is to Succeed" takes a close look at how the firm got out of control and what the partners have done about it. It's impossible to predict economic unknowns, we find out, but it's imperative to consider them in periods of "conquest and glory."

While the Miami architects would have been served well by a strategy that had them sticking to a smaller scale of growth, calculated risks shouldn't be ignored. For thirty years Bob Praegitzer ran a lumber mill in Oregon, but when his operation became one of the biggest in the area, Praegitzer itched for a new challenge. Traditional management enthusiasts would advise the lumberman to investigate business opportunities in related areas—paper products, for example, or trucking. Manufacturing electronic circuit boards, however, would not be a responsible suggestion, but that's just what Praegitzer got himself into. He met up with a fellow whose twenty years of circuit board experience made him somewhat of an expert on those devices but who didn't have the finances or the business acumen to start his own shop.

Both timber and high technology are boom-or-bust industries, and that is where their similarities end. But the process of strategic planning—defining and reaching a market—apparently carried over from lumber to electronics. Praegitzer surveyed the terrain and saw that local electronics plants used about $50 million worth of circuit boards annually, only 10 percent of which came from shops located in Oregon.

"Out on a Limb" investigates how Praegitzer took full advantage of his observations in order to position himself in the high-tech circuit board market. Local suppliers had a clear advantage over out-of-state suppliers, but that wasn't Praegitzer's only tack. Instead of producing boards for the low-end, high-risk market, Praegitzer found his niche in the high end of the market, where demand and profits are comparatively stable. His business is running strong after only three years of operation and his plans call for expansion to handle production backups. The next step, diversification, is still a dream, but Praegitzer plans to become an equipment manufacturer someday, thus removing the latest thorn in his side—reliance on demand from other equipment manufacturers.

We've seen how important a comprehensive strategy is for small companies—particularly in light of what happens when there isn't one. But what about those $200-million operations that seem, at least to the start-up entrepreneur, to be impervious to harm? The planning needs of the mid-size company are surely different from those of the start-up. Who is going to purchase the goods becomes secondary to how the company can keep abreast of new technologies and remain flexible as it continues to grow.

"Mutual Benefits" covers an original plan put into effect by Analog Devices, a company that makes electronic components. Noticing that his company's future growth might not continue to be as dramatic as it has been, Analog chairman Ray Stata developed a plan that would allow his company to benefit from industry innovation without having to formally acquire a pack of smaller companies. With financial help from Standard Oil, Analog has formed partnerships with dozens of smaller companies. For Analog, these new relationships have kept the company on the leading edge of technological innovation. For Analog's small partnerships, new collaborative relationships, both with people from Analog and among themselves, have proven valuable. For all parties, the new partnership seems to be working.

Many people in top management have the talent to devise strategies like the one developed at Analog. That's why they are in top management. The problem for many, though, is an inability to get out of their own way. "Your Own Worst Enemy" reports on ten pointers from turnaround experts Morton H. Scheer and Robert Rosen that can help management get a grip on company operations.

Q: How many Americans have never heard of Trivial Pursuit?

A: Not many—and that is becoming a real headache for the folks who manufacture and supply the new national pastime. The three Canadians who developed the game are sitting pretty, even though they are growing tired of coming up with new questions for future editions. But without a coherent strategy, Trivial Pursuit has caused an epidemic of migraines among the game's manufacturer, distributors, and suppliers. And the relationships between suppliers and producer and between producer and distributors is very sour indeed. "Big Game" investigates some of the casualties of this tremendous leisure-time trend.

The collection of articles in this section was compiled to illustrate that a good business strategy does not necessarily mean a plan for skyrocketing growth. Rather, the role of strategic planning can be to help prepare for growth, to control it, and integrate it. The collection's final article illustrates one result of having no strategy at all.

GROWING STEADY

Hino & Malee Inc., a Chicago-based designer of high-fashion women's clothing, has urged some of its big-name department-store clients to buy less, not more, of its pricey duds. Healthcare Services Group Inc., a firm in Huntingdon Valley, Pennsylvania, that contracts with nursing homes, has twice called a six-month halt to its selling and advertising efforts, in an attempt to discourage new business.

Young companies, led by their founders, turning away good business and turning up cautious? This isn't the way entrepreneurs—bold, brash risk-seekers—are supposed to behave. Or is it?

Howard Charney thinks it is, which is surprising when you consider his own situation. He is a cofounder of 3Com Corporation, a company that lives in a neighborhood—Silicon Valley—and works in an industry—microcomputers—where spectacular growth is commonplace. But Charney and his colleagues, 3Com chairman Bob Metcalfe and chief executive officer Bill Krause, don't fit neatly into the growth-at-any-cost stereotype. Charney, in fact, thinks that the entrepreneur-as-wildcatter is a myth perpetrated by business school professors.

That may be, but the professors are not alone in their mythmaking. The business press—*Inc.* magazine often included—bestows its plaudits and notoriety on entrepreneurs who create the most from the least in the shortest period of time. The investment community, from venture capitalists to institutional portfolio managers, looks for growth the way college admissions officers look for high test scores, and places its bets accordingly. Entrepreneurs themselves, goaded by the press, the market, or simply by pride in their own accomplishments, frequently measure their success by sales-and-revenue curves, and forget about everything else.

The riskiness of such single-mindedness occasionally shows up in the headlines. Osborne Computer Corporation, for a while the darling of Silicon Valley, went from start-up to more than $100 million in sales in only a year and a half before winding up in bankruptcy court. Pizza Time Theatre Inc., brainchild of Atari Corporation founder Nolan Bushnell, grew at a compound annual growth rate of 171 percent for five years—enough to place it for two consecutive years on *Inc.*'s list of the one hundred fastest-growing public companies in the United States—before it, too, filed for protection under Chapter 11.

Such stories alone prompt doubts about top-line growth as a measure of business success, particularly when compared with profitability or productivity. When entrepreneurs and CEOs forget that growth is only one measure among many—when they become fixated on growth and feel compelled by pride or ambition to emulate or top the growth of others—that is when they get into trouble.

But avoiding trouble isn't the only reason for putting growth in its place. More important for a healthy company may be the long-term strategic value of controlling growth just as one controls other variables in the calculus of business. At any given time, no growth, slow growth, or just less growth may be what is called for, if only so that the pace can pick up in the future. Indeed, if holding back today is what will make tomorrow's expansion possible, then to hold back is only good sense.

Whether more than a few growth-oriented companies subscribe to this notion of good sense isn't yet clear. But at least some entrepreneurs believe that growth at any cost is precisely what their competitive situations do not call for. To control growth, they are willing to forgo selling opportunities, limit their market share, and keep money in the bank rather than spend it. The stories of three such companies show why.

Last April, Joan Collins of "Dynasty," and celebrity designers Bill Blass and Giorgio Sant'Angelo joined hundreds of people from the Seventh Avenue fashion industry, all bedecked in the frippery of their trade, for a festive gathering in the Grand Ballroom of the Pierre Hotel in New York City. The occasion was the judging of the first annual More (cigarette) Fashion Awards competition for young designers.

Among the young designers present were Kazuyoshi Hino and Malee Chompoo. Hino, who uses his last name because, he says, Kazuyoshi is too difficult to remember, and Malee, who prefers her first, were one of five finalist designers or design teams chosen from among 250 entrants. They didn't win. But that was all right: The recognition they received at the gathering meant they had arrived in an industry in which status is everything. Their company, Hino & Malee Inc., was indisputably hot. And it was time, by some reckonings, for the pair to shoot for the moon, to create the next fad, to ride high on a wave of trendy fashion.

Hino and Malee, by common consent, have both the design talent and the imagination to go for such goals. But they chose not to try. In fact, the flattering attention they gained at the Pierre—and that they have gained elsewhere on numerous occasions in the past few years—didn't change one iota the way the shy couple does business. Just surviving in the fickle fashion industry is risky enough, in their view, and the two entrepreneurs have studiously avoided taking other chances with their infant enterprise. They would much rather have a solid small company than a shaky larger one.

Their conservatism shows up in any number of areas. Their company has limited its line to a relatively small niche—designer sportswear—in the huge garment industry, and to a distinctive style within that niche. It does no work on speculation: Contrary to industry practice, the Chicago company won't make a garment in its 14,000-square-foot North Side factory until sales representative Tom Hewitt produces a confirmed order for it. If orders exceed the plant's capacity to produce, the company may lose some sales. On the other hand, if orders fall short of expectations, it has invested no labor—which at 25 percent to 30 percent is the largest single component of a garment's cost—in unsold finished goods.

Financially, the company remains as close to a cash-based business as the two partners can keep it. They have financed the company's growth almost exclusively from profits. The only contributed equity in the business is the $2,500 each invested in the first few months to buy fabric for their first collection. A close friend loaned them enough cash to finance Hewitt's first selling foray to Manhattan; they have never borrowed from a bank.

"Next spring," says Hino, "even if we sell nothing, we don't owe anybody anything."

No retailer, no matter how prestigious its name, gets a shipment from Hino & Malee until its credit is approved. At the cost of some lost sales, but in the interest of undamaged profit margins, this prudence in trade-credit approval has kept the company's bad debt rate at less than 1 percent of revenues. Even if a store's credit checks out, Hewitt sometimes persuades store buyers to order less than they think they can sell. He has urged some chains to limit the number of their stores carrying the Hino & Malee label, focusing only on those in urban centers where more fashion-conscious women shop. "When stores like I. Magnin start pushing us into remote locations," says Hewitt, "it makes us a little nervous. So we're saying, 'Why don't you just keep us in three or four, not fifteen or twenty, of your stores?' "

There are sound business reasons for Hewitt's caution: Not all sales are necessarily good sales when a tiny company depends on giant retailers for 60 percent of its business. Department stores routinely ask garment-makers to take back unsold goods at the end of a season. Or they ask manufacturers to contribute "markdown money," cash to compensate the retailer for the lower margins it gets in end-of-season sales. Both of these are bad for the manufacturer's bottom line, and the larger the manufacturer, the more likely the retailer is to seek help. As a tiny business, Hino & Malee can plead a lack of resources should the likes of Bonwit Teller, Bergdorf Goodman, or Lord & Taylor raise the issue.

Growth is also an issue that Hino and Malee are struggling to resolve for themselves: It is a personal as much as a business issue.

Hino, forty-two, came to this country from his native Japan in 1975 and got a job in Chicago working as a pattern maker for a manufacturer of uniforms for Las Vegas casino workers. Malee, a year younger, left Bangkok in 1969 and was a design assistant with a high-fashion apparel company in the same building. When she lost her job he quit his, and in March 1980 they created the company and began selling women's sportswear, designed by Hino and sewn by Malee, from a tiny boutique in the corner of an upscale Chicago beauty salon. Within a year, they had been introduced to Hewitt, who became their full-time rep and moved his showroom from Chicago to the Manhattan fashion capital. Hino's "architecturally" inspired designs began to be shown in Bloomingdale's and other department stores. Sales in fiscal 1982 climbed to $512,000; in 1983 to $1.3 million; and last year to $2.1 million.

Despite these sales figures, Hino & Malee is still almost a mom-and-pop operation. It has no management organization, no strategic planning, and no articulated goals. Hino and Malee themselves are amazed by their success in just four years, and are at the same time frightened by the size and the momentum of the business they have created. They have no experience—in finance, marketing, personnel management, or cocktail-party protocol—and no formal training, either. With their soft, inexpert English, sometimes difficult for the ear to capture, often they can only indicate, not explicate, complex thoughts—as when, for example, Malee says of their business strategy, "We just use our sense."

The pair started the company primarily to give expression to their design ambitions, and Hino, especially, worries that he will become too busy running the business to do the designing. They may hire a president, someone to manage the company, or they could sell the business and stay on in their creative roles. At this point they don't know what they want. But in the meantime, they aren't going to jeopardize their options by trying to move the company beyond their own capabilities, beyond what "sense," as Malee puts it, can manage.

"We could all have smiles on our faces staying between two million and three million dollars [in sales]," says Hewitt. "We don't have to grow to six million. The larger you get, the more vulnerable you are."

The managed-growth strategy that Hino and Malee arrived at by default would make sense to Dan McCartney: A similar strategy has been part of his plan from the outset. Healthcare Services Group, the firm McCartney and Mel Mason founded in 1977, has no direct competitors; it has more capital than it needs; and its market is both receptive and practically untapped. In fact, the main thing—the only thing—holding Healthcare's growth rate in check is McCartney's insistence that the firm stick to its plan, which, while it drives the firm's growth, also constrains it. In his view, the single biggest threat to Healthcare Services' long-term success would be impatience, the temptation to short-circuit the plan. McCartney has proved a patient man.

Healthcare is in the business of selling a solution to a problem. Neither the problem nor the solution is terribly complicated; you just have to see them and recognize the business opportunity, as McCartney and Mason did.

The problem they recognized is that, in most nursing homes, the worst-managed department is usually housekeeping—the people who scrub, clean, and polish. The head nurse has prestige, the chief dietician has prestige, but the top janitor does not. Usually, says McCartney, he is a former floor man who is good with a bucket and mop but has no management experience or training. Housekeeping, consequently, is frequently inefficient and ineffective, and is a constant source of niggling problems to nursing home administrators.

The way to solve the problem, of course, is to replace the bucket-and-mop people with trained, ambitious managers who can hold their own with the nurses and dieticians while motivating the cleaning troops. McCartney figured out how to do that, and he and Mason built a company around the solution.

You attract ambitious people to the job, he reasoned, by making it an early step in a challenging management career, not the last step in a vocation that tends to attract people without other skills or talent. And then you train those ambitious people to do things your way. "I am of the opinion," McCartney says, "that in our industry there is no talent to steal."

After Healthcare signs a contract with a nursing home, it replaces the current chief housekeeper with one of its own trained managers. The working troops technically become employees of Healthcare, not the nursing home, but their wages, fringe benefits, union agreements, and so on remain unchanged. As far as they are concerned, they still work for the nursing home. "The only difference," says McCartney, "is the management."

Even if they have had some experience, all new Healthcare managers go through sixty to ninety days of training, beginning with the basics. They clean patient rooms, then public rooms, and move on to floors. They learn to hire and train new cleaning workers. They supervise specific cleaning crews. They learn administration. After three months or so, if their evaluations are good, they will be made assistant housekeepers at large facilities.

From there, a manager might solo at a smaller home, then take command of a staff of assistants at a bigger institution. Then he or she can progress through training manager, district manager, regional manager, and, as the company's geographic expansion proceeds, take charge of a division.

"We use the same mop handles as everybody else," McCartney says. "The difference is that we can provide a better manager than the facility itself can. Our guy knows that he can move on and up. The facility's own person is stuck there, or at another place just like it."

McCartney's idea works. Last year, its seventh, Healthcare earned pretax income of $1 million on revenues of $8.2 million, from contracts with more than seventy facilities in the Northeast and in Florida. Since 1980, its revenues have grown nearly 45 percent compounded annually, and net earnings have expanded at an annual compound rate of 100 percent over the same period. Just as significant, however, is the firm's 95 percent contract-retention rate. In seven years, only six clients have canceled or failed to renew their contracts, one of them because it went out of business.

The limits to growth for Healthcare have not been market-imposed. "Getting new business," McCartney says, "has been the least of our problems." With the graying of America, the nursing home industry has expanded rapidly, and facility owners apparently are impressed by McCartney's standard argument. "A nursing home may spend, say, two hundred fifty thousand dollars a year on housekeeping," he says, "so I ask them, 'If you had a quarter-of-a-million-dollar business across the street, would you hire Jim the janitor to run it or somebody with some management training?'"

Nor has a lack of capital slowed the firm's growth rate; it is, when things work properly, closer than even Hino & Malee to being a cash-based business. Most client institutions, McCartney says, treat Healthcare's fees just like a payroll expense, writing checks to Healthcare weekly or biweekly, and the firm, in turn, pays its housekeeping employees. If Healthcare has correctly estimated its own costs, it begins collecting a profit from every new client with the very first payment. "When we started the company," McCartney says, "we had to be profitable instantaneously because we had no money." And now it has almost an embarrassment of capital riches: Last year, Healthcare went public, raising $3.5 million.

Indeed the only limit to Healthcare's top-line growth has been the time it takes to recruit and train managers and build the management structure. But this limit is a significant one, and overstepping or ignoring it could be fatal to the firm. "In 1978," McCartney says, "I thought we had started to lose it." Healthcare had enough entry-level managers to staff the facilities it served, but their supervisors, the district managers, were stretched too thin. Because it takes about two years to train a new district manager, in McCartney's view, the firm had to slow down. It did, adding only three accounts that year.

In 1982, Mason and McCartney imposed a six-month selling moratorium on themselves because, once again, the business began to tax management's capacity to manage. Eight new district managers were trained that year. The company has to lose only two or three contracts, McCartney says, to lose its reputation, "so, in retrospect, that [moratorium] was probably the most important decision we've made since going into business."

The shortcuts available to Healthcare are obvious enough. It could reduce the training time for new housekeepers by hiring people with on-the-job experience. It could increase the number of facilities each district manager is responsible for and increase the number of district managers reporting to each regional manager. It could grow by acquiring other companies that deliver a similar service and using their management personnel. Any of these options would speed the growth of Healthcare but might jeopardize McCartney's carefully thought-out strategy. McCartney has considered them but has decided to stick to the original plan.

Sticking to the plan is a precept that Howard Charney and his colleagues at 3Com would endorse—along with Hino and Malee's preference for caution and profitability.

In October 1980, this unusual group of entrepreneurs began approaching California venture capitalists with an unusual business plan. The group included 3Com's prime founder, Bob Metcalfe, formerly with Xerox Corporation; Charney, who is an engineer with an MBA and a law degree; and two others. The plan, instead of projecting spectacular growth and early capture of market share, predicted that the year-old company's share of the potentially huge market for computer networking systems was going to *decline*, from 6.5 percent down to 5 percent, over the next five years.

Declining market share is not something venture capitalists like to see, and it is certainly not the sort of projection Silicon Valley entrepreneurs normally wave around when they are out raising equity capital. "The venture capitalists' reaction," says Bill Krause, now 3Com's president and chief executive officer, "was, 'Come on, what is this? We're looking at maybe a three-billion-dollar market, and you guys are only going to be an eighty-million-dollar company?'"

Still, the venture capitalists came across with $1 million in first-round financing, largely on the strength of the reputations of Metcalfe and his Gang of Four, as the founding group became known, plus a fifth—Krause, a fourteen-year veteran of Hewlett-Packard Company and general manager of HP's General Systems Division, who was recruited by Metcalfe to be 3Com's president. "We liked the team," says Gib Myers, a venture capitalist investor who now sits on 3Com's board, "but we had no great insight about whether Ethernet would win the race."

Metcalfe, with others, had invented Ethernet at Xerox in the early 1970s. It is a system for linking all of a company's computers and computer peripherals (e.g., printers) within an office building into a so-called local area network system (LANS). Networks allow machines to talk to one another, permit people to use electronic mail, let personal-computer users tap data stored in mainframe computers, and encourage other innovations in intraoffice computer use. But before Ethernet or any of the other competing LAN systems could be exploited commercially, there had to be lots of computers that needed connecting. Until 1981, there weren't. "Ethernet was a technology ahead of its time," says Krause. It was a solution waiting for a problem.

Before 1981, companies typically had large mainframe computers, or at most a few minicomputers. There was some business to be done in tying these machines and other terminals together. But Metcalfe and the Gang of Four decided in 1980 to convert 3Com from a consulting firm into a LANS manufacturing business, based on their conviction that the market would change. They didn't know when it would change or who would change it, but somehow, Metcalfe was persuaded, 16-bit personal computers would become ubiquitous. When they did, people would want to link them together, and that would define 3Com's main market.

There were other, conflicting theories. Some people in the industry thought the future lay in linking more terminals to larger minis and mainframes. Others thought the future was in linking together the small, inexpensive 8-bit machines produced by such companies as Apple Computer Inc. And there were other LANS technologies besides Ethernet. So 3Com had plenty of options it could have pursued, some of which promised earlier results and quicker payoffs than the company might achieve by waiting for a hoped-for market to materialize.

"It came down to the two kinds of strategies that one can take in starting a company," says Krause. "In one you build up a large amount of fixed overhead in your engineering, marketing, and manufacturing, and bring your product to market; the risk is that there won't be enough demand for your product to cover that overhead. The second strategy is you let market demand determine your rate of growth and you let your shipments lead your expenses. The risk you take there is that the market may run away from you because you haven't invested fast enough."

3Com chose the latter strategy, in large part because of Krause's conservative predilections.

"Bill Krause might offend some people in our business," says Dick Kramlich, a venture capitalist and one of 3Com's first-round investors, "because he's a little too orderly for them."

Krause's orderliness at 3Com meant that things were done according to plan, not according to impulse. It wasn't always easy—for Krause or for the rest of the company.

Just five months after coming aboard as president, for example, Krause imposed a four-month survival plan on a crew that theretofore was accustomed to living on its entrepreneurial exuberance. Sales of the company's interim products to the limited market that existed in the summer of 1981 hadn't risen as much as the company's monthly planning process, another of Krause's management tools, had anticipated. So Krause imposed a hiring freeze and created a list of specific objectives—customers to be called on, orders to be gotten, distribution channels to be opened—that had to be met.

Charney, currently 3Com's vice-president for engineering and then the vice-president for manufacturing, recalls the reaction: "People in the Valley said, 'Here's this little company that has a million dollars in the bank, that's supposed to be in this really hot market, and yet they're putting in place a four-month survival plan. These guys must be really crazy.' At the time, even I thought we were being paranoid. At first, just having a survival plan created a depression [in the company]. People would ask, 'Why are you putting me through this nightmare?' And Bill would say, 'You know, we don't have a problem today, but if we continue along this path, we're going to have a problem, which is going out of business. So we're going to follow this other path. We're going to tighten the belt, and I'm going to highlight those three things each of you has to do, and we're going to go out and do them.' Companies that are out of control never have survival plans. Why? Because they don't know that they need them."

When sales still didn't develop according to plan, Krause did something businesses in Ohio might be used to, but not those in Silicon Valley. Everybody in the company took a pay cut. "We developed our fifteen-ten-five plan," Krause recalls. "Executive committee members took a fifteen percent cut; exempt employees, ten percent; nonexempt, five percent. We felt that the people most responsible for the fortunes of the company should take the largest pay cut."

While all this was going on, IBM Corporation introduced its 16-bit personal computer and, with that one announcement, created the market 3Com had been waiting for. By the summer of 1982, 3Com's sales were back on track, and that fall its growth began in earnest. The planning, the patience, and the survival plan had all paid off. Now 3Com is on a growth track that, Krause projects, will take it to $100 million in sales by 1987, with a return on stockholders' equity substantially higher than it could have earned if it had consumed capital pursuing other, shorter-term markets, or if it had gone back to the capital markets instead of conserving the cash that it had.

The philosophy—almost the corporate culture—that led to this payoff now seems to permeate 3Com and is reflected in what its executives say when they assess the slow-growth period of the past. "Bill," Charney says, "has an expression, which is, 'Do a few of the right things well.' Doing a few of the right things well is a very good way to run a business, because doing too many things will kill you. You don't have enough resources. Too many small companies die because they attempt fourteen variations on six different themes. That's what 3Com's business plan was—a plan of too many of the wrong things done poorly. That's not to say that we were stupid; it's just to say that we had to grow up, learn to focus on what our business was about, and then concentrate on the two or three things that really needed to be done over the next twelve months."

"My view," says Krause, "was that long-term profitable growth was more important than short-term market share. My theory is that you start out with a set of principles or beliefs, and from those you begin to develop business strategies that are consistent. My purpose in building a business is to create something that will live beyond me. I want people to say they want to join 3Com because it's the best-managed company in Silicon Valley, so I needed to stick with some fundamental principles: make a profit, serve the customer, achieve product leadership, and build a quality organization. They became both conditions of and constraints to our growth. We couldn't take on too broad a market, for example, because how, then, could we be perceived as product leaders? Trying to do too many things might require us to grow faster than our principles would allow us to grow."

"Bill," adds Charney, "would say, 'We don't buy into the philosophy that we'll make profits tomorrow and suck cash today. It's just as easy to make a profit today, and we're not going to fall prey to that intoxicating thought, to put profit off into the future.'"

So far, the fiscal conservatism of people like Krause is only beginning to be reflected elsewhere in Silicon Valley. Top-line growth, points out venture capitalist Myers, is what creates "value" in a company's stock. "Maybe what's changed, though, is how you go about it." There is more pressure today, he acknowledges, to be smarter about not putting too much money into a company too early. And some companies themselves are chary of venture financing precisely because of the superfast growth rates typically demanded by venture investors.

To Charney's way of thinking, however, the lesson couldn't be clearer, both from his own company's experience and the experience of others. "Here's 3Com. It went public in the worst time in years, and its stock went up; it's acknowledged as being a very well-managed company; and it's growing at three hundred percent a year, or whatever. And so you say, 'Well, didn't you miss? You could have grown at five hundred percent a year.' Yeah, yeah . . . but I'm not embarrassed to go to my investors and say that we grew from $4.7 million to $16.7 million this year . . . and we had fifteen percent operating profit in doing so. And I'm still here, and the turnover is low. Maybe there's some lost opportunity, but I find it hard to believe that it's worth the risk."

Other companies' trajectories, he notes, bear out this conclusion. "Fortune [Systems Inc.] made a bet on one computer system with one technology, high flying. They said, 'We're going to staff up to two hundred fifty people; we're gonna raise twenty-six million dollars. I don't care if we are sucking six million a month in negative cash flow.' 3Com took a completely opposite point of view. We said, 'We're going to raise one million dollars. Then, when we kind of think it's all gone, we'll raise another two million dollars. Meanwhile, we'll come out with this little tiny product and see if we can sell it. And if somebody buys it, that'll be great.'

I would say that the probability [of success with Fortune's approach] isn't worth the risk. We have Osborne and Victor and Fortune and Eagle. So we have three or four resounding didn't-make-its. Atari is another. Pizza Time Theatre is another."

But what about the ones that succeeded—Apple Computer, say, or a more recent hot number like Convergent Technologies Inc.? Charney is unshakable. "And then we have Convergent, one which appears to have made it and also took that risk. I don't want to take the Convergent risk as an entrepreneur—that all-or-nothing risk. I just don't think it's worth it.

"The reason I don't is that a more conservative, lower-flying, more controlled growth, more wait-and-see approach has a higher probability of success. I believe it will get you there in the end."

—TOM RICHMAN

"YOU'D BE SURPRISED HOW EASY
IT IS TO SUCCEED"

You have to see the building site through the architect's eyes. To the casual passerby, it is just another construction project, one more pit in the ocher clay of residential Miami. But not to David Wolfberg.

The air is hot today, even in the shaded suburbs, muggy, with gray heads of thunder forming over Biscayne Bay, so Wolfberg stays inside his Mercedes-Benz, air conditioner on high, when he visits the site. He can't afford to muck about in the mud, sweating up the crisp cotton of his monogrammed shirt and getting spots on his polished shoes. Now that Wolfberg/Alvarez & Associates, formerly Wolfberg/Alvarez/Taracido & Associates (WAT), has hit hard times, image is even more important than it was during the glory days of fast growth in the early 1980s.

But even through the tinted window, David Wolfberg sees more than just an imaginary new building—6,000 square feet of offices about to go up for South Miami's Hematology & Oncology Associates, his clients for the job. He sees dollars—and the chance to get his firm moving forward again. In a break with architectural tradition, Wolfberg/Alvarez not only drew the plans, but will also manage the construction—hiring the subcontractors and monitoring cost and quality. If everything goes according to plan, the firm will earn not just the 6 percent architect/engineering fee, but the construction manager's 5 to 10 percent as well. In the future, Wolfberg expects to offer clients even more services: from site selection, environmental reports, and community relations right through to delivery and installation of the furniture and equipment. In time Wolfberg hopes to provide financing, too, or set up joint ventures. Whatever it takes to make his business grow.

About growth, the thirty-seven-year-old chief executive officer considers himself an expert. The company description he gives clients describes Wolfberg/Alvarez as the "fastest-growing" firm in America, and for a time the characterization was believable: WAT soared from sales of $200,000 in 1976 to $6.1 million by 1982, a 2,950 percent growth rate. For two consecutive years it made *Inc.*'s listing of the 500 fastest-growing privately held companies in America; it even hit *Build-*

ing Design & Construction magazine's list of the fifty biggest architectural/engineering (A/E) firms. WAT was celebrated for seizing the technologies and management styles of the future, and its glittering roster of government and private-sector clients reflected its reputation. Virtually overnight it became a national presence, doubling and redoubling staff in a year.

Throughout, Wolfberg basked in the success, convinced that with "inherent skill" like his, business was easy. Then, perhaps inevitably, the growth curve tapered off, slowly at first, then flattening, then plunging downhill. Profits and productivity fell, and the firm that had recently grown so quickly found itself struggling for survival. Yet even that didn't shake Wolfberg's confidence. He had learned his job, he figured, crisis by crisis. The end of growth was just one more lesson in change, albeit the most wrenching.

Now, with the recession behind him, he looks at the yellow-brown hole in the ground and sees only more glorious triumphs. Other architects may scoff. His own staff may be losing faith. But he plans to become the total, modern, market-driven architect—if only he can find the market again.

Few of America's 60,000 architects have found their markets easily in recent years. Profitability among architects has shrunk to an industry average of 3.2 percent of net sales, all this while the nation's architecture schools are annually releasing another 4,900 would-be practitioners into an already glutted market. Good design, most professionals agree, is still the sine qua non of success, but good design isn't enough anymore. Clients are no longer patrons; they have become customers. Design competitions have become price sensitive, with work awarded to the lowest bidder. To survive, architects are being forced to give up the pipe-and-tweed fantasies of exploring art through building, to think of architecture not as a profession but as a business, a service industry.

"I give it five to eight years before the conventional A/E firm is extinct," Wolfberg says flatly. "It just doesn't pay. Other architects can 'pooh pooh' themselves to death."

Not that Wolfberg ever set out to be a businessman. Offered a job running his family's textile-manufacturing business, he chose architecture instead, and helped start WAT specifically to escape the pressures of a business-oriented practice. He and the other frustrated young mavericks who founded the firm in 1976 were idealists, and their objective was to create the New Age A/E firm, a warm and humanistic environment in which creative young talent could thrive.

There were six at the start. Wolfberg, the *wunderkind* design director at Connell, Metcalf & Eddy (now called Connell Associates), a prominent Miami A/E firm, fired for being too cocky, too outspoken— too New York. Julio E. Alvarez, a project electrical engineer at Connell, a Cuban exile, a former employee of the power company, disgusted by the red tape of big companies. Hector Seiglie, who had worked with

Alvarez on occasion; C. David Morton, a solo practitioner with a yen for big projects; and Karl Frese and Manuel Taracido, two more frustrated Connell engineers.

"The whole point was to avoid becoming what we ran away from," Alvarez says. Connell, they felt, dictated design from the bottom line. Connell didn't understand that architects sell *environment*. The distant old men who ran the firm didn't know real design, or care; they spent their time making rules, tightening a corporate chain of command meant to stifle the young and imaginative.

In their company, all six agreed, there would be no bureaucracy, no obsession with profits, and no chasm between management and employees—once they could actually afford employees. The partners would stay involved, rolling up their sleeves and sitting down with blueprints, all six making management decisions in concert. To begin, they aggressively pursued government projects; although that meant filling out reams of forms, at least they could save the cost of four-color brochures and client lunches. On paper, they would vest 51 percent of the business in the firm's Cuban-born partners—Alvarez, Taracido, and Seiglie—so they could check off both "small business" and "minority owned" on all the applications. At first they thought of using a generic name, such as "The Design Group," but settled instead on listing all six names on the letterhead, along with the company's conservative gray and maroon logo.

The fledgling business fell short its first time out, coming in twenty-fourth in a competition to choose twenty-two firms to design Miami's twenty-two new transit stations. It was all politics, Wolfberg steamed, convinced they had been torpedoed by his old bosses at Connell.

For the next three months, until they bid on their second project, the six eked out a living separately from whatever solo work they could find. But when their second chance came up—a new vehicle-maintenance center for the city's trucks and heavy equipment, a $2.6-million garage with a $176,000 design fee—they were ready. The firm's Hispanic partners met with the predominantly minority members of the commission and presented their proposal. And all six partners, with their wives, showed up at the commission hearing.

"I want to win an award with this," the mayor told them when he presented WAT with the job. "You will," Wolfberg replied.

As any businessperson might have predicted, that first success brought the firm's first real crisis. "Once we won the garage, we started spending like drunken sailors," Alvarez remembers. "Then one day there was no money, and that's when the conflict started." The inefficiency of management by consensus would have to go, he told his partners. They needed a CEO, and someone else to manage the cash.

"What do you mean, manage the cash?" one of the partners sneered. "I thought you said there was no money to manage."

But the former idealists had little choice; it was either get down to business or disband. Alvarez began training himself as a financial officer, setting up and monitoring a structured invoice and cash-flow system. Wolfberg became CEO and wrote a business and marketing plan, pledging 12 percent of future sales income to marketing, significantly higher than the industry average. A friendly banker lent them $15,000, and WAT stayed afloat.

Wolfberg sold hard, trying to offset youth and inexperience with local ties, with minority ownership, and, above all, with indefatigable energy. He submitted all of his forms in red folders, so they would stand out on a desk. He spent hours schmoozing with secretaries, trying to convince them to leave the folders on the top of the stack. He tried to anticipate clients' objections. "This time you're not getting somebody's assistant to work on your job, you're getting active participation of the partners," he would tell clients who worried about WAT's small size. "I'm not going to show you pretty pictures," he would say, to disguise the firm's lack of completed projects.

For a while, nothing helped. The partnership's net sales hardly reached $200,000 in that first year. Wolfberg went back to the bank, but WAT's friendly loan officer had been fired. There was no money for partners' salaries; all the partners went nine months without taking a check. The strain began to show. Partners started to drift off, to concentrate on their own projects. The list of names on the letterhead got shorter.

"I became very religious," Wolfberg jokes. "Every time it looked like we would die, a small project would come in through the door. They were dog projects, lots of small renovations, five-hundred-thousand-dollar projects with a thirty-thousand-dollar fee, but at that point we'd take whatever we could get."

By 1979, however, Wolfberg's selling skills and persistence began to pay off. Finally the firm was up and running, with four partners, nineteen other employees, and $579,000 in net sales. The Miami garage was finished; true to Wolfberg's promise, five design awards hung on the wall.

And Wolfberg, the reluctant CEO, started to get frustrated. He wanted more than survival, he wanted growth. Although he didn't know it at the time, that meant he needed computers.

The leap into computers in the fall of 1980 was hardly a rational business decision. Wolfberg didn't even pay much attention when the interviewer from the Army Corps of Engineers asked him if he knew anything about computer graphics. "Sure," he said, and went on talking about the proposed table of organization and equipment.

A table of organization and equipment is, in civilian parlance, a maintenance garage, but this was not just any maintenance garage. WAT was to design twelve different prototype vehicle-maintenance centers, site-adaptable around the world, for the Army. The fee—$500,000—was more than the partnership grossed most years. So when the officer called a month later wanting to modify the contract to specify that the work would be done on computers, Wolfberg didn't hesitate.

"Our biggest customer said we needed a computer, so we went out and bought one. If we had asked a bunch of MBAs to advise us, they would have told us we were crazy. But we didn't ask." Instead, WAT hired a programmer and made a deal for $400,000 worth of hardware, 10 percent down and the balance due in ninety days, the same time the final Army fee came due. "I figured if things went well, it would pay for itself. And if worse came to worse they could just crate it up and take it away."

Computer-aided design and drafting (CADD), by most architects' estimates, is still a technology in search of a function: Systems are not yet well-enough developed to be of much practical use. Wolfberg, although he boasted publicly that CADD would cut design costs to the client by 25 percent, has himself never been enamored of the technology. A computer makes beautiful drawings, he says, but the system threatens his staff, cuts his flexibility, and "really doesn't save me any money." Still, that was all right: Wolfberg never meant to use CADD primarily for design. Instead, he used it as a marketing tool. In that context, he says, "the impact was spectacular."

Completion of the Army project on time, within budget, and on a computer made a name for Wolfberg virtually overnight. Suddenly WAT was swamped with commissions from other high-volume builders. In one month, $2.5 million in fees came through the door, most of it from new clients attracted by the mysterious promise of state-of-the-art architecture. And the work kept coming: fire stations, barracks, and commissaries for the military; corporate headquarters for high-technology companies; a specialized payload handling device for the National Aeronautics and Space Administration's space shuttle—"all clients I wouldn't have gotten without the computer," says Wolfberg. He set up a consulting firm, called AEI CADD, to sell computerized architecture, engineering, and interior design and drafting services. He printed up a glossy brochure to take to trade shows, sweeping in such jobs as an underwater mapping project for Phillips Petroleum Company.

WAT was hot. Now there were never enough bodies for the work, never enough desks for the bodies. The firm kept moving into new offices, first 1,200 square feet, then 2,200, then 4,400, then 8,000. Working at a blackboard, the partners made up a hit list of the talent they could steal from local firms, people like themselves stagnating at places like Connell. Then Wolfberg went on a series of raiding missions, luring forty professionals from his competitors in six months, including nine hired away from Connell in a single three-week blitz.

Hiring them was one thing, Wolfberg admits, absorbing them was another. "When we got to fifty people, we began noticing the big-office syndrome taking hold. There was a lethargy, a tendency to blame the other guy. Not that we were turning into a bad firm; we were turning into a typical firm. We were losing our ability to respond."

It was a time for dramatic moves, and Wolfberg made them. Like most A/E firms, WAT was organized by departments: architecture, electrical engineering, and so forth. A project would move through department after department until it was finished. That was fine when the firm was small, a handful of people working together, but in the white heat of growth it broke down. People assigned to the same project might well be working in different offices. A missed deadline in one department would place the other departments behind schedule, too. Alvarez, watching the invoices, saw disturbing drops in productivity.

Wolfberg tried setting up a stricter organization chart. That didn't help much, and it was dismantled when the grumbling of his new young Turks grew louder. So he decided to try making the business small again. He broke the staff into six teams, specialists from each department under a team leader, and sat them together with their own handful of projects. He turned the team leader into a small-business proprietor, managing the projects and the personnel, acting as prime client contact, sending out invoices and monitoring collections. Each team leader was free to set his own priorities, to trade staff during a crunch, and to help hire more members for his team. Clients liked the instant access the system gave them to every aspect of a project. Employees liked being able to follow a project through to the end.

WAT became a magnet for young talent from across the country. "I'm offering opportunity," Wolfberg would tell prospective recruits. "There are lots of balls lying around. If you want to pick one up and run with it, go ahead." The workload was staggering—nights and weekends were the rule—but so were the opportunities: Young architects and engineers got 10 percent and 15 percent raises, the chance to become team leaders while still in their mid-twenties, the opportunity to manage the design and construction of a forensic hospital, a maximum-security facility for the criminally insane, the first fabric-covered mall in America, or the restoration of the historic Vizcaya Museum and Gardens. Corporate visitors were common; there was a dress code, but there was no quibbling about time clocks, sick days, or taking a sunny afternoon off. And the partners were right in there pitching. Employees called Alvarez "Mr. Alvarez" to his face, and they called Wolfberg "God" behind his back, but the two were "Julio and David" at the softball games and the regular Friday afternoon beer blasts.

By the end of fiscal 1981, a year after WAT leaped in to CADD, productivity was up to $50,000 per employee, 25 percent higher than the industry average, and profits were 13.5 percent of $3.3 million in sales, compared with the industry average of 3.6 percent. The partners introduced "WIP," a work incentive program, promising to distribute all annual profits exceeding 10 percent. They subsequently gave out $100,000 to the staff.

"We were taking the town by storm," Wolfberg remembers. The papers were filled with praise: stories about his garage, his prison, his computer, his style. His in-box was filled with tributes to his "creative use of technology," his "relaxed though thoroughly businesslike attitude," his "professional competency, dependability, and talent."

"If I'd had an MBA, we wouldn't be where we are now," Wolfberg crowed to a local reporter. "I've read all the articles and gone to some of the seminars, and, to be very honest, I think they're mostly garbage.

"Look at how far we have gone. . . . You think creatively and you don't bog yourself down in doing things by the book. Then you'd be surprised how easy it is to be successful."

In 1982, while the papers reported hard times for Miami architects, WAT just kept growing. Sales climbed another 85 percent, up to $6.1 million. Although his firm's profitability was slipping, Wolfberg preached volume, predicting $10 million by 1983. To cap it all off, Wolfberg set his sights on creating new headquarters for the firm. The new offices would be a symbol, concrete proof that WAT had arrived.

As a young architect just out of Ohio State University, Wolfberg had worked in the New Haven practice of Kevin Roche, the architect of record for the United Nations Plaza Hotel and the renovation of the Metropolitan Museum of Art in New York City. He had been impressed that Roche had renovated a decaying mansion for his offices; Wolfberg liked the statement that made. Now, recycling an old telephone switching station into an office for WAT would be his own homage to tradition.

But Wolfberg imagined he could make the building a symbol of much more than just respect for the past. The new building would be his first *project* development: WAT would design, build, manage, and own the property. As such, the building would be a prototype for the many similar ventures he had in mind. Law-plan, he called one such scheme: design, development, and operation of a building specifically geared to lawyers' needs. Med-plan would be a similar arrangement for doctors. "People are looking for a single source of things," he explained. "Doctors don't want to know from interviewing architects and going out for bid and choosing a construction crew and building. They only want to know how much money and how little aggravation."

With these projects, Wolfberg told his staff, he could offer even more opportunity. He had just about reached the ceiling on salaries, he explained, but everyone involved could get a piece of the action with the new office development, once the lawyers worked out the paperwork, and a piece of all the action to come.

The building itself was a triumph, a giant open workroom upstairs for the teams, a huge display room for models and mock-ups next to the computer, space for the bookkeeper, the controller, and WAT's three marketing assistants. WAT moved in.

The recession hit WAT right after the move. The downturn had been going on for a while—the worst recession since the Depression, it was called. Still, Miami fared better than some parts of the country. And WAT had seemed virtually immune. Who else could have grown so fast, come so far, in such otherwise bleak times?

But the recession was only late, not absent. In three fateful weeks in 1982, the firm lost three projects in a row. One project that was delayed was a Miami International Airport central utilities and cogeneration plant; it was a big project, with a $3-million fee. That $3 million alone was almost six months' worth of sales.

Suddenly—even more suddenly than it had grown—WAT was in trouble. And Wolfberg, for once, wasn't sure what to do.

"We were losing money, but we didn't want to let people go," Alvarez remembers. "We kept saying, 'We're going to get a project next month.' It was the intoxication of having won too much. We thought we could do nothing but go up."

With more staff than work, WAT's backlog quickly dropped from a year to two months. Productivity dropped as well. WAT was tied in to long-term commitments for everything from computer equipment to office copiers. Worst of all, the firm's beautifully renovated building, the symbol of its success, was turning out to be a millstone. In addition to the new building's costs, Wolfberg was carrying the lease on his old office, all 8,000 square feet worth. He had used his line of credit for the new space instead of taking out a separate loan. Now, when he turned to the bank for funds, he was turned down cold.

When 1983 sales were down 17 percent from 1982's, Wolfberg and Alvarez had no choice: They had to shed load, dismantling what they had built. First to go were the administrative director, the office manager, and other support staff, "the people you think you need when you're fat," Alvarez says. The marketing team was chopped down to one assistant and two word processors, churning out customized forms. No more trips to conventions. No more overnight packages. Long distance calls were monitored through the switchboard, and all expenses had to be approved in advance. Wolfberg's wife left her full-time position as head of the company's interior design department and became an outside consultant. Alvarez's wife became company counsel.

The softball games and beer blasts withered away as more and more desks emptied out. The young Turks—those who were left— became more and more restless, dispirited, and paranoid. By the beginning of 1984, the company was down to 83 employees, from a high of 154. Miami's other firms began to fill up with old WAT staffers who either had quit or were fired. All carried tales of the broken promises, the crushing workload, and the change that had overtaken the remaining partners.

"People upstairs think we've changed. Well, we have," Alvarez admits. "The recession changed us. There are still some scars left from the downturn. During the period of conquest and glory we were great guys, great leaders. Then we hit the recession. We were no longer growing; the money wasn't flowing in. We had to make hard decisions, like firing the guy who's been playing softball and having a beer with you. That left us with a bitter taste.

"The only thing I resent is that we tried to explain the why in ways no one ever did for us. I knew I wasn't going to make my bank payments if I didn't cut people, but they didn't understand that upstairs. It just made people nervous. They didn't want to hear the truth, they wanted to be comforted.

"So we've become a little secluded. I don't think I can emotionally handle the strain of getting close to these people again."

Today, stepping inside the imposing gray Wolfberg/Alvarez office in suburban Miami is like stepping inside a refuge. Outside it is hot; a Jaguar and a Mercedes, the partners' cars, sit side by side in the parking lot, baking, while traffic rushes by on the busy suburban street. But behind the thick walls it is quiet and cool. A grainy black-and-white blowup of Frank Lloyd Wright hangs behind the reception-ist, frozen in time over a wilting philodendron.

The building also bespeaks an uncertain time for its occupants. The computer blinks and hums away in the back room, but the corridors leading to it are dim, lights off and desks empty. The display room for the models is an echoing cavern. Only two of the original six partners are left, facing each other through the glass walls of their main-floor offices. Alvarez sits beneath a framed letterhead from his grandfather's confiscated Havana business, poring over the daily ex-penses and the weekly invoice forms. Wolfberg still sells hard, but he, like Alvarez, also reads all the incoming and outgoing mail, and checks the weekly reports from the team leaders and the department heads.

Upstairs, away from the partners' closed offices, Wolfberg/Alvarez has changed as well. "It's important for us to be *perceived* as if we're still a big firm," says Wolfberg, but the large workroom feels deserted, with pockets of four or five men clustered in small groups rather than the mobs crowded together during the glory days. Nor do most of the employees sit with their teams any longer. With the staff cuts, quality had started to fall off; the firm was left with too few senior engineers and too many low-priced novices. So Wolfberg reinstituted depart-ments, with department heads responsible for technical accuracy. "But that could change again tomorrow," Wolfberg says. If he has learned anything crisis by crisis, it is the importance of being flexible.

What hasn't changed is Wolfberg's energy and his capacity to spin out strategies, plans, and dreams. No more buckshot marketing, he vows; no more "obsession with volume." Now he will concentrate on profit, aiming at high-payoff/low-labor projects in which his capital investment in computers can make a real difference. He also plans on expanding the services he can offer, just as he is already doing with Hematology & Oncology Associates. "I'm going to be out there offering design, construct, manage, furnish, finance, lease—I'll do whatever you want," he spiels. "Once you get a client, why turn him over to someone else to make money?" Med-plan, he is convinced, is one way to come back, to heal the scars of the struggle, selling busy doctors turnkey architecture. If that doesn't work there is Law-plan, or AEI CADD, his incorporated computer consulting business.

And if these plans don't fly, there is Metro Support Services, which, Wolfberg reports, is "in high gear" for a joint venture with the Wackenhut Corporation to provide forensic hospitals for the public sector—not just to design and build them, but to staff and run them as well, riding the coming wave of privatization.

The recession, Wolfberg claims, "may have been just what we needed." He feels smarter for the trial, and the business may be stronger because of it. Wolfberg/Alvarez shed 54 percent of its expenses while keeping 86 percent of its capacity. The $3-million Miami International Airport plant is back on the board, and for fiscal 1984 Wolfberg expects $5 million to $6 million in sales, with a modest profit. The pared-down staff, with most members in their late twenties to mid-thirties, still racks up impressive numbers. Each professional turns out close to $70,000 in work a year, 75 percent higher than the industry average; team leaders still invoice and collect, with collections averaging forty-three days, about half the time most A/E firms wait. "So I don't think we did anything wrong," Wolfberg says. "With our growth momentum we had always been at the limit. But we landed on our feet, so it wasn't a failure."

Even so, the staff is restless. Team leader Marcel Morlote, in his late twenties, dismisses Wolfberg's new promises as "pie in the sky," but adds, "I don't buy lottery tickets, either. I hope they do something in the immediate future, though, or they'll lose people. Most of the good talent here plans to leave and start their own firms anyway; we're all that kind of people."

"This is still a young firm," agrees Samuel Matthews, a project architect. "In older firms they already have practices for keeping people, but the partners are still struggling with that here. The only really important thing for morale, though, is the perception of where the company is going."

Wolfberg knows how they feel; he was young and impatient once, too. But he is a different man from the young idealist of 1976 or the go-go growth CEO of the early eighties. "Morale has always been bad," he says impatiently. "So what? In the growth period, people complained they were too busy. During the recession, it was no money. Now, it's 'What's my future?'

"I do talk pie in the sky, but my dream is their dream. The most important thing I have to offer is opportunity. I know that. And I know that when the opportunity is gone, I'm going to lose them.

"Let them go start their own firms," he scoffs. "There is a certain delusion about how easy it is to do what we've done. But I'm tired of hearing about the problems of the past. Let's get rid of that baggage. Let's look forward again."

And that, of course, is exactly what he is doing as he looks out the window of his air-conditioned Mercedes at WAT's latest project, the ditch that will one day be doctors' offices. Viewing the site with the eyes not just of an architect but of a man who has learned a lot about business, he shows that his vision, at least, hasn't failed.

"This may *look* like it's just a hole in the ground," he insists, "but it's more, much more."

—CURTIS HARTMAN

OUT ON A LIMB:
Oregon Lumberman Goes High-Tech

It all ended one day, with no fanfare. The trailers laden with Douglas firs that had rumbled past Bob Praegitzer's office stopped coming. There were no more lumberjacks swearing in their cabs, no more power saws buzzing in the yard.

Praegitzer, one of the most successful loggers in western Oregon, moved into a new building 1,000 feet down the road—and, in effect, into a new century as well. After thirty years of felling huge trees, he was jumping into high-technology business of printed circuit boards. It is an industry in which success depends on an exquisitely fine touch: Hundreds of circuit lines, each thinner than a human hair, must be etched onto a glass board. Instead of cumbersome axes and power saws, his instruments would be drilling machines accurate to within one-thousandth of an inch.

To his shocked bankers, who knew Praegitzer as a tough logging man, it seemed that the moon had reversed its orbit around the earth. It was one thing, they felt, to lend him money for timbering the mountain slopes. It was quite another to finance him in a business that they knew nothing about. "My banker," Praegitzer says now, "couldn't understand any business proposal that reached his desk without tree bark on it." His banker might have returned the barb. Unlike hundreds of other high-tech entrepreneurs, whose pedigrees reach back to the computer labs of Massachusetts Institute of Technology or Stanford University, Praegitzer knew almost nothing about the technology of his new venture.

Indeed, only a dizzying boom-and-bust cycle seemed to link logging and circuit boards. Fortunes in logging are made and lost on movements of the housing market. Makers of circuit boards, poised on the fringe of the electronics industry, are even more vulnerable. In the two years since he opened his new plant, Bob Praegitzer has learned much about this similarity—the hard way.

Praegitzer, who is fifty-three, prospered from the ups and downs of the logging business; he says that logging made him financially secure twenty years ago. Even so, he is not a man given to show. His only displays of wealth are his brown Porsche and the recreational vehicle that he drives to Palm Springs, California, or to the Oregon coast to angle for salmon. And although he employs three of his four children, giving them a start in manufacturing and custodial jobs, they labor under his expectation that they, like him, will be self-made.

Dallas, Oregon, where Praegitzer grew up, is a universe removed from the high-tech whirlwind of Silicon Valley. Nestled against the Coastal Range sixty miles south of Portland, it is a rural community in which cows sometimes graze on front lawns. In the fall, one of Praegitzer's associates takes afternoons off to drive a combine.

Praegitzer's first job as a boy was on a local farm, where he earned the $70 he needed in 1944 to buy a green Model A Ford. Only thirteen, he fibbed about his age to obtain a driver's license. During the war, even a vintage Model A was impressive. "Anybody who drove his own car to school was a pretty big wheel," says Praegitzer with a chuckle. A school buddy, Vern Perry, remembers how they used their cars: "We chased girls and drank booze." But Praegitzer had a serious side, too. "When we were kids, there wasn't a lot of money around. Bob always wanted a better life, and he started working for it," says Perry, who now owns his own logging company in Dallas.

Bored by school and fired up by the idea of earning a living, Praegitzer dropped out at age fourteen after the ninth grade. In those glory days of Oregon logging, sawmills hugged the road almost every mile, welcoming burly young men who could handle the huge logs in the yard. Again lying about his age—this time to obtain a work permit—Praegitzer got a job in a sawmill working on the "green chain," pulling cut timber off the line and stacking it.

Praegitzer became a boss at eighteen, and he has never forgotten the experience. Promoted to foreman of a mill work crew despite being the youngest of the group, he found that the men laughed at him when he gave orders. Frustrated, he went to the mill owner, intending to quit. "He said I should go out and fire someone, that if I wanted to be boss I should go fire George," says Praegitzer. "Well, it was a tough thing to do. I went out and told George that we didn't need him any more. From then on I was boss. It was a helluva good lesson in my life."

In 1951, at the age of twenty, Praegitzer quit his job. "I decided that I couldn't stand to work like my father, going to work at the same place at the same time every day for forty years," he says. "I needed a challenge." At the time, two uncles were cutting timber from a 450-acre tract near Dallas, and Praegitzer asked them for the rights to mill the logs. Commitment in hand, he and a partner from school days bought a small portable mill on credit for $1,500.

The partner sold out six months later to Vern Perry, Praegitzer's old buddy; together they borrowed another $8,000 to buy a much larger, stationary sawmill. The new mill was their entry into the big-time logging business, and the two men, still in their early twenties, invested all they had to increase their capacity by 40 percent in only two years. "We just worked hard and didn't spend much money on booze," says Perry.

With a strong market going, the partners felt ready to make their fortune. They hired a hard-working crew of mill hands, who lived with their families close by in a small shantytown of rough lumber and tar paper. Then, one day after work, Perry and Praegitzer went five miles down the road past other mills to look at a stand of timber. Looking back, they saw a column of smoke—and it seemed to be billowing from *their* mill. They raced back in time to see the last of it consumed in flames. Praegitzer is still saddened by the loss nearly thirty years later. "We were ready to cut a fat hog that year, and then the mill burned down," he says mournfuly.

Their insurance was meager, so the pair were suddenly $50,000 in debt. They cut that in half by selling timber. Then Perry quit, feeling he could do better as a paid hand than as an owner. "My accountant said I was crazy to take over the business," Praegitzer says. "But I had faith in myself." Times were hard. "I hunted from necessity," he says. "My kids ate a lot of venison."

His break came when he discovered a niche in the timber business. All the local loggers were cutting the majestic conifers, like Douglas fir; Praegitzer saw a market opening for the smaller and scrubbier hardwoods, such as alder, which are used to make furniture. But at first, he couldn't get the logs to the hardwood mill in Eugene, because the truckers refused to haul them. "The truckers would haul one load and never come back," he says. "They didn't want to be seen with these logs. On the road they'd pass their buddies, who'd be carrying stately Douglas fir, while they'd have brush on their own truck." Other truckers wouldn't even bother loading his wood. "They'd say, 'I'm not going to haul that shit.' They'd see my wood and drive off."

The sawmill eventually sent its own trucks to pick up the wood, and Praegitzer finally made money, netting $21,000 that year and nearly eliminating his debt. That was an important turn in his fortunes: From then on, his business grew, although there were difficulties along the way. In bad economic times, which arrived frequently in the 1970s, he had to lay off some of his roughly 130 employees. He bought a veneer mill in southern Oregon in 1974 but shut it down eighteen months later in a depressed market.

What bothered Praegitzer more than uncertainty, however, was his success. "I'd had visions that I was going to be the biggest logger in the area," he says. "When I was one of the biggest, there wasn't anyplace else to go. The challenge was gone. The excitement was gone." More and more disaffected with logging, he looked around for another business opportunity. He found it, entirely by serendipity. Praegitzer's friend Sally Evans, then a real estate agent, met an engineer named Ed Brown one day in the fall of 1980 at a local watering hole. They got to talking, and Evans asked Brown what he did. Brown, she learned, owned his own circuit-board company. And he was looking for backers.

Ed Brown, who had twenty years of experience in the business, had moved from California to Oregon two years earlier and, with two partners, had started a circuit-board shop called Marion Electronics on a $40,000 shoestring. With so little capital, he had to buy broken or obsolete equipment from the "bone yards"—the backyard dumps—of other board shops. He wanted to inject more capital into the business, and he asked Evans if she knew of anyone who might want to invest.

Within days, Brown met with Praegitzer to give him a tour of his facility. Nothing could have prepared the logger for Brown's ramshackle shop inside an old concrete cherry cannery with a Quonset roof. Because they use large quantities of acids and metals, even the best board shops can smell like a petrochemical plant.

"There was water all over the floors," Praegitzer remembers. "It was a mess. It stank. I was very turned off by the smells. I knew nothing about acids, and here I was walking around with a guy [Brown] who had lost his sight in one eye from acid."

Brown sensed he was in trouble, so he rushed Praegitzer up to Tektronix Inc., the large electronics company in Beaverton, fifty miles away. Tektronix had a much more impressive board shop, filled with shiny stainless steel equipment. For Praegitzer, it was a vision of what a well-capitalized shop could look like.

The two men didn't meet again for several months. Slowly, Praegitzer became more intrigued by the growth potential in electronics. Although circuit-board makers are as invisible to consumers as the folks who supply the buns for a McDonald's hamburger, they produce a sophisticated product that has contributed much to the dramatic miniaturization of electronics. To eliminate individual wires, which take up a lot of room, engineers developed techniques to "print" the wires on the surface of a board as extremely fine lines of conductive material. These printed wires connect hundreds of tiny electronic components plugged into the board. Sophisticated boards—which have helped make possible products from satellites to desktop computers—may have up to twenty-two layers of printed wires.

Figuring he could gain a stake in circuit boards inexpensively, Praegitzer offered Brown a guaranteed $50,000 line of credit at the bank in return for an option to buy 60 percent of the company's stock. But Brown's partners sold out to a Canadian company instead.

Within a few weeks, Brown moved into a back office of Praegitzer's logging shop to draw up a business plan and a layout for a new production facility. Now it was *his* turn to be shocked by an inside look at another industry. "I saw the loggers go in and out," recalls Brown. "They were roughneck guys. They had to talk twice as loud as normal because they still had buzz saws ringing in their ears."

These two men from different worlds, in their marriage of convenience, conducted an informal marketing survey of circuit-board demand in Oregon. They calculated that local electronics plants were using about $50 million worth of circuit boards each year, but only about 10 percent of that came from shops in Oregon. "We were looking at building a three-million-to-five-million-dollar-a-year plant," says Praegitzer, "so there was plenty of market to service."

Geography is an important factor in the business, because circuit boards involve both service and manufacturing. When electronics companies develop a new product, circuit boards are usually the last component designed but among the first needed. Board shops build prototypes, which often require many revisions, and teams from both companies often meet on short notice.

Praegitzer also learned why the circuit-board business has the same kind of boom-and-bust cycle as logging. The total market for circuit boards this year is $4 billion, with a 15 percent annual growth rate, according to Philip Lapin, an associate at Technomic Consultants, a market research firm in Redwood City, California. Half of the dollar volume comes from captive circuit-board shops, owned by electronics companies, which provide boards for their parents. Merchant shops make up the rest of the market, but only three companies— Hadco, Tyco Laboratories, and the Photocircuits Division of Kollmorgen—are in the $100-million-a-year range in annual sales. Only a handful of the 800 or so merchants have sales of more than $5 million a year.

Life for the merchants is a constant balancing act on the precipice. In times of economic expansion, the electronics companies look beyond their captive shops to fill the excess demand. The merchant shops expand their capacity and raise prices sharply. When the economic downturn comes, though, the electronics companies cut off the merchants first; they save the available work for their own shops, which are often able to keep running at full tilt. "That leaves the merchant shops high and dry with even more capacity than they had in the last cycle," says Brian Patterson, president of Kollmorgen Corporation's additive products division. Board makers are battered, too, when specific products go sour. Kollmorgen rode the video game craze for several years, then saw the business nearly disappear. "We lost half our business in a year," says Patterson.

Having learned much of this from Brown, Praegitzer decided to accept Brown's plan to build a state-of-the-art board shop that would aim at the high end of the market. Multilayer circuit boards—used in business computers and other sophisticated equipment—constitute a more stable and profitable market than the relatively simple boards used in many consumer products. Within a few months, Praegitzer's bid for a stake in circuit boards had soared from an option to buy control of Brown's threadbare operation into a $2.5-million investment in a top-of-the-line shop. Praegitzer Industries was born.

By permitting Brown to act as midwife, Praegitzer demonstrated a new management style. He had run the logging company himself, relying on his deep knowledge of the business. He knew little about circuit boards, though, so he delegated most of the decision making. Taking charge of the finances, he ran the rest of the business by consensus, entrusting the technical matters to Brown and other recruits from the circuit-board industry. "I was going on the faith that

Ed Brown could produce people that would make it all possible," he explains.

Praegitzer's banker of fourteen years didn't share his faith and refused to lend him money for the new enterprise—figuring, apparently, that circuit boards had short-circuited his brain. "The business was more Greek to them than it was to me," says Praegitzer, "and it was pretty Greek to me." But another bank in town lent him the money, all guaranteed by his personal assets. "I felt that this plant would be an asset for electronics companies in the area," he says. "I figured I could sell it at a profit if I couldn't make it work." Built on part of the seventy-five acres of industrial land Praegitzer owns in Dallas, the plant opened in October 1981.

Although a recession was then gripping the country, the new company flashed across the sky like a meteor—and for almost as short a time. In Beaverton, Tektronix was having big problems with a merchant shop it was dealing with in California. The company asked Praegitzer Industries if it could produce an important board. Praegitzer said it could, and eventually its engineers shipped the order. Then, like first-time authors submitting a manuscript, they waited with a combination of fear and expectation.

The telephone call finally came. "They said it had failed the simple inspection," recalls Brown. "It felt life-threatening to us, because it was our first product shipped." While the failure seemed devastating to the start-up company, it was hardly noticed at Tektronix, a billion-dollar corporation. "During that time, we were experiencing some really bad performance from some of the people we were dealing with," explains Gene Hendrickson, a general manager at Tektronix's circuit-board manufacturing plant. "If we got a shipment from Praegitzer that didn't work out, it would've seemed like just some noise on the line."

In a surprise move, Tektronix came to Praegitzer with a tantalizing proposal. The company was phasing out its circuit-board shop while building a more modern one, and it thought that Praegitzer Industries had the equipment and talent to help take up the slack. The deal: Tektronix would buy virtually all of Praegitzer's output for the next eighteen months. For Praegitzer, it would be like skiing St. Moritz after an avalanche warning: The ride was sure to be exhilarating, but if the mountain collapsed he would be in real trouble. Before agreeing to do the work, Praegitzer got a commitment from Tektronix not to cut off the work precipitously when the big company opened its new board shop. Instead, Tektronix would reduce the work by only 10 percent a quarter, a rate that would enable Praegitzer to find other customers.

That commitment died in the recession. Its business eroding, Tektronix cut off all of its business with Praegitzer in June 1983. "They warned us about it," says Praegitzer. "We were lax in getting out in the marketplace sooner than we did to drum up new business." Bill Bailey, Praegitzer Industries' vice-president of marketing, adds, "We didn't react quickly enough. We could have said we're not going to take the next order [from Tektronix]. We should have found other customers." It had been a sensational ride for the company, but now the mountain *had* collapsed. Sales plummeted 67 percent in one month. Expensive equipment was idled. The company laid off twenty people, more than a quarter of its workforce. So unprepared was the company that it didn't even have a sales force to scout for new business. Scrambling, two marketing executives hit the road to call on prospective customers.

What really helped save Praegitzer Industries, however, was the vigorous economic recovery, which buoyed the circuit-board business by the late summer of 1983. Within months of losing Tektronix, the company had replaced the business, and then some. "By October," says Praegitzer, "we were well-enough known and the business climate had improved. We were swamped with orders."

At the moment, Praegitzer's business is strong. He expects sales to reach $8.5 million this year, only his third full year of operation, and $25 million two years hence. He is investing another $2.5 million in plant and equipment, and plans to have triple his present capacity by the end of 1985. The reasons for expansion were compelling. The production people argued that they needed more capacity to smooth out bottlenecks and that a line for making prototypes of new boards would be a service to customers. The marketing people pointed to the orders they were turning away because all of the company's present capacity was booked.

Even so, history cautions that what is compelling in circuit boards isn't always wise. By expanding so rapidly, Praegitzer risks trapping himself deeply in the boom-and-bust cycle of the industry. Although the company has contracts that run a year into the future, recessions have often bloodied the business for longer than that.

The company's work in the high-end, multilayer part of the market, which is not highly dependent on fickle consumer spending, may shield it a little from a general downturn. However, Praegitzer Industries still looks vulnerable because it has not diversified its sales by product lines.

Although diversification is a goal, says vice-president Bailey, "right now we're reacting to the market. We don't have to go out and look for work. It comes to us." As a result, the company does half of its business in circuit boards for computers. It does little work in the fast-growing communications market, and at the present time it doesn't have certification for defense work, an area that is growing rapidly under the Reagan Administration's military budgets.

Nor is diversification the only unrealized strategic goal. Bailey says that devoting more than 20 percent of the company's capacity to one customer is "asking for trouble." But Praegitzer Industries now does 50 percent of its business with Hewlett-Packard Company and 25 percent with Tektronix. The business with HP is spread among six different divisions of the company, which lessens the risk. But a deep recession could cut the need for circuit boards throughout HP, or a corporate decision could send the work either in-house or to another supplier.

Troubled by his inherent vulnerability as a supplier, Praegitzer plans to become an equipment manufacturer someday. "As long as you're a subcontractor," he says, "you're dependent on somebody else, on whether your customer's product will sell." He already owns 35 percent of a company that makes industrial printers, and he is looking at other products he can manufacture in-house.

For Praegitzer, who always wanted to be his own boss, that would be another major step in his business career. One metamorphosis in a lifetime apparently isn't enough. Not every business proposal, as he says, has to have tree bark on it—or circuit boards, either.

—STEPHEN SOLOMON

LACK OF FORESIGHT SAGA

Bob Praegitzer is a man who takes big risks, whether changing careers or conducting day-to-day business. Recently, his approach backfired.

In 1981, Praegitzer set out to build a plant for his company, Praegitzer Industries, a manufacturer of printed circuit boards. To finance the plant, he personally took out a five-year, $800,000 mortgage at 16¾ percent from Family Federal Savings & Loan in Dallas, Oregon. Two years later, he wanted additional financing on the property. That, the bank said, would require a new mortgage to replace the old one. And because the old one was thus being terminated, Praegitzer would have to pay a $50,000 prepayment penalty.

Praegitzer devised a risky strategy to avoid the penalty. He would stop payments on the mortgage. Then, on receipt of the bank's demand letter warning of imminent foreclosure, he would pay the outstanding balance and any interest due. Praegitzer figured that the bank's action, short of legal foreclosure, would save him the prepayment penalty.

Family Federal, though, regarded the technical default as a real default. The bank skipped the demand letter and instead filed a formal foreclosure action in the local courthouse.

When the foreclosure action hit the local newspaper, one reader who, by his own account, was "quite surprised and none too happy" was Bill Zurcher, vice-president of Rainier National Bank in Seattle. Rainier was one of several banks negotiating with Praegitzer Industries on an industrial revenue bond issue. Within days, the bank withdrew from the talks because of its concern over the circumstances surrounding the foreclosure action. "I think *bizarre* is a good word for this—it's not normal," says Zurcher.

Praegitzer insists that neither he nor his company is in financial difficulty, but he admits that his ploy to save $50,000 has boomeranged. "If I had known what a god-awful fuss was going to get made of all this, of course I wouldn't have done it," he says.

—NELL MARGOLIS

MUTUAL BENEFITS:
One Company's Profitable Collaboration

Jon Peddie felt vaguely uneasy, perhaps even a little irritated, as he sped along California's Highway 17 last October, on his way from Berkeley to Monterey. With him were two of his top managers from Jupiter Systems, a fledgling maker of high-performance graphics equipment, of which Peddie was founder and president. Their destination was a resort hotel overlooking the Pacific Ocean, where they were to attend some sort of business conference—for what purpose Peddie was not exactly sure. He had made the commitment to go several weeks before, but now he had visions of spending two days in boring meetings followed by boring banquets while, back at the office, a major bid sat waiting to be completed. Quite frankly, the prospect made him apprehensive.

What was this meeting all about, anyway? Peddie knew little about the other participants, their companies, or the businesses they were engaged in. What were they going to talk about? What did they have to say to each other? Why were they even being brought together?

Indeed, they were a disparate group—the founders and managers of ten young technology companies working in fields that seemed only tangentially related. Their products spanned the diverse frontiers of information processing—from superfast integrated circuits to specialized microcomputers to medical imaging systems. Some of the companies had annual revenues approaching the $20-million mark; others had no revenues at all. But appearances notwithstanding, the companies did have at least one thing in common: Each had recently sold a minority equity interest to the host of the two-day gathering in Monterey, a $214-million, Massachusetts-based electronics company by the name of Analog Devices Inc. And therein lies a tale.

Founded in 1965, Analog Devices was in the business of making electronic components for scientific and engineering applications. Over the years, it had managed its growth well, seizing diversification opportunities as they presented themselves and developing most of its new products from within. But about four years ago, as the pace of technological innovation began to quicken, Analog founder and chairman Ray Stata looked ahead and saw trouble. The market for the company's electronic components was changing and changing fast. Within a few years, new products would be available with capabilities that would far surpass those of Analog's old products. Unless the company found better ways to respond to this challenge, he feared that the days of impressive growth would soon be over. "To do what we needed to do," Stata explains, "we had to regain some of the facility and flexibility of a much smaller company." The question was, how to do it?

Stata didn't believe that Analog had the internal resources to respond effectively, and he knew that he could go out and acquire a bunch of young companies only at the risk of losing key talent through defection. Instead, he decided to try something different. "Our idea was to create a series of relationships with promising companies," Stata says.

By "relationships," Stata meant quasi-partnerships—arrangements that would serve both Analog and the companies with which it became involved. Each relationship would have to be nurtured individually, in keeping with the interests of the small company founders and their key employees. Some of the companies might eventually be acquired; others would not. If the approach was going to work, notes Stata, "everything had to be built on mutual benefits."

All of this could, of course, prove expensive. Somehow Analog would have to find the cash to finance the outside investments without undermining its own ability to fund internal product development. Stata and senior vice-president Larry Sullivan decided to approach Standard Oil Company (Indiana), which was a minority shareholder in Analog, and one with diversification ideas of its own. Standard Oil agreed to advance Analog $10 million a year to invest in promising young technology companies. In exchange, the giant oil company would receive options to buy additional shares in Analog at a future date.

With Standard Oil's money, Analog established relationships with the ten companies that gathered in Monterey last October. In a sense, the companies represented Analog's vision of the future, a vision that was still in the process of being defined. With that in mind, Analog had called the conference—to give the far-flung entrepreneurs a chance to explore the ways in which they might learn from each other and the directions in which the various relationships might lead.

The entrepreneurs soon realized that they were part of an unusual experiment. Meeting in a second-floor conference room of the hotel, they began to feel a certain camaraderie. "It was almost as if we were members of a club," Peddie recalls. But what kind of a club? Were they simply pieces in an unorthodox venture capital portfolio? Were they future candidates for acquisition? Or were they pioneers developing an entirely new type of corporate entity? Nobody seemed to know.

Indeed, everyone shared that sense of exploring the unknown— even Ray Stata, who stood up to make some after-dinner remarks following the first day of meetings. "Many of us expected him to raise the flag and talk about how Analog reached the two-hundred-million-dollar mark and grew to three thousand employees," says Peddie. Instead, Stata presented himself as another entrepreneur who, like everyone else in the room, was still searching for solutions. "He told us that he was still muddling through problems one step at a time, much the way he did when he ran a five-million-dollar or ten-million-dollar company. And he said something that made an impression on a lot of us. To be successful, he said, you couldn't just depend on doing things better. You also had to be willing to do things differently."

Sitting in his office in Norwood, Massachusetts, twenty miles south of Boston, Stata elaborated on this message: "I wanted to get across the sense that even as a company gets larger and more mature, it never *really* gets there. You become more professionally managed, only to find that you need to become more entrepreneurial and less formal. There's always another challenge around the corner."

For Analog, the immediate challenge was to learn how to work with a group of developing companies, harnessing their entrepreneurial energy without undermining or crushing the creative forces within them. It was a task that had stymied many large corporations in the past, as Stata was well aware. Analog had one distinct advantage, however: It had been a small, entrepreneurial company itself not so very long ago.

In many ways, the Analog experiment had its roots in the early history of the company—going back to 1965, when Ray Stata teamed up with Matthew Lorber, his former roommate at Massachusetts Institute of Technology, to get into the electronics business. Their idea was to launch the company by producing components known as operational amplifiers (op-amps)—devices used by military contractors, medical-equipment makers, research laboratories, and others to process signals that measure real world conditions, such as temperature and pressure, with a high degree of accuracy.

At the time, preassembled op-amps were in short supply. People who needed such components often wound up making their own. Stata and Lorber figured that they could use their off-the-shelf models as a wedge into the market, allowing them to form strong relationships with customers. "We saw an opportunity to create a very broad customer franchise and to build our name in a particular corner of technology," says Stata.

Given that strong market orientation, it was essential for Analog to have a highly skilled sales force, and Stata proceeded to hire trained engineers to call on prospective customers. Not only could these engineers explain the precise performance parameters of Analog's existing components, they were also knowledgeable enough to alert Analog to the changing needs of customers and to suggest new components for the company's product line.

Back in 1967 and 1968, for example, John Harwood, one of Analog's first sales representatives, had a customer called Technicon Instruments Corporation, in Tarrytown, New York, a maker of electronic medical equipment used in the clinical analysis of blood. In the course of making his sales calls, Harwood became aware of a problem Technicon's engineers were having in the design of an upcoming product. What they needed was a new component that didn't exist—one that could convert readings of light into numbers. Harwood relayed the information to Stata. "I told him about my customer's projected requirements," says Harwood, who still sells for Analog in the New York area. "It was Ray who decided to commit the resources."

Over the years, this was a pattern that repeated itself again and again, and—little by little—Analog's product catalogs began to get thicker.

That same sensitivity to the changing market led to Analog's first acquisition, in 1969. At the time, the minicomputer revolution was gathering momentum, and Stata saw an urgent need for Analog to adjust its product line accordingly. "The same customers who were buying our op-amps needed the ability to translate analog signals into digital signals that computers could read," he recalls. Rather than develop the technology from within, he decided to spend about $1 million for a small company, Pastoriza Electronics Inc., that had pioneered in the development of analog-to-digital conversion devices.

That year brought another decision with even more far-reaching implications: the move into manufacturing integrated circuits. Again, Stata looked at changes in technology—this time, the trend toward smaller and more complex electronic components. His conclusion was that Analog would have to become a player in the emerging market for silicon chips, or it would almost certainly pay a price in future growth. The capital investment would be in the millions of dollars, a huge bite for the company, which had annual sales of about $9 million at the time. But Stata considered the move so important that he was determined to raise the capital one way or another—and eventually did so through an initial public offering.

To enter the semiconductor business, Analog took an unusual approach that, in some respects, foreshadowed its future experiment with Jupiter Systems and the other participants in the Monterey conference. Instead of developing the new capability from within or acquiring an existing company, Stata worked out a deal with a talented team of young engineers from another Massachusetts company. "They had the technology, and we gave them the capital to form a new company," Stata recalls. The new company was called Nova Devices Inc. It started out with initial equity of about $2 million—and the use of Analog's aggressive marketing organization. In addition, Stata negotiated with Nova's founders for options to buy the rest of the business as it achieved success in an emerging new field.

"Our goal was to become a market leader," says Stata. "So we figured that the least risky approach was to get some of the best people in the world working on our team." The gamble paid off. Analog completed its purchase of Nova Devices in 1971. In 1973, its semiconductors represented about 25 percent of sales totaling $22 million.

In the late 1970s, two major areas of concern began to converge, both of which affected Analog's ability to identify and react to changes in technology. On the one hand, the company was finding it harder and harder to finance the costs of research and development without undermining the expansion of the more established product areas. Then again, even when the capital was available, management had trouble recruiting and training all the different experts it needed.

As far as the capital problem was concerned, the situation was aggravated by the sorry state of the stock market at the time, which pretty much ruled out a secondary public offering. "The stock market was essentially dead in 1976 and 1977," recalls senior vice-president Larry Sullivan. So, in the summer of 1977, Analog worked out an equity deal with Standard Oil, which invested $5 million, receiving 15 percent of Analog's stock in exchange.

The shortage of trained experts, however, posed an altogether different sort of problem—one, moreover, that money alone could not solve. It manifested itself in Analog's apparent inability to develop certain products—for example, a new line of electronic converters that could process high-frequency video information for use in CAT scanners and other high-speed instrumentation. The company had attempted twice to develop the expertise internally, and twice it had failed. "We were discovering that there was a substantial gap between what we knew and what we needed to know," says Stata.

Eventually, Analog solved that particular problem by acquiring, in late 1978, a small ($3 million a year) company in North Carolina named Computer Labs Inc. But as Stata and his top managers began to formulate plans for the 1980s and beyond, they realized that this was only one in a growing list of new areas in which Analog needed comparable expertise.

Not that the company was in any immediate trouble. On the contrary, it appeared to be at the peak of health, with annual sales fast approaching the $100-million mark. Within a few years, however, various breakthroughs in technology—the introduction of very-large-scale integrated circuits and the like—would dramatically alter the marketplace, reducing the cost of processing systems and thereby inhibiting the growth of Analog's basic business in assembled components and linear chips. Already some customers were beginning to demand more than just components. Down the road, as the cost of powerful circuits plummeted, more and more customers would be looking for complete systems to process analog information—systems that would, in effect, allow them to automate their laboratories and factories.

"The lines between systems and components were beginning to blur," says Stata. "If we saw life as only a component company, we knew we'd be losing out."

During the winter of 1979–80, a task force of Analog's top executives and engineers got together for a few hours every Saturday morning to map out an approach to the challenges ahead. They soon realized that there were all kinds of fields the company should move into, or at least know about—from advanced chip design, to peripheral devices, to microcomputer engineering. Unfortunately, Analog did not have the resources to pursue so many things at once. "All of our cash and all of our people—even new people we would hire—were going to be tied up expanding the businesses we were already in," Stata notes. "And there were some important internal diversifications that we needed to support as well." Yet Analog could not afford to ignore the coming changes in the market. "We knew we needed to cross a lot of new frontiers so we could maintain parity with competitors."

In an effort to find a solution, Stata and Sullivan flew to Chicago in June of 1980 for a meeting with executives from Standard Oil, to whom they explained their predicament. "They told us about the areas they felt they should be moving into," recalls Gordon C. McKeague, president of Amoco Technologies Company, a subsidiary of Standard Oil. "And the vision they had for the electronics industry seemed to make a lot of sense."

Later that summer, Standard Oil agreed to collaborate with Analog in an unusual type of joint venture. Analog would set up a new subsidiary, called Analog Devices Enterprises (ADE), which would make investments in small companies in important areas of technology. The money for the investments, up to $10 million each year, would be furnished by Standard Oil, which would receive preferred stock convertible after five years to common shares in Analog, based on the amount of investment money advanced to the new subsidiary.

"We now had an extra source of money," Stata notes. The next step was to locate the companies to invest in.

ADE got started in the fall of 1980 much as any new venture capital firm would: With money and an eye for talent, it began looking for deals in promising niches of technology. But unlike a venture firm, ADE had goals that were not strictly financial. "Analog had its own diversification shopping list," says Sullivan, who headed up the effort. "We were looking for situations that seemed to smell right."

The first such situation presented itself in the form of a team of Utah engineers who approached Analog for seed capital to produce digital signal processing circuits. "We were familiar with the field," recalls Bob Boole, ADE's director of venture analysis and Analog's former head of corporate marketing. "What they had, and what we wanted, was a different process for making high-speed circuits." Sullivan and Boole studied the proposal and ran it by an advisory panel made up of Analog's own marketing and engineering people—whereupon they wasted no time in deciding to invest $700,000. The agreement left open the possibility that the Utah group might eventually sell the company, called Signal Processing Circuits Inc. (SPCI), to Analog. (In fact, they did just that.)

With one investment in hand, Sullivan and Boole continued to search for opportunities in other areas of importance to Analog's future. They were particularly interested in the new field of array processors, peripheral devices used for boosting the number-crunching capabilities of minicomputers. Such devices had many potential applications for Analog's customers. They could, for instance, be used to enhance computer-aided design by making it possible to test a new product's structural soundness almost instantly, in so-called real time.

For more than a year, Boole and Sullivan scoured the East and West coasts for the right company. "We talked to everyone who would talk to us—in all, about eight or nine different possibilities, including possible start-ups," says Boole. Along the way, they learned a lot about the emerging industry and its players, but "we had a hard time finding the right mix of product and people."

Then, one day, they noticed a product advertisement placed by a company called CNR Inc. in a technical publication. Through it, Boole contacted Peter Alexander, the architect of an unusually fast array processor. ADE agreed to invest $1.5 million—to pay CNR for the rights to the design and to capitalize the new business formed by Alexander. In return, Analog received a modest share of equity in the new company, called Numerix Corporation.

Another area that seemed to hold promise for Analog was digital image processing, a technology that uses computers to assist in interpreting medical and earth-resources photographs. Early in 1981, Sullivan and Boole set out to locate a vehicle for participating in this field, and soon stumbled on a whole nest of image-processing specialists in and around Silicon Valley. On an impulse, Boole decided to phone Richard Ashcroft, president of International Imaging Systems Inc. (I²S), in Milpitas, California, to see if Ashcroft had any interest in talking with him.

At the time, I²S was six years old, with $6 million a year in revenues and a passel of cash problems. Ashcroft, a marketing man with a background in engineering, was spending much of his time exploring options with venture capitalists. "We had known Analog [only] as a component vendor," he says. But the more he learned about Analog's entrepreneurial operating style and its ambitions for the future, the more intrigued he became with the possibility of developing a long-term relationship. "They could give us money and advice like a good venture capitalist, and they could also provide technical support for our products and the resources of a large company.

In June of 1981, ADE invested $3 million in I²S, receiving about 45 percent of its equity in return. "Dick Ashcroft and his people helped us understand the potential for the business," says Boole. "We knew about the current applications for image processing. But they made us aware of whole new areas that we could help them develop in the future."

Indeed, the search for investment opportunities was taking them in a variety of unexpected directions, leading them to technological areas of which they had been unaware. They discovered, for instance, that the users of array processors had very specialized software needs, and that meeting those needs would help the market develop more fully. The insight prompted Analog's decision, in late 1982, to invest $500,000 in Quantitative Technology Corporation, a new company in Portland, Oregon. "When we started out, we had no idea that software was such an important concern," explains Sullivan. "But after a year in the business, we were getting smarter."

Through its exposure to image processing, Analog also had learned of the importance of high-resolution computer graphics for sophisticated industrial applications. So Boole began looking at and contacting companies in the field. Then, in the summer of 1982, he attended a computer graphics trade show in Boston, where he encountered Jupiter Systems. "Bob Boole saw our product demonstration and he was very up-front," recalls Jon Peddie. "He said Analog was interested in graphics and was making selective investments in related technologies."

As it happened, Jupiter had nearly exhausted the start-up capital from its founders, and Peddie was already in touch with a number of financing sources. As he explored the various possibilities, he became more and more interested in ADE. Sullivan and Boole had many years of marketing and financial experience between them, and they understood the dynamics of building a technology company and the difficulty of achieving success in any market. Moreover, in contrast to many of the venture capitalists Peddie had met, they were forthright about Analog's corporate objectives, without being heavy-handed or arrogant. "Most venture capitalists come in and *tell* you how much money you need," says Peddie. "They have their sights set on taking the company public. [Sullivan and Boole] made it clear that they might be interested in acquiring us someday if everything worked out, but we, as the founders, would always be free to change our minds if it didn't feel right. Nobody would pressure us to do something we weren't comfortable with. They seemed more interested in growing a tree than a weed." The discussions culminated in a $2-million deal in June 1983, which gave ADE about a fifth of Jupiter's equity and an opportunity to buy more in the future if Jupiter decides to give up more equity.

Meanwhile, ADE was also making investments in companies it had no intention of ever acquiring. Since 1982, for example, it has put $3 million into Charles River Data Systems Inc., of Framingham, Massachusetts. The company, founded in 1973, had recently begun making specialized microcomputers for scientists and engineers. Its first such computer was designed around a powerful new microprocessor—Motorola Inc.'s 68000 chip—that gave it the processing capabilities of much costlier systems. Charles River's young founder and president, Rick Shapiro, had made plain his intention to take his company public someday. He was therefore not the least bit interested in selling out to Analog, or anyone else for that matter. On the other hand, ADE could not ignore Charles River's technology, which was bound to affect Analog's traditional market. "We knew that this type of computer would have an impact on our business," says Sullivan. "So we decided to get involved with Charles River Data simply to learn about where the industry was going."

ADE took a similar approach to GigaBit Logic, a Newbury Park, California, start-up that was developing new, high-speed chips made of a substance called gallium arsenide for applications in computers. Like Shapiro at Charles River Data, GigaBit founder and president Fred Blum wanted his company to remain independent. Analog respected that position. "We talked to them about their objectives, and we came up with an arrangement that had something for both of us," says Sullivan. ADE agreed to invest $1.5 million to help GigaBit gear up for production. In addition to equity, Analog obtained the rights to market some of the new gallium arsenide semiconductors as soon as they became available and, in the future, to produce its own semiconductors in noncompetitive products using GigaBit's proprietary technology.

Whatever Analog's long-term goals were with regard to specific companies, it was committed to making the relationships work. And it still is. To some degree, after all, they share a common future. So it is in Analog's own interest to see that these companies thrive.

Toward that end, Sullivan and Boole have joined the boards of directors of several portfolio companies and have arranged for other Analog executives to do likewise. At meetings and in telephone conversations, they offer ideas on subjects ranging from how to buy test equipment to how to hire key personnel. "We make comments, and we try to give the entrepreneurs the resources they need," explains Sullivan. "But we don't tell them what to do. It's up to them to run the business. If it doesn't make sense, they won't do it."

When specific problems arise, Sullivan and Boole often refer the entrepreneurs to experts at Analog. "There's a tremendous amount of experience within that company," says Jupiter's Peddie. "Even in areas where they haven't been totally successful, they've learned lessons that they're willing to share."

In addition, Analog has encouraged the companies to collaborate. As young businesses in related technologies, they frequently face similar challenges. Last summer, for example, both I²S and Numerix wanted to expand their marketing efforts in the oil industry, but neither could justify the expense of hiring a full-time, Houston-based salesperson. "I suggested that they talk to each other," says Sullivan, a director of both companies. They did—and decided to get together and hire a salesperson between them.

It was the desire to explore further synergy that led Analog to call the Monterey meeting last fall. And, in fact, as the entrepreneurs discussed their businesses over a two-day period, they began to discover a variety of overlapping interests. There was talk of other joint sales and marketing efforts and of combining on volume purchases of components, such as memory chips, to qualify for lower rates. Some of the companies even explored the possibility of buying from and selling to one another. And all of them traded ideas on ways to motivate and reward their employees as their businesses grow in the years ahead.

"Monterey provided a forum for everyone to get to know one another," says Sullivan, who helped host the event. "And there was an awful lot of mixing."

The October meeting, however, offered no clear answers to the fundamental questions at the heart of Analog's experiment. How much independence, for example, will the portfolio companies have if and when they are acquired? And what incentives can Analog provide to encourage the people who created the companies to stay on as part of a much larger business organization?

Analog is still searching for answers to these questions. During recent visits to I²S and other affiliated companies, Stata has been talking with groups of employees about the importance of mutual benefits in any successful relationship. Analog would be foolish, he contends, to exercise an option to buy any portfolio company without the full backing of its people. "We're not interested in forcing a shotgun marriage on anyone. The onus is really on us to create the type of environment that people want to be part of."

As for Analog itself, Stata has no illusions about the challenges ahead. "We don't know what will happen as we grow from two hundred million dollars to five hundred million dollars and larger—whether we'll be able to fight off rigor mortis and bureaucratic diseases. But through all of these affiliations, we're trying as hard as we can to be a company that maintains the vitality and flexibility of a much smaller business."

It will, of course, be years before the results are in. In the meantime, the mere fact that Analog is trying bears witness to the strength of its entrepreneurial spirit. "This is really unplowed ground," says Stata. "And if we succeed, we will have untied a Gordian knot."

—BRUCE G. POSNER

YOUR OWN WORST ENEMY

Would you pay a consultant $75,000 or more for knowledge you already have? There are those who do, in frustration or desperation. The consultants they pay are specialists in corporate rescues and turnarounds. One such specialist is Morton H. Scheer, president of Service Resources Corporation in New York City, who defines the problem in this way: "I don't care what they want to call it in Washington. We're in a major recession. For our clients, it's a question of survival."

Scheer and his partner, Robert Rosen, have been turnaround consultants for fourteen years. Both insist that the bottom-line problem is always top management. "The typical client," explains Scheer, "is an entrepreneur who has been in the same business for many years. His strength is in sales or production, seldom finance. Most of the people around him grew up with him and his business, and they are close—so close the chief executive can't bring himself to suddenly get tough."

"By the time we get his call, he's already in deep trouble," says Rosen. "We never get an early call. It's always a case of crisis management."

"Many managers just can't believe that anyone knows any more about their business than they do. And in a lot of ways they're right; we're not geniuses with some whiz-kid solutions," says Scheer. "All we sell is common sense, but there are a lot of managers who just will not take advice until it's almost too late."

In an interview with *Inc.*, conducted by freelance writer John J. McNamara, Jr., Scheer and Rosen were asked how small businesses can avoid the need for turnaround specialists and succeed in an economy punctured by corporate setbacks. Their advice is summed up in these ten "dos and don'ts" for management.

1. Set up a realistic cost system, and keep it updated.

We have had clients who start their cost system by saying, "This is what the product has to sell for. We've got to beat our competition." That is unrealistic. For all you know, your competition may be *giving* it away. Realistic costing must cover all of the items that go into your product, even some of the interest. After that, if you can't get your price, walk away. There is no sense going broke on volume.

A while back, we were asked by some lenders to help a cutting-tool manufacturer, a client whose raw materials were exotic steels and whose labor was very skilled and expensive. Ten years before, the manufacturer's accountants had set up a costing system whereby retail pricing was adjusted on the basis of the increases in the monthly federal figures for inflation. It was neither a realistic nor a sufficient adjustment; the manufacturer was losing his shirt. Further, he had bought an expensive plant and elaborate machinery. We got him back to health by advising him to sell the plant and equipment and subcontract for the supply of his base products. He is no longer an original equipment manufacturer, but he now has a simple, profitable business by adding 35 percent to 45 percent to his known costs.

Also, remember that it is the little things that can get you. Cost out and control your waste fully. For example, many people forget that a round piece from a flat bolt has an inherent 25 percent loss. Take a hard and careful look at what you are throwing away. We once had a paint-manufacturing client who was discarding $400,000 or more of what he thought were unusable pigments. We convinced him to install a spectrograph machine that enabled him to blend this waste into other usable shades. He reduced his waste to nothing. Furthermore, he had been spending nearly $100,000 for trucking and disposal. Where you can't reduce or eliminate waste, don't forget the cost of ultimate disposal with all the new environmental regulations.

2. *Review expenses regularly. Keep them in line with actual business.*

Let your expenses increase only as actual sales increase. Before you decide to put on a big sales push, take a hard look at what you did last year; work up a budget estimate of what the push is really going to cost; and be sure the goals are attainable. Hold the fixed costs, such as general and administrative, where they are. Keep a lid on production costs. Expect selling expenses such as travel and entertainment to go up, but stay on top of them. Check your budgeted and actual expenses monthly—don't wait for year-end surprises.

Too many small businesses do exactly the opposite. They set a big sales goal and hire new salespeople to achieve that goal. At year end, when they don't make it, they wonder how they got hurt. There can be a lot of pitfalls to an unrealistic sales push. Beware of the "order takers" and salespeople who move your product with gimmicks, volume discounts, price concessions, and consignment deals—sometimes with management's permission, but often without. To meet their goals, your own people can get you into deals of which you are unaware.

3. *Keep up on your market yourself, and see what is selling.*

If your company is going to stay on top, you need to get away from your desk, get into the market, and see what is selling. No matter how far up you are in management, you must always work at sales.

In most small businesses, the chief executive officer is the person who built the company. In the process, he established personal relationships with the buyers of his product. But as the company grew, these buyers began to deal more and more with new and unfamiliar salespeople than with the CEO. That shouldn't be allowed to happen—the CEO must continue to cultivate his early contacts.

4. Insist on monthly financials generated internally.

Many managers don't learn the financial facts until long after the period is closed. Too many self-made CEOs look on their financial and administrative people as dead overhead and don't confide in them. In some smaller companies, the CEO still signs the checks, so the financial and administrative people may feel intimidated. Ideally, the chief executive should have a triumverate of managers immediately below him—the finance manager, the production manager, and the sales manager—all on an equal footing. Too often they are not equal, and the financial manager is the low person on the totem pole.

5. Include the cost of money in your cost of goods sold.

That may defy standard accounting principles, but you just can't leave the cost of money as a below-the-line item anymore. In the past year, most small companies have paid 18 percent to 19 percent or more to borrow. In the old days of cheap money, it probably made sense to keep interest out of the cost of goods. But today, even for companies operating on a 35 percent gross margin, the cost of money could amount to 12 percent to 15 percent of the item sold. We recommend adding another line to the costing sheets and throwing in a major portion of that 18 percent money cost.

6. Don't fall in love with inventory; it costs money to carry it.

There is nothing wrong with being back-ordered ten to thirty days. A "same-day shipment" inventory is very costly. If your inventory is seasonal, dispose of it seasonally. Many managers postpone the write-down of closeouts, believing that inventory will make them look good with their lenders. A knowledgeable lender can walk through a plant and spot dated inventory in no time. If you keep holding on to it, the loss will be larger later.

7. Create individual profit centers by product line.

This will enable you to identify marginal or unprofitable lines. You can determine whether your loss leaders are really necessary to sell a whole line. Too often they just aren't worth it. An individual accounting of each product line will soon tell you.

Not long ago, we were working with a photographic-equipment distributor who was handling fifty different lines. When we got through our analysis, product line by product line, it was obvious that the most prestigious lines were the least profitable. We got the distributor to cut back to the eighteen lines on which he was really making money. And it worked, with a funny twist. The most prestigious German lens manufacturer couldn't believe it when he was told he might be dropped. The manufacturer had been getting paid by letter of credit on shipping documents, and that front-end interest really hurt our client. When the German manufacturer saw that our client was serious about dropping the line, it switched the terms to consignment, and the line became profitable.

8. Insist on daily reporting from your production people.

If production schedules are not met, find out why. Many managers have no clear picture of what is coming off their production lines. A recent client, a filter manufacturer, was continually late on deliveries and getting into a cash bind. We learned that upper management had never investigated the problems. So we had all the manufacturing machinery brought up to full repair, installed output counters on every piece, and ran an eight-hour, nonstop full-capacity test. When we got through, management set 80 percent of that production capacity as a realistic goal—and it has held up. In addition, the production people now know what is expected of them.

9. Call meetings with key managers at least once a week.

The meetings should include sales, finance, and production managers, as well as administration. In most troubled companies, this just doesn't happen.

Your meeting format should permit a free flow of ideas. If all your key people understand and can comment on your company's problems, you will be surprised how many useful ideas they come up with. Force the communication—and don't skip the meeting just because there seems to be nothing to discuss. Some sessions will simply be briefer than others.

10. Treat your outside advisers like insiders.

Use your outside professionals continuously, and that includes your attorney and accountant.

Have your accountant review your financials at least twice, and preferably four times, a year. You need outside assurance of the accuracy of your internal numbers. Also, these days a company can't really make a move without fully considering the tax consequences.

Never surprise your lenders. Keep them informed of where you stand and what you will need well ahead of time. Meet with them several times a year. Keep them furnished with updated financials, and discuss your new products and potential customers with them. Most important of all, don't hold back bad news from them.

As a dividend to the list of dos and don'ts, Scheer offers this final word of advice: "Don't use the economy as an excuse. Recessions call for even tighter management. The well-managed business will survive."

BIG GAME:
The Trivial Pursuit Craze
Hits Suppliers

"**W**e've worked hard to get here, and now we're on a treadmill keeping up," says Scott Abbott. "You don't just cash in your chips and walk away." It is July 1984, and for the past sixteen days, Abbott, Chris Haney, and Haney's brother John have been secluded in a room at the Ascot Inn in suburban Toronto, the vertical blinds drawn against the seductive summer sky. There they have been crafting their sixth set of 6,000 questions—their second edition on general topics—for players of Trivial Pursuit.

Abbott mans the computer, editing out questions that have appeared in earlier editions. Some of the new questions seem too obscure even for trivia buffs. . . . Where can you find the hundred thousandth piano made by Steinway & Sons? (The White House.) Others pass through without a smile from their creators. . . . What chemical is most widely used to keep swimming pools clean? (Chlorine.)

"We're through a lot of our richest material," says Chris Haney on an afternoon in which the drone of questions is punctuated by too many silences.

He is a big, rumpled man of thirty-four, a high school dropout who later became photo editor for the *Gazette* in Montreal. He invented Trivial Pursuit with Abbott, thirty-five, a trim former sports editor for Canadian Press, who is equally quick with a biting remark or an infectious laugh. Each owns 22 percent of the company they formed, Horn Abbot Ltd. Their partners, with 18 percent each, are John Haney, thirty-eight, a former hockey player, bit actor, and bookstore manager, and Ed Werner, thirty-five, a lawyer who played hockey with John at Colgate University and in Europe.

After work, when they gather in the bar across the hall, the flashes of humor characteristic of their game come frequently as they savor stories of past years and questions of past weeks. . . . Who ran unopposed in the 1984 Hawaiian Democratic primary and finished second? ("We were going to put "Fighting Fritz Mondale.")

They speak of the freedom their wealth has brought—their company's royalties will, they say, "very conservatively" exceed $50 million this year. But earlier, closeted in a motel room beneath two imitation candelabra chandeliers, they seemed bored. The pursuit of trivia has begun to look a lot like work.

"This plant can be thought of as a big machine. It has a capacity geared for the games of Selchow and Righter—Parcheesi and Scrabble. Well, Trivial Pursuit comes along and demands four times that, five times that. You say, 'Put on a night shift.' Well, we don't have room for supplies."

Bob Bohnenberger joined Selchow & Righter Company, the U.S. producer of Trivial Pursuit, thirty-five years ago as a bookkeeper. He is now vice-president of production at the Holbrook, Long Island, plant. "I don't have room for more than two days of boxes," he says. "I try to keep a week's supply of cards, a week's supply of boards, a week's supply of plastic. . . . It's not just numbers on a piece of paper. There's a tremendous amount of volume here."

The process looks deceptively simple. A stack of elegant-looking, navy blue setup boxes is piled at the head of a forty-five-foot conveyer belt. A worker opens a box and puts in a sheet of waxed paper. As the box passes down the line, other hands put in game platforms, two boxes of question cards, a bag of plastic pieces and a die, a square, double-folded playing board, and lastly, a code card and instruction sheet. The box is checked and closed. A machine wraps the box in shrink-film, and another worker carts the games away.

In February of this year, with Selchow & Righter producing 63,000 games of Trivial Pursuit a week, back orders had passed a million. By August, back orders had reached 11 million games, and sales projections surpassed 20 million.

To handle the load, Bohnenberger decided to contract out much of the manufacturing operation. "There is no way with our staff [almost doubled in a year, from 80 to 150] and with our plant [100,000 square feet] that we could have increased production capacity tenfold without doing what I did," he says. Indeed, the Trivial Pursuit games expected to be sold in the United States this year alone will consume more than 70 million pounds of a special paper stock; will require the printing, cutting, collating, and boxing of more than 20 billion cards; and will enlist 2,000 to 3,000 workers at more than two dozen suppliers.

To put all this in perspective, consider that, in 1983, toy manufacturers nationwide shipped a total of $201 million of children's and adult board games to retailers and wholesalers. This year, if Selchow & Righter meets its projections, it will sell very nearly twice that much of a single game. Its revenues are projected to jump from $40 million in 1983 to more than $400 million in 1984.

"We have bought some new equipment but not on a grand scale," says Bohnenberger. "We haven't bought collating machines and cutting machines. We didn't bring in plastic molds. . . . This is a nice clean place. We've worked very much like a family through these years. We have a very good rapport with our people. We do what we do best."

"I am waiting for the day to get even with them. It's easier for me to reach the Kremlin in Moscow than it is to reach this company. They don't call you back. It takes them thirty days to call you back." Speaking is the president of a company that distributes games wholesale. He says he has been shipping Selchow & Righter games for thirty years, and in big numbers—more than 100,000 a year before Trivial Pursuit even came on the market.

"I believe really deeply that this item was put in the wrong hands," he says, requesting anonymity. "It's an old-line company that has been in the business for many years and has not progressed. It has been far surpassed in new business, far surpassed in promotion, in creativity, and especially in terms of customer relations. It is a backward company. It would have been out of business many years ago if it hadn't been for Scrabble."

He ticks off a list of complaints: surly shipping agents, salesmen who don't call back, and a price structure that, he says, gives no break on the listed wholesale of $19 for the complete game—not even to distributors who buy in bulk. "I can get merchandise from the Orient as fast as I can get it from them for anything—Scrabble, Parcheesi, you name it. They'll have an order for months and months for one hundred thousand pieces and a little retailer calls up for a few dozen and will get it before I do—and it's my customer. They'll say they haven't shipped for weeks and weeks. Well, that's a lie. The *retailer* gets it. My credibility has been hurt tremendously with retailers. My salesmen have had to go into stores and say, 'We can't get six pieces.' The answer comes back, 'What do you mean? We got seventy-two yesterday.' I used to talk to their salesman every week. Now he never calls back."

"I have a guy who wants to use the [trademark] on etched crystal. I have a guy who wants to do a brass box for the game. I've got a guy who wants to do tablecloths."

Since opening the doors of Horn Abbot Merchandising in April, president Randy Gillen, a former law partner of Ed Werner's, has been swamped with proposals to put the name, artwork, and questions of Trivial Pursuit on everything from highball glasses to umbrellas.

"Including the fifteen requests for T-shirts, there have easily been over a thousand phone calls, and it's getting worse," says Gillen. "I'm to the point now where I'm sending out letters in which I say, 'I am not an SOB and I am not ignoring you, but I just don't have time now to get back to you.' I just don't know how many of these licenses we'll be able to get in place by Christmas sales."

At the moment, Quillmark, a division of Random House Inc., is producing four types of Trivial Pursuit calendars, a memo pad, and an appointment book. Collegiate-Pacific Companies, in Totowa, New Jersey, is doing the T-shirts.

"I don't think any of us involved with this game really understood what the potential was," Gillen says as he talks of products to come—pine and oak tables with the gameboard etched in; a 14-karat, electroplated playing set; Trivial Pursuit linens; Trivial Pursuit athletic apparel. Rejected are "chintzy-looking school supplies" and "a cheap-looking carrying case," but, says Gillen, "frankly, I'd look at anything." Quality, he insists, is the key. "That's our style. Things for the upstairs portion of the department store where the expensive stuff is."

"I'm a troubleshooter," says Joe Cornacchia, who works out of a makeshift office on the fifth floor of a narrow brick building three blocks east of Manhattan's Washington Square Park. He is a graphic engineer and president of his family business, Cornacchia Press Inc. "I enjoy putting pieces together, making it work. It's dealing."

Since September 1982, he has been doing just that for Trivial Pursuit. First, says Cornacchia—who has done "odd jobs" for Selchow & Righter since the early 1960s—Bob Bohnenberger asked him to estimate manufacturing costs. Then he asked him to find a printer for 10,000 sets of cards, then 30,000, then 100,000, then millions. Orders for games followed, growing and growing through the first half of 1984: 15 million at George Banta Company in Menasha, Wisconsin; 3.7 million at Toronto's Chieftain Products Inc., the Canadian manufacturer of Trivial Pursuit; 2 million at Western Publishing Company in Racine, Wisconsin.

In the fall of 1982, Cornacchia approached fifty printers before he could find one that would handle an order for just 30,000 card sets for the game. The next problem was finding a way to handle the 1,000 cards contained in each game and subsidiary set of Trivial Pursuit. "We had to decide how to cut them, how to collate them, how to pick them up," says Cornacchia. "I've got big hands. How does a girl on an assembly line handle thousands and thousands of cards without dropping them all over the floor?

"My nature is always pie in the sky," adds Cornacchia. "I was always doubling what Selchow wanted. Around the time of the [American] Toy Fair [in February 1983], Selchow said they could use thirty thousand card sets a week. So I went back to Banta and said, 'We better plan for sixty thousand.' In the fall I went to Selchow and said, 'Let me do thirty thousand games for you complete. You may need help.' They said, 'Don't be silly, we can do three million games. . . . In the meantime, I get word from Canada [that they are selling 2.3 million games]. I said, 'We will sell twenty-five million.' Selchow was still figuring four or five."

In 1983, Cornacchia assembled 30,000 games complete. A year later, his three submanufacturers turned out that many every few hours. "When I had all the cards I needed, I didn't have enough plastic.

When I had enough plastic, I didn't have enough cards. And when I had both, I didn't have enough boards."

Hating to have to constantly fly on commercial airlines around the country, Cornacchia spent $3 million to buy his own ten-seater, twin-engine turboprop. "The toughest part was waiting to see if it really would happen," says Cornacchia. "Would it sell? Am I doing all this work flying all over the country for nothing? I had stopped doing any other work for anyone. If it had dropped dead, I had nothing. That was two years ago. And where are we now? Is it going to sell out? Is it going to die? Where are we going to be next year? I have a three-month lead time. Should I buy dice?"

"You always get the nuts coming out of the woodwork who say they've invented this before, who say, 'This is our game—we invented it in Ireland in 1974 but never showed it to anyone,'" says Jim Carson, a patent lawyer with McBeth & Johnson in Toronto. "And, of course, you do get these funny things where people don't like the questions written about them. There is the question, 'What's the nickname of the L.A. Rams cheerleaders?' The answer is, 'The Embraceable Ewes.' Well, they didn't like that. Horn Abbot got a letter saying it wasn't in line with their image of clean-cut American girls."

"I'm not aware of any question that's been replaced because of a complaint," he adds. "Chris is sort of irreverent, but I don't think there's been any libel, any untruths."

Carson got involved with Trivial Pursuit in September 1981, when he was approached by Ed Werner, an old law school friend with a new idea. Carson says he did "the standard things we do for every client." He filed for a design patent on the board, a trademark on the name "Trivial Pursuit," and copyrights for the questions and answers, the board design, and the game's graphics. He took on the work for expenses only, a practice that continued into mid-1982.

"In the beginning there was nothing [to do], but now there's tons," says Carson, whose billing to Horn Abbot will be well in excess of $100,000 this year. "I suppose some days I get tired of trivial matters."

Close to half of what Carson does for Horn Abbot is to see that the game's copyrights, trademark, and patent are protected—first in Canada, then in the United States, and now in at least thirty-two countries around the world. The inventors jealously guard the name of their creation, as Carson was quick to inform a bar owner who borrowed it in British Columbia, and a real estate company in Oakville, Ontario, which used the name in a trivia promotion that had nothing to do with playing the game.

Three dozen or more trivia games have flooded the market since Trivial Pursuit's success. Most, Carson says, have been "legitimate" competitors. Others "have actually ripped off questions from the Genus [master] game." Of equal concern to Carson—and to Selchow & Righter's law firm, which is suing—are two companies that are marketing trivia cards specifically for play with the Trivial Pursuit board: Trivia-

Sense Inc., in Minneapolis, and Decipher Inc., in Norfolk, Virginia. "If you subscribe to the idea that Scott, Chris, and John have a little magic in the way they write questions—especially the questions for the first edition—then why let the public be disappointed by people who imitate those cards and hurt the potential success of future games?" asks Carson.

"We don't think it's a rip-off, but more like an add-on," counters Peter Zollo, coinventor of Trivia-Sense cards. "It's the same thing as buying a computer. One question is, How much compatible software can you add on? . . . It's just a new set of cards to be used with Trivial Pursuit. We think what we're doing is increasing the longevity of their game."

"Our type of paper is very tight," says Joe Lukowski, general sales manager of bleached paperboard for Federal Paper Board Company in Montvale, New Jersey. In late 1983, Federal promised Cornacchia about 40 million pounds of a special card stock, 10-point Carolina Coated Bristol, covered on both sides with a clay that gives it a glossy finish and a smooth printing surface. The order was for nearly 20 percent of the capacity of the only machine in the country capable of milling and coating both sides of the paper in one operation. But it still wasn't enough.

"They've revised their figures upward and upward, and we can't go any further. We can't just walk away from our regular customers. You know, this is sort of a flash-in-the-pan thing."

"We had landed other business, but nothing anywhere near close to that," Dennis Lowry recalls, laughing. He is plant manager of Northern Plastics in Elroy, Wisconsin. "And we had three presses. One was even running. We had four full-time people and two part-time people." He laughs again.

In the late fall of 1983, Joe Cornacchia flew into Elroy, population 1,513, to meet with Lowry. "They had advertised in the *Wall Street Journal*," recalls Cornacchia," and I called this guy and said, 'Do you need work?' He said, 'Yeah,' so I flew in. . . . There was nothing there. It looked like a steel building completely empty, with one machine sitting in the corner. I said, 'Are you guys for real?' They said, 'We have three hundred or more people who will come to work tomorrow.' I advanced them the money for the plastic bags. I advanced them money for the plastic. I put up money for the molds. They started running and the product was good.

"All my life I've always visited a plant before I give them work," Cornacchia continues. "You make a judgment. Either they can do it or they can't do it. I just thought these guys could do it. . . . I don't know if you want to print that. It sounds a little flaky. But the reason I liked this plant being empty is that most plastic people have customers, so they can't commit to something like this without throwing out their customers. Well, these guys had nothing. I knew they could commit wholeheartedly."

As the operation has grown nationwide, so has the magnitude of the problems. "The usual," says Larry Ormson, president of Northern Plastics. "When you are going twenty-four hours a day, there is no overtime." Before Cornacchia came along, Ormson had invested about $820,000 in equipment for a business he had never worked in, just so he could return to the hometown he had grown up in as the fifteenth of seventeen children.

Northern Plastics now has 140 employees and eight presses running full tilt. Six more are on order. And the doors never shut. "We are open seven days a week, twenty-four hours a day," says Lowry. "We couldn't teach anyone to close the doors, so we keep them open." Every twelve seconds, the injection plastic molds at the plant produce twelve swizzle sticks—each attached to one of six plastic disks that go in a game of Trivial Pursuit.

"I just heard about it yesterday," says Bernard Graham, an insurance dealer visiting from Caracas, Venezuela. He reaches for the All-Star Sports edition on one of the two six-foot-high bookcases of trivia games at the Barnes & Noble Sales Annex on Fifth Avenue in Manhattan. "Someone I know played it and liked it very much. . . . No, I'm not a game player normally." Graham has not been stopped by the prominently displayed orange and black sign: "Master Game Trivial Pursuit is temporarily out of stock."

Does he know what he is about to spend $22.95 on? "I have no idea. Can you play the game without the master? It's cards? Six thousand cards?" After soliciting advice from another customer, Graham, not a sports fan, grabs the maroon box of the Baby Boomer edition and leaves.

"Believe me, it's no fun" says Dick Locher, Selchow & Righter's vice-president of sales. "I take my work home at night for the luxury of doing it without interruption. Otherwise I'd never get anything done. I spend the days trying to placate customers."

He hasn't always succeeded. "I think our credibility in the marketplace has suffered a great deal this year." Locher talks very fast: Dozens of callers are awaiting answers. "On the one hand, we are producing a highly desirable item. On the other, we are frustrating customers with our uncertainties. You are forced to say, 'I think it will be so and so,' but in effect you are saying, 'I don't know.' You can't be sure, because you don't know if there will be a break in the supply line; you don't know if the assembly will break down. It adds up to a horror story of our inability to give hard information to anyone."

To make matters worse, says Locher, "everyone wants it at once. It is just a situation where nerves are frayed and people aren't thinking coolly. There's just an unbelievable amount of pressure. Our priorities are first in, first out, as fast as we can. The oldest orders should go first. We haven't stopped taking orders from anybody."

Meanwhile, the distribution pipeline sometimes gets clogged. "California is a problem. Texas is a problem. Oklahoma is a problem. . . . Things are happening so fast we just try to cope with each problem as it comes up. Sometimes you aren't aware that a certain area hasn't gotten shipments for a few weeks."

Now, in midsummer, a potentially more ominous problem is developing. Locher has told his company that it will sell 24 million games, based on the number that have been ordered, but some of the orders have begun to dissolve. "In areas where the game is getting more in evidence, where maybe five stores in town have it, all of a sudden these guys who placed tremendous orders are canceling them or cutting them in half. There's a certain amount of sandbagging. People are ordering eight thousand, and we don't know if they really want four thousand. When you are making them as quickly as we are, you can get in trouble real quickly."

"Customers would be calling every week and I had nothing," recalls Karen Shutt, owner of the Kings Crown Inc. store in Overland Park, Kansas. "Finally, I just gave them their money back." Shutt received her first order in late June—three months later than promised and too late for several customers who had paid $45 each in advance, expecting April 11 delivery. She had limited her order to only a dozen games because local distributors were demanding $27.99, more than the retail price charged by some of the big chains in the area.

"We haven't seen one since before Christmas," laments Shelton Yee, general manager of Gamemasters of San Francisco. It is late July and he has been waiting to place an order since the end of last year. "Every time I call the company, they say to call back next month. They don't have to deal with people looking for it, demanding it, screaming at you and saying, 'You are hiding it.' Our retail operation has had about fifty calls a day. There's been a little slackening lately, but not much."

"The big quantities are being sold as loss leaders in the chains," says Tom Driscoll, then general manager of The Game Player in Houston. "It will go as low as twenty-three dollars. The Sears, the Targets, the Penneys will drop an order for one hundred fifty thousand pieces, and that takes care of what Selchow and Righter can give. We can't get it directly from the factory, so we've got to find a wholesaler. I have yet to see what a month's supply is. I can't get enough games."

But even being a small wholesaler of adventure games hasn't helped Yee. "We've seen none," he repeats. "We have standing orders with our distributors, and we've seen none. We've been promised by distributors and by Selchow and Righter. They can't keep their promise."

"For someone to do the kind of volume Trivial Pursuit is doing is simply unprecedented," says Bruce Jones, vice-president of marketing at Parker Brothers. "Even something like Rubik's Cube didn't do the kind of numbers they are talking about. It's reminded people again that games are, and can be, very profitable."

In February 1982, at the American Toy Fair, Parker Brothers was one of several companies that sent Haney and Abbott packing when they were desperately trying to peddle their game. Last year, General Mills Inc.—of which Parker Brothers is a division—paid an advance to distribute Trivial Pursuit overseas. Parker Brothers has developed its own trivia game, called People Weekly. "It's selling extremely well right now," says Jones. "It's our best introduction this year."

"I think you've got to have a gimmick now," says Scott Robinson, president of Baron/Scott Enterprises Inc., which, in August, introduced a music trivia game, Rock 'n' Roll Replay, complete with two tape cassettes with five-second snatches of blasts from the past. Robinson's other game is called Sexual Trivia, with questions like, Is keeping a condom in a wallet a good idea? (No, because body heat breaks down the rubber.) "It's extremely educational," says Robinson, who nonetheless doubts that the game will be adopted by schools, since players win by collecting orgasms.

"We spent four hundred thousand dollars researching why Americans would spend one billion dollars on anything," says Ken Paradiso, marketing manager for Professional Software Inc., in Needham, Massachusetts. The study discovered "psychological flaws" in Trivial Pursuit, such as the inventors' decision not to set up a system of handicapping. Professional Software's Trivia Fever, a $39.95 retail software package compatible with the Commodore 64 home computer and the IBM Personal Computer and PC jr., earned its name by selling 200,000 copies to retailers in its first six weeks, according to Paradiso.

"We are conservative, we are cautious, we consider things very carefully, all the options," says sixty-two-year-old Dick Selchow, who six years ago took over as president of Selchow & Righter, the oldest privately owned game company in the United States. "We are not a promotional house. We are a staple manufacturing house, and our hallmark is that we try to select things that will be around awhile.

"We've made a big step upward by attempting such a thing," he says, referring to Trivial Pursuit. "I think we have shown we can handle things of bigger scope." This year, for the first time, Selchow & Righter will enter the preschool market with a line of toys called Scrabble Brand People. And there is talk of a line of wooden toys and of buying a subsidiary plastics plant.

Selchow is a polite, formal executive who dresses in muted suits. He is a vestryman of his church. His favorite game, he says, is Parcheesi, the company's oldest. According to his résumé, he also enjoys a good game of Scrabble with his mother-in-law.

Selchow & Righter was the choice of Haney and Abbott because they wanted to be associated with Scrabble. "In my mind," Chris

Haney says, "it's one of the most dignified games around." Still, he recalls their first meeting with Selchow & Righter executives on September 22, 1982: "It was 'Saturday Night Live' meets 'The Lawrence Welk Show.' "

Although Horn Abbot retained editorial control of all cards, a few questions in the master game's 6,000 questions and answers offended Selchow. About fifteen in the Canadian edition were either sanitized or dropped, and a practice of screening continued in subsequent editions. One Baby Boomer question that disappeared: How many months pregnant was Nancy Davis when she walked down the aisle with Ronald Reagan? Answer: Two and a half. Selchow says simply, "There are very few I recall being changed."

"This is a very important card set for us," says Chris Haney. "It's our acid test for the future. We're hoping to repeat the success of the first edition."

Today, the creators of Trivial Pursuit are millionaires, talking of boats and mansions; of blue-chip stock and the sixty acres of grape-growing land they own a half interest in; of the one-hour television special they are coproducing to air on ABC. It is just about two years since Haney, feeding his family on $200 a week and the receipts of bottle returns, suffered a nervous breakdown as the first major shipment of games was about to be assembled. The anxiety attacks recur, and he will not appear on live television. And it is just two and a half years since he and his three partners committed themselves to $250,000 for a game the experts scoffed at. They went away from the 1982 toy fairs in the United States and Canada with fewer than 500 orders.

Their game, which chides the world's newsmakers and teases the public's recall of the tidbits of the past, is sprinkled with carefully measured portions of the irreverence its authors still cultivate as a way of being—or, at least, as a way of appearing. "Nothing is sacred," says Haney.

Nothing, that is, but their game. Perhaps that is why he sneers at the new industry of imitators ("gnats swiping at an elephant"); why he bristles at complaints about their game's answers ("We are so high-profile people just want to nail us to the cross"); why he chafes when asked how long and how often their game can be played before it becomes a piece of trivia itself ("That's not a fair question"). And, perhaps it is why they are spending their summer in the Holiday Inn–chic of a suburban Toronto motel, thinking of questions for a new edition.

"We are working on the next best-selling game in history in that room right now," boasts Chris Haney, four or five beers into the evening. In an industry in which, in the words of one analyst, "there is no future," they want their championship season to linger.

—GERALD LANSON

PART
III

LESSONS FOR CONTROLLING GROWTH

"**W**ouldn't you like someone to come into your room in the morning and say, 'O great and omniscient one, are you ready for your coffee?'" asks Pong inventor and notorious entrepreneur Nolan Bushnell.

Perhaps that is a dream for the very rich and idle—those who can afford to pay $2,000 for a robot manservant. One doubts, though, that even a Rockefeller or a Getty would find such an expenditure conscionable. Nevertheless, Bushnell poured $1 million into the development of a domestic robot he envisioned would become all the rage. It did not.

Part III of *The Best of* Inc. *Guide to Business Strategy* looks at what has lead to the decline of two companies that, from the look of things, had everything going for them. In fact, both Provincetown-Boston Airlines (PBA) and Bushnell's Pizza Time Theatres looked so good in the early eighties, one might have thought that only a meticulously plotted sabotage could bring either company down. And that, in a sense, is what happened with both enterprises. Part III will also show how another company managed to recover from a spree of acquiring and consolidating that, it later turned out, nearly sent the parent company to bankruptcy court.

Back in March of 1983 we first reported on the business strategy of Nolan Bushnell. By then a fabulously rich and successful businessman, Bushnell was focusing his energies on investing in a handful of high-tech start-ups. His was no ordinary venture capital scheme. Bushnell's idea was that the cost of starting a business could be reduced if the new business shared space, office supplies, and utilities with other start-ups. Bushnell's role would be to oversee these new companies by housing his own in the same building. In this way he had control over what was and was not being developed. "Nolan

Bushnell: The Pied Piper of Sunnyvale" looks in on Bushnell's strategy and the ever optimistic "guru of Silicon Valley."

Some nineteen months after we reported on Bushnell's original and daring strategy for empire building, it started to come unglued. What went wrong? Was his investment strategy invalid? Did he spread himself too thin? Was he losing his touch? "When the Magic Goes" reviews the days when Bushnell guided one product, and then one company, through the marketplace. He operated from instinct—which was usually right on the money—and took on new projects at a manageable pace. But soon he was at the helm of several businesses, yet he still ran things, it seemed, more from hunches than anything else. His business decisions seemed to make less and less sense the more confident he became. Where there had once been an imaginative inventor, there was now a short-sighted autocrat who failed to read the signals in the marketplace or listen to his associates.

The ego and management problems that have come to characterize Bushnell's enterprises—and many others in Silicon Valley—are not exclusive to genius inventors turned adventurous businessman. Even family-owned, tradition-bound companies can fall victim to hyperbole. Our third piece, "PBA: A Tale of Two Airlines," surveys the philosophical and strategic changes that occurred when that company was passed from father to sons.

When we first reported on PBA in 1983, John Van Arsdale, Jr., who grew up in his father's planes, was busily increasing PBA's fleet, the number of cities it would service, and the overall level of expertise that would, he surmised, come to characterize his company. PBA was never considered a fiercely competitive airline, and the senior Van Arsdale wanted it that way. His philosophy was to corner a particular market and stay there. John, Jr., saw things in a different light, and he openly and aggressively took on other commuter airlines previously considered peers rather than competitors. Though the changes made by John, Jr., and his brother Peter made their father nervous, they appeared to be working well for PBA. Revenues climbed steadily and the number of routes grew from six to twenty-four in two years. PBA was flying high.

Two years later, however, PBA was in very serious trouble, only some of which was financial. The FAA cited the airline with a total of 160 violations, and it wan't just a few careless employees who were responsible. John, Jr., himself was accused of violating FAA regulations when he failed to land a plane he was piloting after detecting a maintenance problem, and of then falsifying records to cover his tracks—not a very responsible act for a CEO. "Tailspin" looks into what went on at PBA that allowed such carelessness to thrive. John, Jr.'s, failure to delegate responsibility, we find out, was partially responsible for the swift decline of PBA. But the airline also suffered a streak of terrible luck. In the end, a feather could have knocked it over.

Our final piece, "The Once and Future King," demonstrates that the misguided energies of an overoptimistic CEO needn't end in bankruptcy court. For 195 years Frank Sands' family owned and operated a company that sold baking flour in the New England area, but flour usage among families had fallen off sharply, causing concern in the industry, particularly among small companies. To keep his company healthy, Sands reasoned, he would invest in bakery supplies other than ordinary flour. And so he did. Inside of ten years, Frank Sands acquired three small companies in the baking business and formed a distributing deal with a fourth. And just as Sands was itching to go into semiretirement, his empire started to crumble. By turning back to the company's historic roots—King Arthur Flour—Sands was able to save his company and return to his regional market.

Demonstrating enthusiasm over growth and success is no sin. These *Inc.* articles have been compiled to illustrate how too much confidence can destroy a company—and how such uncontrolled growth can be leashed.

NOLAN BUSHNELL:
The Pied Piper of Sunnyvale

Two bearded tinkerers with electronic gadgets getting together to discuss the future is not, by Silicon Valley standards, extraordinary. So when entrepreneur Nolan Bushnell, founder of Atari Inc. and creator of the world's first coin-operated video game, sat down with engineer John Vurich, inventor of the world's first computerized pinball machine, northern California's blasé technology community took small notice. Nor was anyone surprised when, in March 1980, the two game makers opened a new garage shop in Sunnyvale, even though the enterprise was auspiciously located only a few feet down the street from where Atari had started eight years before.

Yet the coventure, Axlon, Inc., is apt to be pivotal in the annals of high-tech finance. It was Bushnell's first start-up since he sold Atari for $28 million to Warner Communications Inc. (along with Pizza Time Theatre, a division Bushnell later bought back) in 1976. Now barely three years old, Axlon bears the distinctive marks of its progenitor. It has no fewer than nine computer-peripheral products up and selling. One is a mass-marketed handheld terminal that plugs into telephones, another, a small, OEM-vended, solid-state device that expands microcomputer memories. Both are offspring of Bushnell's hyperactive and playful imagination, one avenue of which aspires to the ultimate peripheral—a shirt-pocket, intelligent terminal.

The undertaking has sparked even wider aspirations. Bushnell seeded two additional companies—Magnum Microwave Corporation, a manufacturer of microwave components and systems for satellite communication, and Compower Corporation, maker of switching-power supplies for computers. Both, like Axlon, are fully operational. And in December 1981, Bushnell formally became sole proprietor of Catalyst Technologies, a holding company of some half dozen additional Bushnell start-ups huddled like newborn rabbits in his Sunnyvale warren. "Investing in companies only fifty feet away," reflects Bushnell on the new brood, in which he reportedly has sunk nearly $10 million, "is very handy."

Bushnell conceives, bankrolls, staffs, and guides the enterprises from scratch, one by one. As it is born, each company is housed in a room or two at 1287 Lawrence Station Road in Sunnyvale, the incubator established especially for properly breeding little companies and sending them out to face the rigors of the marketplace. The expertise force-fed by Catalyst's brain trust, the thinking goes, will prevent these companies from making typical start-up mistakes and bring them to profitability all the sooner.

Predictably, the Catalyst companies are mainly in such consumer markets as home robots, electronic shop-at-home systems, a computer camp for children, and high-resolution television. Like any bettor on a roll, Utah-raised Bushnell (who worked his way through college playing poker until he lost his entire tuition in one game and swore off gambling) is in the process of confidently compounding his gains. And the increment of the $15 million nest egg with which he left Atari may turn out to be geometric. Still-private Axlon, for example, is already profitable, with sales that multiplied eightfold, from $500,000 in 1981 to an estimated $4 million in 1982.

In Catalyst's sparsely appointed building, the prototypical company represents a Bushnell whim given flesh. And that whim—a sense of market-*cum*-technology that, Bushnell admits, is as much intuitive as studied—comes only in extra-large size. Bushnell's musings dauntlessly roam not simply to niches but to entire new industries. For that reason, he is a magnet for an array of bright engineers and executives eager to leave comfortable jobs and homes for the chance to be in on the launching of an engaging and often playful adventure. "Nolan senses where the technology is going and how it can be taken advantage of," says Catalyst's president Lawrence Calof, the attorney who renegotiated Bushnell's employment agreement with Atari. A commanding figure with a ready smile, Bushnell exudes a sort of Pied Piper of Sunnyvale attractiveness. "I've never met a person who has more ideas than [Nolan] does," enthuses John B. Anderson, executive vice-president and a former Atari vice-president for administration. "He attracts a lot of people, and *they* have ideas of their own."

Bushnell doesn't invest just in businesses: He recently brought in a "very, very bright kid" he had run across in Los Angeles. Eventually, Bushnell says, he will find something for the young man to do. And on the side, Bushnell set up for his father-in-law an elite (except for some video games near the bar) Valley restaurant, which has become an area mecca for forging high-tech business deals over lunch.

At first, Bushnell intended to make Catalyst a public company based on 1980's so-called Heizer Act, which made nonprivate investment corporations more feasible. But, dismayed by the subsequently poor showing of Heizer stock on the American Stock Exchange, management concluded that the public wasn't patient enough to wait the usual five years or so for a venture capital deal to produce returns. Besides, Bushnell's concept of pursuing offbeat technologies and squeezing them into novel packages was apt to seem dubious in the public eye. "This," admits Calof, "is truly risk capital—as risky as you can get." Even so, he anticipates return on investment from seed money in as little as three years, and at multiples of as much as 1,000 times the original investment. That is a rate of return that more than a few public investors would be willing to take a chance on. But they won't get the opportunity until a Catalyst company goes public farther down the road—if, indeed, any does.

Given a Bushnell inspiration, Catalyst sets up a company (usually a Subchapter-S corporation) with a handful of people deemed capable of converting imagination to reality. The brainpower comes mostly from people Bushnell knows down in the Valley. Many are restive employees of other companies who would like to work in a small group (and field the opportunity to strike it rich through stock options and the like).

"They come knocking on our door," says Anderson, "and we offer them the opportunity to do something new and exciting." Bushnell's vision for consumer robots (he foresees 1 percent of American households having one by 1985 and a vast market by 1990) took shape in a suite of Catalyst offices in October 1981, with five staffers—all engineers. Not until the project was approaching prototype-stage a year later were a marketer and operating officer hired and supplied with a rudimentary business plan.

By centralizing Catalyst condenses the rote part of setting up shop—the first several months that are bogged down in a search for space, buying furniture, evaluating telephone systems, and figuring out employee benefits. To launch its companies efficiently, Catalyst's turnkey operation supplies not only the requisite cash but also a set of desks, a notebook with all essential organizational documents, and a core of seasoned administrators and advisers. A company that taps this pool is charged accordingly but doesn't have to carry more G&A (general and administrative overhead) than it needs. "Here you can have one-third of a person working for you," explains Bushnell. "On the outside, people don't come in thirds."

And the number of petty details that tend to irritate infant businesses are kept to a minimum. Bushnell is convinced, for example, that every greenhorn entrepreneur who goes to a bank will come back with the wrong kind of checkbook. Additional homespun schooling is dispensed (often via in-house video) on such quintessential seed matters as taxes, stock options, patent law, and accounting. "I've never gotten fair value from an accounting department," Bushnell sympathizes. "It's a monkey on your back. It doesn't contribute to marketing. I'll guarantee that no Catalyst company will ever get as cheap accounting as it's getting now."

Another synergistic advantage of having everybody in one spot comes through Catalyst's frequent courtyard klatches. Among the chickens (a gift for Bushnell's thirty-ninth birthday) that roam as freely as in a *Grapes of Wrath* kitchen, ideas and problems are batted around by building denizens (some residents aren't Catalyst companies, but simply tenants whose rent helps cash flow). Theoretically, such elbow-rubbing enhances the pace of progress more than if each company were out on its own. Management may find, for instance, that some collective purchasing items may cut costs, and typical entrepreneurial errors are kept to a minimum.

If all this doesn't do the trick, the Grand Council of the Empire, as Catalystians call it, meets every month. These executives and senior members, including Bushnell; Calof; Anderson; E. Beirne Shuffle, treasurer; and Robert Allen, Jr., financial analyst, keep an eye on the nestlings and set them right when they stray. Although a founding precept is to have all operations close by initially, one Bushnell ambition, says Calof, is to populate Silicon Valley with Catalyst offspring.

Although a Catalyst company has all the earmarks of entrepreneurship, the difference is that nobody within it is an owner; at the start, Catalyst—or more specifically, Bushnell—is. If a company needs second-phase financing, outside investors may be let in later. A few months after Catalyst's 1981 seeding of Androbot Inc. with about $1 million, a sum quickly used up by the home-robot company on capital equipment and research, Androbot sold 400,000 shares of convertible preferred stock for another $1 million to an individual and was putting together a $1.5 million research and development syndication partnership to develop a robot "brain" (see "Will the Robot Be Father to the Industry," page 000). About to be weaned from Catalyst's services and sent off on its own, Androbot is seeking another $2 million from outside investors. Catalyst expects to shorten the R&D cycle to six months to a year, and to use up $500,000 to $1 million during that phase.

Even though they aren't owners, Catalyst company employees are made to *feel* they are. "We instill fire in their eyes," Bushnell proclaims. "The entrepreneurial flame burns as brightly as if the business were their own." And, indeed, some of it is. In addition to the autonomy granted by Catalyst (each company's management is expected to make virtually all its operating decisions, guided only by the inescapable sense that Bushnell is looking on), one poker that stokes the embers is lavish income potential. For example, both Androbot's president and chief operating officer are already major shareholders of the corporation and have been granted stock options that will be amply rewarding should the company take off. Says Androbot president Thomas Frisina, "Nolan conveys the impression to all the presidents that it's their baby. If we hit, we get a lot out of it; if we screw up, we'll be out of a job."

For a while, Catalyst Technologies was probably the only institution in Silicon Valley without an overdesigned logo out front. Although it had existed since December 1981, it wasn't until ten months later that anyone got around to putting up a sign. But it really didn't matter, since the shortcuts and expertise within can't be characterized anyway. Bushnell is the real catalyst. Says Axlon's Vurich, "Nolan makes new things happen. To do it efficiently, to make his ideas become reality, he put everything under one roof. If you have lots of ideas, it's the logical way."

"Nolan is the vision," Calof extols. "He's the spirit of this operation. Anybody can sit around and come up with ideas all day, but we're *doing* things here—lots of different things. This place has to be flexible, or it isn't going to work."

The first all-Catalyst company to leave the premises and operate on its own will be Androbot, due to depart this spring, a scant eighteen months after it was started. "Two weeks after we're gone," Frisina notes, "one of Nolan's other ideas is going to be in this space, incubating like we did."

There is no doubt that innovative products will be waiting in line. Bushnell seems not only willing but anxious to bankroll leading-edge projects. Big companies like Warner Communications "don't have the guts" to innovate any longer, he feels. The conservative cycle that businesses are following these days is that they wait for their products to peak before daring to undertake a new venture. Bushnell is less patient. For one thing, he promises that on October 1, 1983—the moment his agreement not to compete with Atari expires—"I'm going to be back in the game business." The corporate beneficiary of this reentry into video games (with three-dimensional playing fields, he hints) will probably be Pizza Time Theatre, a 1978 start-up in whose operation Bushnell is still closely involved.

"If I were still at Atari," Bushnell declares, "I'd have all these things going on at once. But now they're afraid of failure. Yet every new product runs that risk."

Will the Robot Be Father to the Industry?

The first born-at-Catalyst company that will be nudged over the side of the nest on the assumption that it will fly is Androbot Inc., scheduled for eviction this spring. Although barely out of swaddling clothes, Androbot's 1984 business plan aspires to sales of no less than $25 million. Founded with a handful of engineers let loose in a Catalyst Technologies lab, Androbot now has thirty employees—and one product, a homely three-foot-tall home robot called Topo that was introduced in the plastic flesh at the Consumer Electronics Show in Las Vegas this past January.

It is a loveable product that Nolan Bushnell believes will be irresistible to U.S. householders. Bushnell may be wrong about an untestable market. But with a record of good guessing that includes the development and marketing of Pong, the computer game that presaged today's multibillion-dollar video madness, a person would need long odds to bet against Topo and its younger but more sophisticated brother, Bob, whose three internal computers are under development at Androbot.

At least three other manufacturers agree: They are each rushing a competing product to market. In December, Heath Company, a Zenith Radio Corporation subsidiary, introduced its twenty-inch

($1,500 in kit form; $2,500 assembled), R2D2esque Hero 1 on national TV and is expecting sales of 8,000 to 10,000 units this first year. Mail-order specialist Hammacher Schlemmer was writing dozens of orders for $8,000 Jenus, a nearly human-size, smiling (via a CRT), articulated domestic (with a vacuum cleaner mode) under development by Robotics International Corporation, of Jackson, Michigan. Mitsubishi in Japan is said to be close to market as well. Although so far essentially a plaything, even the basic product doesn't come cheap or fast: Androbot is well into its second year and second million dollars' worth of development, and Heath admits to having spent more than $1 million in three years for its own project. And as of January, Hammacher's customers had yet to see the real thing.

Each robot is remarkably different in looks and engineering solutions. Ingeniously, armless Topo gets about on two angled wheels, for example, while one-armed Hero 1 has the conventional three wheels, and Jenus two drive wheels and two casters. But all share one characteristic: They don't really think for themselves. Humans have to tell them what to do or "coach" them through simple programs. Topo is radio-controlled; equipped with electronic sensors, Hero 1 can be programmed to repeat predetermined functions, including picking up a newspaper.

Slated for production this spring to sell for about $2,500, Andro-bot's Bob (for "brain on board") will make many of its own decisions. Bob will be guided by ultrasonic and infrared systems that create the basis for artificial intelligence, however rudimentary, operating independent of radio control or an umbilicus. Given a roomful of people—whom "friendly" Bob seeks out through delicate heat sensors that can distinguish between a human and a light bulb—the robot may act unpredictably, claims Androbot president Thomas Frisina. "He might sing, dance, or tell jokes." Bob will also be able to make his way from room to room checking for fire or robbers while autonomously changing course according to an electronic "reading" of the environment. To entertain kids, the machine will play hide-and-seek for hours.

Like the robots it creates, Androbot will feel its way cautiously in the marketplace, as consumer reaction dictates the next steps. In 1983, there won't be advertising, and the robots will be marketed selectively. In 1984, though, plans call for all-out promotion. "By then we'll know how to build the product, and we'll be able to define market needs," explains Frisina, an erstwhile stereo-components marketer and old friend of Catalyst president Lawrence Calof, who brought him in last fall to run the company. For an inexperienced chief executive officer, it is a sobering responsibility, especially as it is Bushnell's capital that will remain very much at risk. But the challenge delights Frisina. "It gives me the chance to be an entrepreneur," he beams, "and relieves me of the liabilities."

Product Fallout

"Shake the tree and something is bound to fall out" was the inspiration, such as it is, behind Nolan Bushnell's 1980 funding of Axlon Inc. The tree happened to be particularly thick with the fruits of Bushnell's fertile mind, and sure enough, oaks from acorns are growing: Peripheral-maker Axlon had 1982 sales of $3 million to $5 million, up from $500,000 the year before.

The sprouting of Axlon was virtually predestined. A computer drifter in search of the action, John Vurich's main attraction, as far as Bushnell was concerned, was possessing the sensibilities for having invented microcomputer-controlled pinball. Summoning Vurich, who had left Atari in January 1979 because he "didn't see their computer going where I wanted," Bushnell proposed that the two start a company.

And so they did. Axlon was Bushnell's first seeding since Atari eight years before, setting the stage for Catalyst Technologies. Bushnell put in most of the money simply because "he had more than I did," recalls Vurich, now chief executive officer. (Since then, only one other investor—Charles Ying, founder of Atex Inc.—has been admitted.) Bushnell's idea for their first product was an order-it-yourself computer terminal for fast-food restaurants. Customers would view mouth-watering options and punch in their choice. Axlon built a prototype, but Vurich was discouraged by the size of the investment needed to hook into existing cash-register systems. "Don't despair, John," said Bushnell. "This one may not be a winner, but we'll get some products out of it.

However vague, Bushnell's words proved to be wise counsel. Serendipitously, Vurich had expanded the memory of an Atari computer for that project and decided to market the new board. Since then, more than 30,000 have been sold to computer users. Rampower, as the device was named, became the company's first bread-and-butter product. Rampower, along with Ramdisk, is a compact, solid-state peripheral acting as the equivalent of two disk drives. With it, says Vurich, "we can turn an Apple into the fastest computer you've ever seen."

Bushnell's next concept was also restaurant-oriented: a small, alphanumeric walkie-talkie–like instrument with which a waiter or waitress could relay orders directly into the kitchen by pushing buttons. Again, Vurich built some prototypes and pressed them into action. But it turned out that without a display, a server got no reassuring feedback. To construct a reliable display required putting in a microprocessor and a two-way radio, resulting in an unacceptably bulky instrument.

Give up? Never. Bushnell and Vurich decided they would try to construct a tiny, dumb terminal from what they had so far. Out came the Datalink, a handheld interactive data handler that can talk to base computers or plug into information services via telephone. Vurich was quick to grasp the mass-marketing implications. At National Semiconductor "I sat next to a guy who delivered six million calculators at a cost of less than a dollar each," he remembers. "It wasn't the greatest calculator, but it sure shows you what volume can do." At press time, Axlon was negotiating an order from a bank for more than half a million Datalinks and has struck a deal with a brokerage firm whose customers will be able to buy or sell stocks directly by computer.

Axlon's product line is now devoted to what Vurich calls the "electronic wallet"—miniaturized communications and data processing devices that people will carry around with them. As Axlon expands, Bushnell ensures that the corporate wallet doesn't get too thin. "Nolan is good at giving us direction," Vurich admits. "Making sure a small company doesn't make big mistakes is critical."

—ROBERT A. MAMIS

WHEN THE MAGIC GOES

The adoring crowd of 300 engineers, executives, and reporters fell silent. They had gathered this Friday night in the bright new site of Sente Technologies Inc., in Milpitas, California, to pay tribute to their leader, a man many of them regarded as the philosopher-king of Silicon Valley. In the last decade, he had founded an industry and parlayed seemingly outlandish ideas into not one but two multimillion-dollar companies. Now he stood before them, puffing on his pipe and flashing his puckish grin.

"My name is Nolan Bushnell, but I'm not God," he told them. "I need to build factories."

If not God, then Prometheus—about to be unbound. At midnight on September 30, 1983, a seven-year noncompete agreement, which Bushnell had signed when he sold his pioneering Atari Inc. video-game company to Warner Communications Inc. in 1976, was due to expire, and a grand party had been organized to celebrate his release. Streamers and banners adorned the walls and ceilings. Bushnell mingled gregariously, clutching a can of Budweiser and a little blue notebook with a picture of a clown on its cover. Waving the notebook about like a wand, he declared that it was bulging with ideas for video games far more creative than anything then on the market.

"The game business, much like the music business or the carnival business, gets in your blood," he pronounced. "For the past several years, I have been scribbling down ideas, waiting for today." Sente, the latest in his series of glamorous enterprises would carry the video-game torch into the future. "My grandchildren and their grandchildren will still be playing video games."

The crowd believed. This was vintage Nolan Bushnell, the Valley's fun-loving, boyish genius, who summoned successful companies like rabbits from a top hat. After Atari had come Pizza Time Theatres Inc., a restaurant chain that expanded so rapidly it twice made *Inc.*'s list of the one hundred fastest-growing public companies in America. After Pizza Time came Androbot Inc., which had dazzled the press and the public with a mechanical-man prototype named Bob. There were others, too—each one a piece of its creator's entrancing vision.

123

As for the creator himself, his charisma was unmatched anywhere in the entrepreneurial wonderland of Silicon Valley. "Nolan walks in the front door with that smile on his face and puffin' on that pipe, and it's like a whirling dervish walked in," says the former president of a Bushnell company. "People's hair stands on end. Their eyes get like saucers. And they flock around him like J. C. the Man just walked in."

Such, indeed, was his reception at the Milpitas party on that magic night in 1983. Only six months later, however, the magic was gone. By then, Pizza Time Theatres had filed for protection under Chapter 11 of the Federal Bankruptcy Code. Androbot, touted by Merrill Lynch in the summer of 1983 as one of the country's hottest new issues, had lost more than $4 million. Sente itself had been sold to Bally Manufacturing Corporation in a desperate attempt to raise cash for the parent company. And Nolan Bushnell had lost around $5 million from his own pocket, plus many millions more in the paper value of his stocks.

How did it happen? In answering the question, it is tempting to see Bushnell as he was in Milpitas, clutching his clown notebook and smiling under a shower of accolades: a sort of overindulged child prodigy. But there is more both to the man and to the collapse of his corporate domain. Bushnell's companies weren't ordinary start-ups built around one or another market opportunity. There was a unifying theme to them, a mixture of technology and fantasy that Bushnell hoped would elevate him to the status of entertainment mogul, the Walt Disney of the eighties, an entrepreneurial sorcerer whose visions permeated American life. That he ultimately turned out to be the sorcerer's apprentice, overwhelmed by his creations rather than in control of them, is his tragedy.

The story of the collapse is also a parable for Silicon Valley, a region increasingly obsessed with technology and troubled by the swift punishments now being meted out in the marketplace. Even more than Apple Computer Inc.'s Steven Jobs or Intel Corporation's Robert Noyce, Bushnell was the spiritual leader of Silicon Valley. He believed, still believes, that one day all of America will in some ways resemble the Valley, a suburban Oz built from California redwood and Spanish tile, where giant billboards advertise computer spreadsheet programs and where the gas stations run promotional programs with names like "Protech." New technology has always been at the center of Bushnell's entrepreneurial vision; like others in the Valley he came to believe it would never fail him. That he was wrong seems no small lesson in a decade that will likely be remembered not for its wars or its cultural artifacts, but for the dazzling technology it has unleashed.

The picture in the newspaper captured Bushnell immersed in a hot tub next to a beautiful girl who could pass for half his age. Clutching his pipe, his face hidden behind a ragged beard, Bushnell looked in 1976 like a high-tech Hugh Hefner.

The image did not sit well with the directors of Warner Communications as they pondered the wisdom of acquiring Bushnell's Atari company. Warner's film and record divisions reportedly were doing poorly at the time, and the entertainment conglomerate desperately needed a strong performer. Atari was that, all right, but the video-game industry—which Bushnell had virtually created when he invented Pong, an electronic tennis game—was in its infancy, and while it was growing fast, some considered it a fad. Disney and MCA, two of Warner's richest competitors, had already passed up the chance to acquire Atari. And now Atari's founder and chairman, a lapsed Mormon, was wallowing in hot tubs like a blissed-out Hollywood star.

If Bushnell was not yet a national celebrity, he was made one by Warner's decision in late 1976 to ignore his antics and buy out Atari for $28 million. Only thirty-three, he was now a rich man, with a personal fortune totaling some $15 million (his share of Atari's sale price) plus a stake in Warner Communications. And Atari was a highly visible company on the cutting edge of a popular new consumer industry. At the same time, of course, Silicon Valley itself was becoming an American Eden of technological genius and entrepreneurial daring.

Bushnell had taken to this garden like a man escaping the desert. Born to a religious middle-class family on the dreary flats of the Great Salt Lake, Bushnell arrived in California a conventional electronics engineer, with a wife, kids, and a suburban tract house. But in the early seventies, he began to tinker with new lifestyles as well as new ideas. On New Year's Day, 1974, just as Atari was beginning its explosive growth, Bushnell left his family. After the sale of Atari, he took to flying around the country in his own Lear jet and sailing on a yacht called *Pong*. He bought a sixteen-acre northern California estate surrounded by old stone walls and complete with riding stables, a swimming pool, and tennis courts. He also acquired homes in Paris and in Aspen, Colorado.

Atari, too, became an emblem of the Valley's promise. Employees showed up for work at the company's Los Gatos headquarters at all hours of the morning, often dressed in blue jeans and T-shirts. At Pajaro Dunes, a coastal vacation resort, company executives gathered regularly for open bull sessions, where new, often wild ideas were bandied about in the ocean breezes.

Bushnell was the immensely popular leader of these New Age shock troops, and his growing legend attracted the Valley's most precious human resource: engineers. Trained in electrical engineering at the University of Utah, Bushnell had designed Atari's first video games himself, laboring with logic boards and a black-and-white television in a converted bedroom of his house. He had faith also, the wild entrepreneurial faith to keep plugging away when his earliest inventions were scorned by investors. As Atari grew, he became less involved with hands-on engineering, but his enthusiasm for the company's technology burned brighter than ever. "The day you go to lunch without playing a game to decide who pays, you know the game has lost your interest," Bushnell explained to a *Washington Post* reporter who asked him about Atari's success. It was the kind of answer that endeared him to some of Silicon Valley's most talented engineers, who would later follow Bushnell from company to company as his empire grew.

He was not a good manager. He admitted it, and few resented it. It seemed a beguiling corollary to his creativity. Besides, his other half, his partner, Joe Keenan, did have managerial talent.

By the late seventies, however, the company was growing so fast that Keenan by himself could scarcely contain it. "Absolute chaos," said venture capitalist Don Valentine, one of Atari's underwriters, describing Bushnell's video-game company at this time. Some of the problems stemmed from the marketing of Atari's Video Computer System (VCS), the home console unit Bushnell had been developing when he sold the company to Warner in 1976. After the acquisition, Warner put up $120 million to develop and market the system, and Atari brought it out in the fall of 1977. Sales were sluggish at first, and remained flat through 1978, leaving Atari up to its ears in unsold consoles.

In late 1978, with the crisis worsening, Emanuel Gerard, the Warner executive who had engineered the Atari buyout, proposed a reorganization. Bushnell would remain a director of Atari but would be replaced by Keenan as chairman. Raymond Kassar, then in charge of the company's home-games division, would take over as chief executive officer.

Bushnell was dead set against the plan. The slow sales of the VCS were due to overpricing, he argued. Gerard countered that Bushnell had little experience in, and knew even less about, the national marketing of consumer electronics products—a charge that was at least half true. The nasty climax came at a November budget meeting in New York City, in which Bushnell and Gerard showered each other with obscenities. A few days later, Bushnell was ousted from Atari. The following month, he resigned from the company's board.

And so the break with Atari was complete. Bushnell immediately set about building Pizza Time Theatres—his second great success and his first great failure.

"I'm sort of a honeybee. I like to fly from flower to flower and pollinate them." The words actually belonged to Walt Disney, and the fact that Bushnell quoted them so frequently reflected nothing so much as his profound identification with the great wizard of family entertainment. After college, Bushnell had tried to land a job with Disney but was turned down; later, in search of a buyer for Atari, he had turned to Disney again in the hope that he might become a part of his favorite company. But Disney's people weren't interested. Unable to join them, Bushnell decided to beat them. Maybe it was only a bit of whimsy that, to take on the proprietors of Mickey Mouse and Donald Duck, he would let loose a rat. But a rat it was, by the name of Chuck E. Cheese.

The first Chuck E. Cheese Pizza Time Theatre opened in May 1977, in San Jose, California, as a division of Atari. Early growth was slow: Eighteen months later, only six new restaurants had opened. Shortly before his final battle with the powers at Warner, however, Bushnell had bought back full rights to Pizza Time for $500,000. When he left Atari in early 1979, he set off to devote his full energies to the animation of Chuck E. Cheese.

Although the Disney influence was obvious from the outset, Bushnell's Pizza Time Theatre restaurants more nearly resemble Las Vegas casinos for kids than Walt's sublime fantasyland. In the theater dining room, families sit at picnic tables and devour pizza while a cast of large animal robot characters, let by head rat Chuck E. Cheese, performs loud cabaret routines based on original songs and dialogue. The music is punctuated by buzzes, bells, and whistles emanating from the nearby Fantasy Forest Game Preserve, an average 2,500 square feet of arcade games, video games, and kiddie rides. Most restaurants also sport a merchandise booth, where T-shirts and toys are peddled to customers.

What Bushnell seemed to admire most about Walt Disney was the reach of his company's entertainment empire. Indeed, he regarded the Disney company as a Pizza Time competitor and took a close interest in its new ventures and overall performance. Yet as much as he was fascinated with Disney's success, he didn't follow Disney's formula. As Pizza Time Theatres' identity evolved, it always retained the atmosphere of a neon-lit, cacophonous summer carnival—much like the Utah amusement park where Bushnell himself had worked as a youth, hustling the crowd into milk-bottle-throw and ring-toss booths. Where Disney's fantasies were always distinguished by their innocence, Bushnell's never quite lost the undertone of hucksterism.

Hucksterism, of course, has never stopped kids from dragging their parents to arcades, and they promptly began dragging those same parents to Pizza Time Theatres. Chuck E. Cheese aside, the restaurants' early success owed much to the flowering of the video-game business, which Bushnell had seeded almost a decade before. Now, as Pizza Time rolled out, video games were becoming an $8-billion-a-year industry. In the first two years after Bushnell left Atari, the number of Pizza Time restaurants grew more than twelvefold, from seven to eighty-eight. About half were company-owned, the rest franchised. In April 1981, Pizza Time went public, issuing 1.1 million shares at $15. Within a year, as the chain mushroomed to 204 outlets in thirty-five states and three foreign countries, the price of the stock more than doubled.

As chairman of Pizza Time's board of directors with a substantial ownership interest in the company, Bushnell was now one of the richest men in Silicon Valley. "Business is the ultimate game in which you keep score with money," he was fond of saying, and he was a big winner once again. The only question was what rabbit—or rat—the sorcerer would pull out of his hat next.

Soon after Pizza Time Theatres had reached the height of its success, Bushnell went to lunch with Herb Caen, the well-known *San Francisco Chronicle* columnist. Bushnell arrived at the appointed place, a ritzy San Francisco restaurant, in a limousine. He sat down at a quiet table and, as Caen later reported, exclaimed, "I'm mad for robotics!"

Caen soon gathered that the robots Bushnell had in mind were *personal* robots, household helpers designed for consumers, not the usual industrial variety. Why, Caen inquired, would anybody want to pay some $2,000 for a robot?

"Companionship!" Bushnell exclaimed again. "Robots are good company. Nice to have somebody around the house. Suppose you're watching a football game on TV and you don't want to walk into the next room to get your pipe or a beer. You don't want to press a button for one of the servants, either. So you get the robot to do it.

"And then there's the ego thing. Wouldn't you like someone to come into your room in the morning and say, 'O great and omniscient one, are you ready for your coffee?'"

Madness was perhaps an accurate description of Bushnell's attitude toward robots. For years, he had longed to build and market robots, but he had never managed to translate this fantasy into a sound business plan. Then, in the fall of 1981, a group of ex-Atari engineers approached him about funding a robot company. The group was led by Walter Hammeken, who had worked as an executive at several Silicon Valley companies, and included Jack Larson, who had been a key Bushnell employee at Atari.

The group had lots of enthusiasm but no money. Bushnell had both. He agreed to form a company, line up investors, and pay the engineers' salaries while he went to work on a marketing plan. "I guess that's the way the idea became his," says Larson.

Androbot Inc., as the company was called, was more than just a fun new plaything for Bushnell: It was part of the entrepreneur's evolving strategy for the eighties, his attempt to build an entertainment and consumer-product empire to rival Disney or even Warner Communications in size and scope. Pizza Time, for the moment, was the centerpiece of this strategy, Bushnell's point of entry into the hearts and minds of consumers. But Pizza Time was already a triumphant success, and Joe Keenan, who had left Atari, was running it on a day-to-day basis just as he had Atari.

Bushnell needed a new challenge, and Androbot could provide it. But, he wondered, why work with just one company at a time? His long-term vision called for many companies. Moreover, Hammeken's team wasn't the only group of Valley entrepreneurs to seek his money and expertise those days. And so, in late 1981, Bushnell formed a proprietorship that he called Catalyst Technologies. It was one of the most innovative business ideas ever seen in Silicon Valley.

Catalyst was conceived as a protective holding company that would eventually mass-produce not products but small high-technology enterprises. In early 1982, it began to provide wide-ranging support to a number of start-ups. Initially the support was to include seed capital, business plans, office space, accounting, and other operating services. Later, when the sponsored company was ready to fly on its own, it would get a second round of venture financing.

Androbot was the first Catalyst company and Bushnell's favorite. Fueled by a $1-million investment that he arranged, it moved into the Catalyst building even before heat and electricity had been hooked up. Bushnell spent increasing amounts of time there, consulting with the engineers and developing a marketing plan. He was excited about the prospect of building truly personal robots, friendly mechanical pets that would sell for $1,500 to $2,000 and could fetch a beer when the owner "didn't want to press a button for one of the servants."

As it happened, Walter Hammeken had had quite a different idea: He wanted to build industrial robots, perhaps to serve as mobile guards or fire-watchers in plants and warehouses. Bushnell, however, was not to be stopped, and this time around it was he who owned the company. After a series of what Hammeken calls "severe disagreements," Hammeken left the company abruptly.

With Hammeken gone, Bushnell plowed full speed ahead. He recruited a new president for the company: Tom Frisina, a Los Angeles sales executive with a strong background in consumer electronics marketing but no experience in Androbot's kind of engineering. Frisina recalls that his own attitude at the time was: "I know what makes people tick in homes. I know how to motivate them to buy things. Let's build some personal robots that can satisfy people in their homes. And let's not worry about how difficult they are to build, because we'll find some way of licking the problems."

That, of course, was the Nolan Bushnell way.

Hundreds of people were crowded onto the Las Vegas hotel convention floor, milling from exhibit to exhibit at the January 1983 Consumer Electronics Show (CES). Many of the visitors were congregated near Androbot's booth. There, the darling of the entire show, a three-foot-tall electronic creature named Bob, was walking purposefully about, talking to the guests and following them around like a three-year-old child. Bob was Androbot's first prototype. When Bushnell had unveiled him to 200 reporters from around the world at the start of the show, the reaction was electric: It was as if everybody's science-fiction fantasy had materialized on a makeshift stage in a Vegas hotel. Bushnell, who was manning the Androbot booth with Frisina and Catalyst president Larry Calof, rubbed his beard and said, "You know, this is going to be the next Atari."

When the executives returned to California, they were in high spirits. Bushnell called a meeting to discuss how the company should proceed, and told Frisina that he wanted to develop ten different robots over the next twelve months. Some would be as intelligent and mobile as Bob, others would be less sophisticated but could plug into a personal computer; still others would be targeted to educational markets. Bushnell also wanted to draft a business plan that could be used to raise $13 million. Although the company had not yet sold a single robot, Bushnell wanted to take Androbot public.

Frisina had also been seduced by the adulatory crowds at CES. But as the executive responsible for implementing Bushnell's ambitious plans, he worried that Nolan wanted too much too soon. Ten products, he told Bushnell, was too many. "I should have taken a strong stand at that point," Frisina recalls in hindsight. "I should have said, 'Nolan, it's hard enough to do one product right in a start-up.'" Instead, Frisina compromised with Bushnell, committing the company to develop four separate products with nonoverlapping technologies. Bushnell, for his part, was satisfied with the compromise and not at all worried that four new robots was too many. He says now that he believed in early 1983 "that the lower-end three products were a real slam dunk." Slam dunk. As easy as that.

But even as he revved up Androbot for its public offering that summer, he was simultaneously preparing to make a Napoleonic return to the video-game business, following the seven-year exile imposed by the noncompete agreement with Warner. The vehicle was to be Sente Technologies, a company he had named with care. The name "Atari" comes from the Japanese game Go, and describes a move similar to check in chess. As Bushnell's publicists relentlessly pointed out, "Sente" is the only move in Go that can overtake "Atari." The noncompete agreement would expire in October 1983. Now, in January, just after he returned from the celebratory CES in Vegas, Bushnell closed a deal to buy the assets of Videa Inc., a game software company run by ex-Atari engineers, for $2.2 million. Bushnell made Videa and its engineers a part of Sente, and set the whole operation up as a wholly owned subsidiary of Pizza Time Theatres.

It must have seemed to him, back in the winter of 1983, that all of his maneuverings finally were coming together into the grand master strategy, a *tour de force* of technological and entrepreneurial wizardry. Video games, in Bushnell's estimation, were the key to Pizza Time's success. But because of the noncompete agreement, Pizza Time had been little more than a national game distributor, in effect a middleman for the companies like Warner that manufactured the games. In October, though, Bushnell would be free to create his own games and distribute them exclusively through hundreds of Pizza Time restaurants. What's more, Bushnell did not intend to sell his Sente video games, as most other game manufacturers did; instead, he would lease the games' hardware and software to distributors and retailers.

The model for the entire system was the pre-1950 film industry. Back then, the major movie studios not only controlled the pictures they produced, they owned the theaters as well. "It was such a good business that it ultimately was broken up by the Justice Department," Bushnell says. "I felt that the analogy was such a powerful one, of having unique, exclusive products in a retail establishment, that it was just an overwhelming profit potential." And indeed, if one accepted the idea that video games were equivalent to motion pictures, Bushnell's new empire would have it all: theaters, games, even a pizza concession.

"We're talking about bedazzling new games that will also be educational. We're talking about putting a player inside the video game. What we come up with will be well worth waiting for," Bushnell proclaimed. Even Androbot had a crucial place in the entertainment juggernaut he planned to unleash. At the same time he introduced his revolutionary new video games, Bushnell intended to debut robot table service in Pizza Time Theatres. Such an innovation, he said, would be "astounding."

The truth about magic is that is works: A man's fantasies can change the world. But the truth about the world is that it won't stay under anyone's spell for long. As early as the summer and fall of 1982, sales at Pizza Time's restaurants were "relatively flat," and in mid-March of 1983 the company warned that first-quarter earnings would be lower because of a 20 percent drop from the previous year in average store sales. Pizza Time executives blamed the hit movie *E.T.* and exceptionally rainy weather for the poor showing. In fact, the flat sales reflected a national waning of interest in video games. Despite Pizza Time's explanations, the price of the company's stock dropped dramatically; the *Wall Street Journal*'s "Heard on the Street" column reported analysts' concerns that Pizza Time's concept was wearing thin with consumers. The analysts, said Bushnell, "have their heads up their asses. . . . you're talking to fools, or people who are totally misinformed."

He could not so easily dismiss the lawsuit filed by Atari around the same time. The suit charged that he was violating his noncompete agreement by priming Sente Technologies for entry into the videogame business. Bushnell settled the suit in May, but the litigation hampered his efforts to get Sente off the ground.

At Androbot, too, there were signs that all might not go according to Bushnell's plan. The Las Vegas CES had proven to Bushnell that there was tremendous interest in consumer robots, but the show hadn't demonstrated the existence of a market. Moreover, Bob was nowhere near ready for manufacturing. As a "brains on board" robot—that is, one whose memory and functions are entirely self-contained—Bob presented monumental engineering problems, particularly if it were to sell for $2,000 or less. And once the glow of the CES reception had faded, no one at the company was entirely certain what tasks Bob should be programmed to perform. "That's when the question came," a former engineering supervisor recalls. " 'Great. It looks terrific. It's fun. But what will it do?' "

The more Frisina's sizable marketing staff tried to find out what consumers wanted from a robot, the more problems it created for the engineers. Consumers wanted a robot to wash windows or mow the lawn. If they wanted a pet, Frisina's research seemed to indicate, they would go to the pound and save $2,000. Bushnell himself was aware that the robot somehow needed to be useful, but occasional remarks—like the one about pushing buttons for a servant—suggested that his understanding of ordinary consumers' needs might be limited.

In any event, there was no way Androbot's engineers could come up with a manufacturable robotic handyman under the gun of a six-month deadline. Some of them doubted they could create such a product in six years. Bushnell's decision to create four different robots simultaneously, moreover, had sown dissension among the engineers. By the new, post-CES schedule, Androbot's first product would be a "brains off board" robot named Topo—a creature that needed a personal computer to operate it. It was hoped that Topo would be sent to market in late spring, carrying a price tag of $800.

But few of the Androbot engineers were interested in Topo; they had signed on to build a real robot, not a computer accessory. In addition, precious engineering resources were now being diverted to develop the company's two other products: Fred, a brains-off-board robot targeted for the educational market; and Androman, a more ambitious consumer robot, described as a kind of three-dimensional video game. Two camps of engineers began to form around Topo and Bob, severing the spirit of camaraderie and adventure that had characterized Androbot before CES. This splintering led to quality-control problems: When the prototype of Topo was finally marketed in May, a large number of the robots were "dead on arrival," and many others quickly developed engineering snafus.

Bushnell was largely unaware of the dissension; he and Androbot's other top executives were preoccupied with financing the company. Frisina, Androbot's ostensible day-to-day leader, spent three solid months working almost exclusively on taking Androbot public. He, too, lost touch with product development.

Bushnell, however, had good reason to raise cash quickly: Androbot was burning his own money at a rate of several hundred thousand dollars a month. Frisina's business plan called for Androbot to go through about $10 million before the company broke even. Without outside financing, most of that would be Bushnell's money. A successful public offering would repay him about $2 million of what he had loaned Androbot. So Bushnell approached his investment bankers at Merrill Lynch, who in turn introduced Frisina to the firm's Capital Markets Group.

"It was pretty heady," Frisina recalls. "[Going public and getting rich] is the Valley philosophy. That's what makes this place tick. . . .

The Merrill Lynch guys looked at the Androbot issue as a great way of getting into the high-tech [market] and making a real stand for themselves. These guys had been accustomed to dealing with smoke-stack America all their lives. And they wanted desperately to get into the Valley and make their mark."

As it happened, this was not the time for anyone to make his mark in the Valley. The first sign of the coming high-tech stock collapse appeared in early June of 1983, when Activision Inc., which at the time of registration was $17, came out at $12 and dropped to $9 in only six weeks. In July, just as Androbot's IPO window (the one-month period in which details of a new stock offering are circulated to investors) began, the electronic game and home computer industry began to crumble. Atari, Coleco, Mattel, and Texas Instruments all reported losses or disappointing earnings. Then word of serious troubles at Osborne Computer Corporation sent a sudden chill through the high-tech market. Retail investors had initially shown great interest in Androbot's $10 issue, but Frisina and Bushnell soon found that institutional investors wouldn't touch it. The offering was scheduled for the first week of August 1983. That week, Merrill Lynch withdrew the offering.

"And there we were, sitting with one hundred and five employees, four products, and we were running out of money," Frisina remembers.

For a long time, Nolan Bushnell's head had been high above this gathering storm. Now, for the first time in his professional life, things began to look desperate. In May 1983, Pizza Time Theatres had sold $50 million worth of 8.25 percent convertible debentures, partly to finance its accelerating growth. A month later the company was forced to announce that it would do no better than break even for the second quarter of 1983, and that its research "indicated that our customers want better service and an improved food product." In July, stockholders were told that Pizza Time hadn't broken even in its second quarter after all. Rather, it reported a loss of more than $3 million.

"I was not planning to spend a significant amount of time at Pizza Time," Bushnell recalls. "I thought it was pretty much on automatic pilot. Then right after the middle of the year, it was very obvious that things were wildly wrong."

Wildly wrong, indeed. While fashioning a plan to make Pizza Time Theatres the center of a family-entertainment empire, Bushnell had forgotten about one thing—pizza. By the spring of 1983, it was apparent that the company's "cardboard" pizza, as a former top Pizza Time executive described it, was turning customers away. So was the accelerating national decline in enthusiasm for video games; in just a few years, the industry had seen sales drop by $4 billion annually. Without a quality food product to fall back on, Pizza Time was rocked by the collapse. Declining customer counts at its restaurants, moreover, gave credence to speculation that consumers, especially parents, were tiring of Chuck E. Cheese and his friends.

While Bushnell was spending a great deal of his time at Catalyst, Joe Keenan and Pizza Time's board of directors were trying to respond to the assault on the company's revenues. They closed unprofitable stores, reevaluated their growth plans, and introduced a new pizza recipe. The 200-restaurant chain, insisted Bushnell, was "never a food concept." He wanted to attack the problems on his own terms, and he moved quickly to unveil his last weapon, Sente Technologies. Games— new and better video games—were the one remaining hope for his grand strategy.

Nolan Bushnell thrust his pipe into the air. "Free at last, free at last! Thank God I'm free at last!"

The crowd at Sente's launching party in Milpitas on September 30 whooped and hollered. But if the party represented one of Bushnell's last opportunities to bask in the glory of his accomplishments, it was also a well-orchestrated attempt to distract public attention from the problems that were leading Pizza Time Theatres toward disaster. In early September 1983, Joe Keenan had announced his resignation as CEO "for personal reasons," and had moved to an office at Catalyst to pursue other projects. Bushnell had retaken day-to-day control of Pizza Time's operations and had announced a major reorganization of the company into four divisions: restaurants, Sente, Zapp's, and Kadabrascope. Zapp's was a singles-bar restaurant concept in early development; Kadabrascope was an animation project that Bushnell hoped would develop state-of-the-art cartoons for Pizza Time restaurants. During 1983, he bought a $1.5-million computer for the division and hired a team headed by a renowned ex-Disney animator named Jack Nichols to run it.

What was taking place backstage, however, was a story considerably more dramatic. With Androbot decimated and Pizza Time bleeding cash, all that remained of Bushnell's grand strategy was Sente. But few, even within his own company, shared his nearly obsessive belief that Sente's games could save the day. Keenan, in particular, disagreed sharply with Bushnell's intention to lease his video games rather than sell them, a decision that would do little for the company's cash-flow problems. Keenan argued that Pizza Time was in no position to bank on the long-term success of the games, that it needed to get its money out of Sente as fast as possible. But Bushnell was not about to mortgage the future of his entertainment empire. He suggested a compromise: Sell the games' hardware to distributors but rent the games themselves as replacement software cartridges, like movies on videotape. Keenan remained adamant: The company could no longer afford to engage in marketing experiments. There was, in the words of one company director, "a lot of conflict." The conflict led Keenan to resign.

"Maybe Nolan really expected a masterstroke with Sente," reflects Steve Lieberman, a Minneapolis video-game distributor and a Pizza Time director who resigned in December 1983. "In fact, it's really difficult to mix a manufacturing with a restaurant business, especially when the restaurant business has indigestion."

Lieberman was not alone in this view. By the time Bushnell took over as CEO, he was at odds with both his board of directors and his top executives. "It was pretty much Nolan versus the world," says Randall Pike, at the time the executive vice-president who coordinated Pizza Time's four divisions. "What we needed was to get a good food product in here. But his time all went toward Sente and the games."

The games. Where were they? By all accounts, Bushnell is one of the most dedicated, hardest-working executives in Silicon Valley. But there was not enough time in the day for him to exercise the kind of managerial control he seemed bent on at Pizza Time, Androbot, and Sente. His days were split inconsistently among the three companies and numerous other demands. Yet the more his companies spiraled downward, the less he was willing to delegate key decisions.

The previous winter, when he had first plotted the ambitious strategy that was now unraveling around him, Bushnell had planned to unveil Sente's first video games in October. Engineering delays and the Atari lawsuit sabotaged that idea. A new debut was set for December 9. Over at Sente, a team led by Ed Rotberg was toiling furiously to make that deadline with a game called Snakepit. As time grew short, Pizza Time's cash problems were making Rotberg's job increasingly difficult. Tools and parts he ordered simply wouldn't show up. When he called suppliers to check on the delay, he often found that Pizza Time hadn't paid its bill in six months.

The company was now losing money at a rate of nearly $20 million a month. Customer counts at company-owned restaurants were plummeting. Randall Pike, Bushnell's second-in-command, was recommending that they shut down the vastly unproductive Kadabrascope division and sell off the Zapp's singles restaurants. But Bushnell refused to let Kadabrascope go. A Christmas cartoon would excite some holiday business at the restaurants, he argued, and Kadabrascope's cash needs were "minuscule" compared to the restaurant division.

Instead, Bushnell convened his board with increasing frequency— once a week, at the peak of the crisis—to wrangle over the company's problems. They met at Pizza Time's Sunnyvale headquarters where, for three or four hours at a time, Bushnell sat puffing on his pipe as he debated with the directors about how to keep Pizza Time from sinking. Some directors felt that Bushnell listened to their arguments and appeared to agree with their suggestions—then when the board would reconvene the following week, it often seemed that nothing had changed. But what could they do? With 19 percent of Pizza Time's outstanding stock, Bushnell clearly represented ownership.

"Some of us heard things and interpreted them one way, and others of us heard things and interpreted them another way," says former board member Don Valentine, who owned 185,000 shares of Pizza Time worth more than $5 million at its peak. "Was it frustrating?

Yes. . . . From my point of view, Nolan was just another player."
Valentine refused to say why he resigned from the board in December,
as did InterWest Partners venture capitalist Wallace Hawley. Steve
Lieberman says he resigned because "board members shouldn't be in
the position of running the company," and because he felt an increasing conflict of interest as a Pizza Time director and independent video-
game distributor.

"How are you sleeping?" a Pizza Time executive asked Bushnell
one morning at the height of the crisis.

"I'm sleeping fine," Bushnell replied nonchalantly. Other men
might have cracked under the stress. By then, Bushnell was working
sixteen-hour days. Androbot was in the midst of massive layoffs and a
bloody purge of part of the Frisina management team. Other Catalyst
companies were proving to be a disappointment. These included Cine-
mavision Ltd., a big-screen TV company; and Axlon Inc., which made
an unsuccessful data communications device. Over at Pizza Time, it
was looking more and more as if Bushnell's beloved Sente would have
to be sold, after all, in order to stave off a bankruptcy filing.

Nevertheless Bushnell pressed on with his plans. "Nolan is a very
optimistic guy," Randall Pike explains. "He always seemed to think
something brilliant was going to happen—tomorrow. He tended to look
primarily at the upsides and not quantify the risks. . . . [Pizza Time's
restaurant problems were] sort of dull to him. There wasn't a quick
high-tech answer to the problems."

Bushnell offers his own explanation. "I am not a person that sits
around wringing his hands. I take a lot of personal responsibility for
whatever happens, both good and bad. The Pizza Time situation, being
my first what I'd call 'failure,' was a real disappointment. But I'm
pretty resilient."

Back in early 1983, when he seemed at the top of the world,
Bushnell was asked by *Success* magazine about the temporal nature of
achievement and ambition. He puffed contemplatively on his pipe and
told the story of Steve McQueen's character in the movie *The Cincin-
nati Kid*: "He always beats the little black guy pitching coins, but then
he loses the big game, and goes back, and the little guy beats him.
Suddenly he can't beat anybody. I think of that often, y'know. . . ."

The end to Nolan Bushnell's big game, when it came, was merci-
fully swift. Bushnell had argued that December would be the month
Pizza Time turned around. In past years, the company's business had
been relatively slow during October and November, after kids returned
to school, and had picked up again dramatically during the holiday
season. In December, moreover, Sente's Snakepit video game would
debut, and Kadabrascope's Chuck E. Cheese Christmas cartoon would
be distributed to Pizza Time restaurants. The combination, Bushnell
believed, would attract hordes of customers.

The hordes never came. Nobody noticed the Chuck E. Cheese
cartoon. The Snakepit game, unveiled to the press in Milpitas on

December 9, was not a flop, but it was hardly a success. Cash problems continued to worsen: Between September and December, Pizza Time lost more than $75 million, over $12 per share. Shortly after the first of the year, Bushnell announced his resignation as Pizza Time's CEO. "When there wasn't the recovery," Bushnell explains now, "I said, 'Okay, maybe I don't have what it takes in this particular situation.' And also . . . other fish had to be fried."

By now, though, Androbot, too, was pretty well cooked. After the public offering was rescinded in August, Bushnell took greater control over the company's day-to-day operations. By January, most of Androbot's original founders were gone, as was much of Frisina's eager marketing team. Fred, the educational robot, hadn't gotten out of the engineering lab. Androman was sold for $1 million to, of all places, Atari, but the deal subsequently fell apart.

Bushnell retained a tiny engineering crew at Androbot, which continues even now to work on robot products. He fully intends to reintroduce one of them within the next several years—"after what I would call a 'false start.'" The debacle, he adds, was a matter of too little money. "It's the only time I've been four and a half million dollars short on the cost of development. Hindsight, I probably wouldn't have done one of the products."

He predicts that Sente, too, will rise from the ashes. When Bushnell quit Pizza Time, Randall Pike took over as CEO. His first act was to shut down Kadabrascope. A few weeks later, Sente was sold to Chicago-based Bally Manufacturing. Bushnell remains Sente's chairman.

Even the $3.5-million sale of Sente, though, was not enough to save Pizza Time. "We had hoped Sente would be a bigger asset," Pike says. "In fact, it didn't turn out that way." At the end of March, Pike resigned. On March 28, 1984, Pizza Time Theatres filed for protection from its creditors under Chapter 11 of the federal bankruptcy laws. It owned 5,000 creditors more than $100 million. In anticipation of the filing, several institutional investors in Pizza Time filed a class action suit against the company's officers and directors, charging that they knowingly deceived the public about Pizza Time's condition when they sold the $50 million in debentures in May 1983.

What has Bushnell learned from all this? In the face of a failure that would rock most entrepreneurs to their souls, he observes, "It was a good, serious lesson in spreading yourself too thin. I think the Pizza Time experience was very valuable to me. I think it's important to really understand time budgeting a little bit better, and to find some ways to monitor and to intercede at earlier times.

"I really think that, looking back, I basically delegated too much responsibility in Pizza Time at too soon a period."

Bushnell says that—despite losing at least $5 million in the Pizza Time and Androbot fiascos alone—his personal solvency has not yet been threatened. "Well, I can't say it doesn't hurt. But I have transcended that, and in fact, and this will sound very utopian, but I've always felt that I'd rather lose my money than [that of the] people who have invested in me. Fundamentally, my pride is more important to me than my money."

Since resigning from Pizza Time Theatres, Bushnell has busied himself at Androbot and Catalyst, where several companies are ready to launch products in 1984 and 1985. He has also been working to expand the Catalyst concept around the globe and expects to announce an offshore Catalyst proprietorship soon. "We think the Catalyst concept is working so well . . . we're expanding it and training it for various places," he says. "In fact, if we wanted to, we could probably set up three or four in the next little while."

One of Androbot's successors as the Great Catalyst Hope is a company called Etak Inc., which is working on a computer navigation system for automobiles. It works like a magic carpet: A driver has a television monitor on his dashboard that displays electronic maps of the area he is in. A blip on the screen indicates where he is going, and another blip shows where he is now. "All you really have to do is drive toward it [the blip]," Bushnell says. Once asked why anyone would spend $2,000—the anticipated initial retail price—for such a device, Bushnell explained, "Let's say you're in your car and you want to go to dinner. You've got this box on the dash. You punch in 'Japanese,' then 'cheap,' then 'good sushi.' The box takes over and guides you to a place."

Where Etak will guide Nolan Bushnell seems these days a little beside the point.

—STEVE COLL

PBA: A Tale of Two Airlines

Peter Van Arsdale had the game won from the start. His competitors at the negotiating table wore business suits. Van Arsdale wore a pilot's uniform with shoes shined and nameplate burnished. They sat fingering calculators. He had the numbers in his head. They were new to aviation, station managers for fledgling carriers struggling to survive the rigors of deregulation. He came from three generations of aviators. As president of Provincetown-Boston Airline Inc. (PBA), he was representing arguably the oldest and most consistently profitable commuter airline in the United States.

It wasn't much of a battle—in the past few months most of his competitors had approached Van Arsdale for a job—but by the end of the meeting he had saved PBA some $8,000 a year on its share of the new commuter terminal being built in Sarasota, Florida, enough, he thought, to justify the one-hour flight up from the company's home base in Naples, Florida. And he enjoys getting into the trenches, particularly if it will show up on the bottom line.

Profiting from hands-on management is nothing new for PBA. Begun by John Van Arsdale, Sr., in 1949 as the successor to Cape Cod Flying Service and run by his sons since 1980, chairman and chief executive officer John Van Arsdale, Jr., and president Peter Van Arsdale, the company has shown a profit for each of its thirty-three years.

The 1980s haven't brought prosperity to the airline industry. Recession, the air traffic controllers' strike, and escalating fuel and labor costs have all taken a toll. Among the major carriers, Braniff International Corporation went under, and Delta Air Lines Inc. reported a loss for the first time in twenty-five years. Among the regionals, Air New England Inc. folded, and high-flying Air Florida Systems Inc., which had reported a $5.1 million profit in fiscal 1980, lost $14.7 million in the 1982 first quarter alone.

But PBA has thrived. Revenues in 1981 rose to $18 million from $12 million; revenues for the first three quarters of 1982 reached $25 million. The company has expanded from six routes to twenty-four, adding service to seventeen cities—new markets that accounted for almost half of PBA's 53 percent growth in the number of passengers carried in 1981. In August 1982, PBA boosted its passenger boardings

100 percent from the August 1981 level, to 102,815, becoming the first of the regional airlines to board more than 100,000 passengers in a single month. And even with such dynamic growth, the bottom line has still shown profit: $127,000 before taxes in 1981 ($267,000 after taxes because of investment tax credits) and a projected $250,000 for 1982.

"We're not tremendously profitable," John Van Arsdale, Jr., says. "Just consistently profitable—regardless of what we confront."

John Van Arsdale, Sr., gave his sons a commuter carrier unique in the United States, one that violates many of the established rules for airline success:

• PBA flies a largely resort trade. It alternates between dual seasonal markets, concentrating on Massachusetts' Cape Cod and island vacationers from Boston, New Bedford, Massachusetts, and New York in the summer and on sun-seekers along Florida's Gulf Coast in the winter. "The nice thing about the airline business is that your capital assets are highly transportable," John, Jr., says. While PBA doesn't abandon routes during the off-season, it relocates 50 percent of its aircraft, some 70 percent of capacity, north in summer and south in winter.

• Conventional wisdom stresses the value of modern, fuel-efficient equipment for ease of operation and maintenance. But the backbone of the PBA fleet is made up of aging aircraft: six Martin 404s and twelve Douglas DC-3s (including "Old 36," with more hours in the air than any other commercial aircraft still in operation), all of which had seen long service with a multitude of previous owners.

• Conventional wisdom touts the value of having a limited number of aircraft types. Instead, PBA has five. Along with the thirty-passenger DC-3s and the forty-four-passenger Martins, the airline flies twenty-seven nine-passenger Cessna 402s, four fifty-eight-passenger Nihon YS-lls, and seven nineteen-passenger Bandeirantes.

It is these anomalies, however, that give PBA its greatest competitive advantage, the ability to balance capacity and demand. Passengers holding PBA tickets rarely know on what size plane they will fly; advance reservations, time of day, major airline feed, and gut feeling determine what equipment will be rolled out to the gate. No prospective passenger is ever turned away. There is no overbooking. Load factors, the ratio of seats occupied to the number of seats available, stay high. While PBA can cut costs during light traffic periods by flying smaller planes, the airline keeps extra equipment on hand to fly additional sections of each flight if so much as one would-be fare shows up.

But the PBA story is really a tale of two airlines, a story of changing generations and a changing business environment, of changing opportunities and strategies that built on the old while embracing the new. For thirty-one years John Van Arsdale, Sr., ran PBA cautiously, buying old planes to fly in monopoly markets, growing slowly, and avoiding debt. But the 1978 passage of the Airline Deregulation Act doomed that strategy. Deregulation allowed major carriers to drop routes at will, routes that then became potential markets for any commuter line that was willing to enter the competitive fray.

"Dad's philosophy was to entrench yourself and avoid competition," says John, Jr. "When someone would threaten to come in on top of Dad he would run to the state public service commissions, the Civil Aeronautics Board, and the FAA [Federal Aviation Administration] to complain. That's the way things were done back then.

"But *we* were younger. We were willing to take risks. And we're not afraid of competition—in fact, we're pretty awesome competition ourselves."

"The Old Man," employees call him. More formally, "Old Man Van." Now two years retired, John Van Arsdale, Sr., has attained the status of fondly remembered myth. Persistent, they call him. And visionary.

Flying made John Van Arsdale ill, but when he was a boy, before his father was killed in a crash at the Hyannis, Massachusetts, airport, father and son flew together in a biplane. "When I'd feel myself getting sick I'd signal him, and he'd turn the plane upside down and I'd let it all go," he remembers.

He struggled, burp bag in hand, to get his private pilot's license. Then he washed out of flight training in World War II and saw service as a weatherman instead. Convinced that, sickness notwithstanding, commercial aviation was where his professional future lay, he set up Cape Cod Flying Service outside of Hyannis in 1946, repairing the runway himself, buying the planes, hiring instructors to train GI-Bill veterans, and enrolling at his own school to get his commercial license at government expense.

Moving to Provincetown, Massachusetts, in 1948, he saw increased demand for charter service between the Cape Cod resort town and Boston. So he started Provincetown-Boston Airline, with inaugural service on November 30, 1949. He chose the name, he says, "so I wouldn't have to tell people where I flew."

The airline's pattern was set with his first route. Like most of PBA's flights today, the Provincetown-Boston run was over water, cutting 120 land miles to 45 air miles, shortening what was then a five-hour drive to a thirty-minute flight. He instituted mixed fleet/demand scheduling, rolling out a two-seat Luscomb for one passenger, a Piper Clipper for two, and a Stinson Voyager for three. He moved his family to Provincetown so he would become the "local" airline. "There's only one way to run a small airline successfully," he argues. "You've got to live in the community, make it your home base, get to know everybody." PBA today still bases its personnel in whatever town they serve.

Provincetown-Boston was a pioneer: It had a dirt runway, a jerry-built terminal, and a wind sock and a radio, rather than radar and navigation aids. Mom Van Arsdale sold tickets. Pop Van Arsdale flew the planes. The four children, too, were expected to pitch in, starting at age twelve as assistant linemen, picking up cigarette butts around the airport. John and Peter both started learning to fly at fourteen, soloed at sixteen, and were licensed as private pilots at seventeen and as commercial pilots at eighteen.

"It was primitive, really something," John, Jr., says. "Sometimes an employee would stick his head outside and listen for the plane, then direct the pilot home by radio. He might say, 'You sound like you're getting a little too far to the west,' and the guy would turn east, and the next thing you'd know, you'd see this plane come drifting over the airport." Provincetown-Boston operated only during the summer tourist season, so each spring new pilots would have to be hired. "And when the weather was bad you couldn't send them out. My father would climb on the airplane and go to Boston, 'cause he knew his way back and these other guys didn't."

In the winter of 1957, looking for more efficient use of equipment and personnel, Van Arsdale and his wife drove through Florida, searching for carriers having similar seasonal problems and with which Provincetown-Boston might ally. Naples Airlines, on Florida's Gulf Coast, was the solution. For three years the two companies leased planes and traded personnel, until the city of Naples refused to renew the owner's airport lease. So in 1960, Van Arsdale bought Naples Airlines out and became a dual-market carrier.

Although John, Jr., and Peter spent time away from the family business after college—John in the budget and accounting office of the Marines and Peter flirting with a banking career on the West Coast—by 1974 they were firmly established as their father's successors. John was vice-president of administration, Peter, assistant vice-president. Their father signed a buy/sell agreement with them both, promising to retire on January 1, 1980.

But when the day came, the Old Man had changed his mind. The post-deregulation transition was incomplete, he said. He wanted another year. He stepped down to the post of vice-president—naming John, Jr., chairman and CEO and Peter president—but he held 30 percent of the stock.

"My father was determined to call all the shots," John, Jr., remembers. "And you can hardly blame him. He founded the company. He ran it for thirty-one years, working seven days a week." He had reason to feel proprietary. From 2,495 passengers in 1947, the airline had grown to 314,619 passengers. By 1980 the mom-and-pop operation employed 230 people. The philosophy had stayed constant for thirty-one years: good service, reasonable fares, and monopoly markets.

But in the post-deregulation era the boys felt it was time to test their competitive strength. It was a philosophical difference that came to a practical head over their decision to go into the Marathon-Miami market, a route served by then-booming Air Florida.

Their father was in Washington when they were approached by the Marathon Chamber of Commerce. Ocean Reef Airways Inc., operating as an Air Florida commuter line on a so-called wet lease—a lease not just of planes but of pilots, flight crews, and all operational personnel as well—had cut service to Marathon, Florida, to two flights a day. Traffic was down 30 percent in one year. But as a tourist center, Marathon depended on that traffic. So the city fathers turned to PBA for help. A visit to Marathon convinced the boys that, with stimulation, the market could be profitable for them, yielding some 40,000 to 50,000 passengers a year. And there was a further temptation: Air Florida's terminal lease had expired, and the Marathon airport officials agreed to give the Van Arsdales exclusive rights.

Peter recalls that C. Edward Acker—then chairman of Air Florida, now chairman of Pan American World Airways Inc.—called up his office when he heard they would be competitive. Acker was pleasant, welcoming them to Marathon, Peter says, although insisting "it isn't much of a market." In twenty minutes, having heard that Air Florida had been evicted from the terminal and forced to set up shop in a rented trailer, Acker called back, livid.

"It's never a very pleasant experience to get evicted, I guess," Peter says, grinning. "Ed's got a big ego. He's not used to getting kicked out on his ass."

Acker today acknowledges the Van Arsdales as "good, smart, stable operators" and "tough competition." And he is politely forgiving about the terminal switch, calling the move "misled" and saying that "even the Van Arsdale boys would admit they overstepped."

The Van Arsdales, however, remain unabashed. "It was dirty pool, sure," John admits happily. "But that's the way it's played. The losing guys are always the gentlemanly competitors."

After thirty-one years of flying exclusive routes, Provincetown-Boston was about to enter its first market war. But the family battle would come first. When the senior Van Arsdale returned to Naples from his trip to Washington, he was incensed.

"He said we were crazy," John remembers. "He demanded that we either conform with all his wishes until January 1, 1981, and stop this expansion and all the other foolishness or redeem all his stock and buy him out immediately.

"It really was a case of him or us. He felt that we were squanderers, too flashy, too eager to try new stuff. But when we said 'We'll take option two,' I think he was secretly relieved."

Once in control, John, Jr., and Peter went after Marathon with a vengeance. Air Florida had been flying two trips a day—three trips in season. Provincetown-Boston—now known as PBA—would fly five. Air Florida's fare was $37. PBA's would be $27. There would be T-shirts for townspeople and a flood of ad revenue for the papers. On February

29, the boys threw an inaugural party for 300 civic leaders, travel agents, and other airline representatives.

The first flight took off, as scheduled, ten hours after the party ended. Then the competition began in earnest. Air Florida increased its flights to seven and cut its fare to $26, estimated by John, Jr., because of the wet-lease arrangement, to be some $7 below cost. PBA cut its fare to $19. "And then," says John, "we both just stood there trying to bleed each other." Acker and the Van Arsdales battled over schedules as well, each repeatedly moving departure times a few minutes ahead of the other to come up first on travel agents' computers. Traffic at the Marathon airport soared to 2,779 passengers in November, up 100 percent from the previous November, with PBA winning the competitive battle. "Air Florida had developed a poor reputation by not serving the community," Peter says. "And we were the good guys." By December, traffic was up again, to 3,691 passengers—2,217 of whom rode PBA. Although both airlines flew nineteen passenger planes during the winter, demand scheduling gave PBA a marketing advantage: They never turned a passenger away because a flight was full. PBA also used thirty-seaters "or whatever the hell we needed," recalls Peter. When spring came and traffic dropped, the mixed fleet enabled PBA to fly smaller nine-passenger Cessnas, operating at half the competition's cost.

John, Jr., and Peter were quick to put their own stamp on the airline, changing some of their father's most cherished policies. He had bought surplus planes at a low price and depreciation, with small interest payments and tax credits, and with high maintenance and low utilization. The new generation flipped the card, adding new planes with a high purchase price and depreciation, large interest payments and tax credits, low maintenance, and high utilization. One week after their father retired, John and Peter signed for two Bandeirantes, the first turbo-props in the fleet. "Dad had gone thirty years without flying one," John jokes. "We went one week."

Their father had avoided any major debt. By the end of the year, PBA had bought two more Bandeirantes—for $1.5 million each, with $225,000 down and 7.5 percent financing—and five more Cessnas— $225,000 each, 15 percent down, and 12.5 percent financing. There was new construction as well: the Van Arsdale Memorial Maintenance Hangar, so called "because my father said it would be built only over his dead body," John, Jr., explains, and two new passenger terminals.

"We started to get in a pretty tight cash position then," John, Jr., remembers. "My dad came by in July and said, 'You're never going to make it. You'll be two million dollars short.' That scared the hell out of me.

"I'll never forget December 31 of that year. I was sitting in the office writing a letter when the monthly figures came in—I hadn't known until then that we were going to make it."

But make it they did—profits of $1.5 million on $12.5 million total revenues.

And they would win the Marathon battle, too, although it would be their longest competitive struggle. Air Florida pulled out of the Marathon market on December 1, 1981.

The PBA offices stand at the entrance to the old airport terminal in Naples, looking like a ramshackle prefab motel unit. The company logo—a white seagull over the red letters PBA on a blue field—is on the door. It hangs above a no-smoking sign, a legacy of John and Peter's days of picking up cigarette butts. Inside, the tiny paneled warrens are crowded with people and typewriters and countless towers of paper on either edge of collapse. An oil portrait of the Old Man hangs on one wall. On the other, a painted plaque proclaims the family credo: "The Lord Giveth, the Government Taketh Away."

Monday through Saturday, from nine in the morning to seven at night, the brothers are at work. Whatever else their father taught them, the value of hard work was always primary. "Dad was a classic entrepreneur, a one-man show," Peter says. The elder Van Arsdale—who today edits the PBA newsletter—had tried to do everything himself: planning, marketing, scheduling, even loading bags and pasting up his own ads. With expansion, however, John, Jr., and Peter have had to departmentalize and delegate. Today there is a vice-president and general manager, vice-president of maintenance, vice-president for operations, and vice-president for finance, as well as a computer for payroll, maintenance, and inventory. John, Jr., and Peter have divided executive responsibility by personal inclination: John likes the change of seasons, so he oversees northern operations. Peter likes the sun, so he stays south. John likes marketing, Peter finance, so John sets schedules and Peter sets fares. They handle all customer complaints personally.

Like their father, both still fly. Resort markets mean traffic and demand surges, not only in season but around weekends and holidays. Management that can grab a plane and carry a load makes it easier to meet the promise of unlimited seats.

"When I don't get called on to fly occasionally, I figure we're overstaffed," John says. "Besides, you can sit in your goddamn office each day and think everything is going well, but you've got to get out and see for yourself. Your whole life with an airline is trying to catch the screw-ups before they happen.

"The key to good management is to set an example that starts at the top. At PBA everybody gets their hands dirty.

"We continually stress to our employees that we're not an airline. We're a service organization. Airlines mean waiting lists and overbooking and unhelpful people. But a service organization operates for the good of the customers—that means everyone pulling together."

The staff of 500 is considerably younger than when Van Arsdale, Sr., ran the operation. Turnover is low, and promotion is from within. Motivation, John says, is easy: "Our employees see that we're a young, aggressive, and growing company, with the opportunity for real upward mobility."

The strategy for that continued growth is hatched in John's chaotic office, with the brothers sitting on either side of the messy desk, pictures of the fleet on the wall, and John's dog dozing in the corner. "You have to change your thinking continually," Peter says. "You're lucky if a five-year plan is good for six months."

"Instead of planning we react," John agrees. "We sit back, make ourselves strong, and wait for opportunities."

One such opportunity—and two more violations of their father's policies—brought six more cities into the PBA network in 1981. In the fall of 1980, Air New England, a certificated carrier transporting close to 600,000 passengers a year, announced that it was dropping service to New Bedford, service that had a federal subsidy, a Civil Aeronautics Board program used to ensure essential service to a market. John, Jr., saw the opportunity New Bedford offered. It could be a door to La Guardia International Airport in New York City and out to Martha's Vineyard and Nantucket as well, a chance to battle it out with Air New England for the lucrative vacation trade. But his father had always argued that it was "suicide" to compete with a certificated carrier and bad business to accept a government subsidy.

According to Joe Mullin, the CAB's eastern regional director, PBA had to be "enticed" to file an application for the subsidy. "John had the businessman's wariness about getting involved with the federal government," Mullin recalls. "But he changed his mind when I pointed out that if he were not the carrier, then some other carrier would be subsidized in his neck of the woods."

"We felt that there was potential in New Bedford," John, Jr., remembers, "but the market was very, very soft. Our problem was that we were competing with Air New England, which was very heavily subsidized [$6.1 million in 1981] and, as a result, could take a forty-passenger plane with all the amenities and run it against my nine-passenger plane without having to watch the bottom line."

CAB subsidies are awarded on the basis of an airline's experience and available equipment, as well as how much money it requests. Not only was PBA the lowest of four bids—$799,225 during the first year, $420,783 the second—it could promise unlimited seats as well as service by the turbo-prop planes it had bought after John, Sr.'s, retirement. Van Arsdale's strategy was to make New Bedford a hub, "a mini Atlanta," from which he could shuttle flights to New York, Boston, Martha's Vineyard, and Nantucket. His eyes weren't only on the New Bedford business, however, but also on Air New England's passengers throughout the region.

Unlike Air New England, which used subsidies to cover operating costs, PBA put its subsidy into capital construction. "You could never compete with Air New England unless you had the facilities," John, Jr., argues. "So we took our subsidy money and spent it on buildings, advertising, and maintenance facilities."

PBA's entrance into the market was carefully planned, starting six months before service was to begin. Seventy people were hired and based in New Bedford, to make PBA the "local" carrier. Advertising started three months before the first flight. A month later, schedules appeared in the *Official Airline Guide*. As in Marathon, service was kicked off with a party for the media, travel agents, and city fathers.

Unlike the situation in Marathon, where PBA was invited in, the New Bedford Airport Commission had initially favored another carrier for the CAB award. Today, however, Mullin of the CAB calls PBA service "a smashing success story, which I cite throughout the region." And New Bedford Municipal Airport manager Isidore Eisner has become a PBA devotee. "This airline is fantastic," Eisner says. "It is run by professionals versus men with pencils in their ears. Air New England's service was completely undependable. And Nor East Commuter wasn't above canceling a flight if they had only two people on board."

Service began on April 26, 1981. During PBA's first nine months the company carried 13,660 passengers through New Bedford, 221 percent more traffic carried through New Bedford than in the similar 1980 period. That summer saw another fare war as well, with Air New England dropping its price for the lucrative New York–Nantucket flight from $79 to $53 to compete with PBA.

During the summer of 1981, however, the air controllers went out on strike. When the Professional Air Traffic Controllers Organization walked out, PBA had just taken delivery of three new planes, besides starting its New Bedford service. PBA lost $125,000 in the first week of the strike alone. For ten days it couldn't get a slot in or out of La Guardia airport in New York City; the number of Boston flights was cut in half. "The only good thing was that it hit us hard, but it hit Air New England even harder," John, Jr., says. PBA kept as many flights in the air as possible, flying on visual flight rules out of Boston. "Air New England had the option to fly VFR, too," he says, "but they canceled their flights instead. So they had airplanes sitting on the ground and customers coming over to fly with us."

Air New England, beset with labor problems and anticipating the strike, announced in July that it was canceling its flights to Nantucket, Martha's Vineyard, and Hyannis out of New York and Boston. In October 1981, the airline ceased operation altogether. In August 1982, Will's Air, another island competitor, filed for protection under Chapter 11 of the bankruptcy law. The market belonged to PBA.

Indeed, by the end of 1982, it seemed that PBA had come full circle. Of twenty-four routes flown, only Miami–Key West is still competitive. There was an attack on the Naples market by Air Florida—Acker out for revenge, the Van Arsdales say—but it lasted only seven months. Once again, PBA flies monopoly markets.

Expansion also seems to have slowed. John, Jr., expects a 20 percent increase in the number of passengers in the North next year but plans no new markets. Although the carrier had hoped to enter several northern Florida cities this winter, it was thwarted by FAA restrictions on new slots.

Having absorbed a great deal of debt to fund expansion, John, Jr., and Peter now find themselves also returning to their father's policy of low debt and cash payment. PBA reports $15 million in debt, with a 4-to-1 debt/equity ratio. "And we're knocking about five hundred thousand dollars off each month," John, Jr. says. "Within four years we'll be debt-free again."

PBA foresees no new competition for its routes in New England. John, Jr., has heard no start-up rumors. "And if they don't get started early, you can write them off," he says. In Florida, the same FAA moratorium on granting new slots that foiled PBA's expansion plans meant no one could begin competing with them in the South either. Ed Acker had made noises about starting a Pan Am feeder, but, given that carrier's troubles, the talk has died down.

"So I've got at least a year to become more entrenched," John, Jr., says. "In another year, I'll be the familiar carrier in all my markets. This is a period to improve our training program, our professionalism, and our creativity. If I do a good job for people, they're not even going to think about riding the competition, if there is any. They're going to say, 'Hey, call PBA.'

"We treat all our exclusive markets as if they were competitive. And to protect those markets we're willing to go as low as we need to go. So anyone who's thinking of trying to get in had better think a long, long time.

"I used to love to play Monopoly as a kid. If you play your cards right, you can maneuver yourself into a no-lose situation. If you own Boardwalk and Park Place, sooner or later someone is going to land on your space.

"There's no monopoly in this business anymore. Anyone can come in against you. But it's still the same game."

What It Costs to Run an Airline

While the strategy of matching capacity to demand using five airplane types seems simple enough, the plan could have expensive implications. What do you do with the aircraft that doesn't match demand on a certain flight? The usual rule of airline management is high utilization, a rule PBA breaks often for much of its equipment. The secret is buying used equipment that you can pay off fairly quickly. According to John Van Arsdale, Jr., chief executive officer, "You got to own 'em if you're going to park 'em."

As an example, Van Arsdale says that if you were paying $30,000 a month for a Bandeirante, or roughly $1,000 a day, and flew it five hours a day, it would cost you $200 dollars an hour toward principal and interest. If you flew it ten hours a day it would cost only $100 dollars an hour. Your operating costs go down as your hours of operation go up.

On the other hand, PBA owns its fleet of twelve DC-3s outright, all purchased for $20,000 to $120,000 and refurbished for up to $150,000 each. The problem is that if you fly a DC-3 hard, it can cost $25,000 a month just in maintenance. The more hours it flies, the more it costs.

The key is to "fly it full, then park it the rest of the time because you don't owe a dime on the airplane," says Van Arsdale. "What you target is high utilization of your expensive equipment and low utilization, high load factors, of your inexpensive equipment."

Van Arsdale is still a well-known tire-kicker around the used airplane markets, and he sees an advantage in both new and used airplanes. Although the seven Bandeirante airplanes were purchased new, representing a $10-million investment, PBA recently bought four fifty-eight-passenger YS-11s for $6 million from Piedmont Aviation Inc. Spare parts cost an added $500,000. In contrast, the de Havilland Dash 7, a plane with comparable capacity, cost $6.5 million new, and its spare parts cost $1 million extra. It is suggested that a minimum of two aircraft be purchased. PBA recently bought another used Cessna 402 (bringing the size of its fleet to sixty-three planes) for $150,000, compared with $375,000 for a new plane.

"It's a question of our tax situation and our financial situation," says Van Arsdale. "We buy new when we need the tax advantage, and we buy used when we see a financial advantage."

The busier the airline, however, the more new planes make sense. "When your utilization gets up too high, your solution is to buy efficient, new airplanes. At that point you've got enough business to keep the new airplanes going," says Van Arsdale.

PBA expects to pay off its present debt within four years then go back into debt for five new thirty-passenger Embraer Brasilia aircraft at $5 million each, scheduled for delivery in 1986.

"We need to do this to get the investment tax credits and depreciation to keep us from paying incredible taxes," says Van Arsdale. "You don't want to be debt-free at 7.5 percent."

Another factor in the choice of airplanes, one with a big impact on PBA's profitability, is the availability and price of fuel. The company's planes burn about 5 million gallons of fuel annually, costing $6.3 million in 1982, 22 percent of expenses. (A major airline's fuel would be a much larger portion of its expenses because of longer flights.)

One of the advantages of the Bandeirante and YS-11 is that they burn jet fuel, at $1.07 a gallon, rather than aviation gasoline, at around twice that price in New York. PBA has other schemes for lowering its fuel bill. After paying $1.75 a gallon for aviation gas in Boston, Van Arsdale bought two tanker trucks at $42,000 and $15,000 respectively. They allow him to buy fuel at the wholesale price of $1.30 a gallon, store it in a tank for 4¢ a gallon, and truck it onto the ramp, avoiding the Boston airport retail rate. In New York, he encouraged Texaco to write a favorable contract with him by leaving $75,000 on deposit.

The other major expense, amounting to 25 percent of all expenses, is labor. While the captain of a DC-9 for a major airline may earn about $90,000, at PBA, a nonunion carrier, the captain of a YS-11 earns $35 to $40 an hour, with a guarantee of seventy-five hours a month. The guarantee, which Van Arsdale says he chokes on now and then, works out to a base salary of $31,000. However, during peak season, PBA pilots fly the legal maximum one hundred hours a month, which means that nobody makes just the base salary. PBA's top pilot is paid $40,000 a year.

Why the Commuter Airlines Are Flying High

Although the effects of deregulation on the entire airline industry have been mixed, the new climate of competition has brought brighter skies for many small commuter carriers besides PBA.

"Deregulation has been very much a positive thing for small commuter airlines," says Patrick V. Murphy, Jr., who is associate director of the Bureau of Domestic Aviation, part of the Civil Aeronautics Board. "It allows them to move into gaps left when larger carriers leave routes. The smaller ones have the flexibility to move in quickly. So, a big plus has been market opportunity."

Before the Airline Deregulation Act of 1978, airlines needed permission from the Civil Aeronautics Board to adopt routes or change fares. Markets were tight, pricing was regulated, and the airlines were almost like utilities. Now, with the lifting of restrictions, commuter lines have flourished in a freer environment that allows them to muscle into new territory and set their own prices.

"It's been terrific," says Marden E. Leaver, a spokesman for United Air Lines Inc. "It's the first time in years that airlines are in a free-market environment, which is the name of the game in America."

The total number of commuter carriers in operation, about 260, still hasn't changed since deregulation. But, according to Tulinda Deegan of the Regional Airline Association, commuter lines carried about 20 million passengers in 1982, almost twice as many as in 1977. "The thing that has changed incredibly is the number of passengers served," Deegan said. "The [commuter] lines in business are thriving."

A major factor for the burgeoning business in commuter carriers has been the revamping of federal subsidies to airlines. The long-running Section 406 subsidy, which was used to underwrite service to remote or unprofitable points, is gradually being phased out by deregulation, prompting larger trunk carriers to leave the routes up for grabs. Replacing Section 406 is a new program, Section 419, which provides funds for carriers to take over already established routes that have been abandoned. The shift in subsidies has benefited commuter carriers that are agile and aggressive.

"It's very much free enterprise now," says Bruce Hicks, a spokesman for Continental Air Lines Inc. "The small commuter airlines reflect the true entrepreneurs in the airline industry."

However, if deregulation has given airline executives the freedom to succeed, it has also given them the freedom to fail. Suddenly thrust into a laissez-faire slugfest, managers now need marketing and pricing skills that were never before necessary. And, just as airlines were accommodating themselves to a looser marketplace, the air traffic controllers' strike hit in August 1981, damping an expansion that was just gathering steam. The cumulative effects of the strike, a worsening recession, and rising fuel prices made management mistakes very costly.

Two salient examples of poor managment under deregulation are the bankruptcies of two regional commuter carriers on the West Coast, Golden Gate Airlines and Swift Aire. Both airlines were controlled by financier Justin Colin, who embarked on an ambitious project to expand routes and purchase equipment. Although he poured a reported $25 million of his own wealth into both companies, they crumbled in the fall of 1981 under the twin pressures of restricted travel because of the strike by the Professional Air Traffic Controllers Organization and a huge debt burden.

"Mr. Colin, in his zeal, didn't do things properly," admits James Lightsey, who was a top executive at both airlines at different times. "But on the other side of the coin, you don't want to miss opportunity. Unfortunately, while he was expanding, and his cash flow was critical, Patco came along. He had taken a risk, but the strike upset the apple cart."

Regulatory officials, however, are less charitable. Paul Gretch, deputy director of the Bureau of International Aviation at the CAB, bluntly states that "they were very, very poorly managed airlines. They had very bad reputations. It is a classic bad-management story."

Gretch argues that the two commuter carriers expanded too rapidly into new routes, without doing such preliminary work as advertising and preparing travel agents. He also says they juggled fares and schedules too frequently, in an attempt to undercut the competition, and purchased too many planes based on overly optimistic projections of flight volume. "They weren't necessarily victims of market forces. . . . The loud message here [at the CAB] was that they were mismanaged."

CAB chairman Dan McKinnon summarizes it, saying that "deregulation gave [airlines] the chance to make wise decisions or to make mistakes. Those that made mistakes fared poorly."

The demise of Air New England is another example of fatal mistakes made under the new ground rules of deregulation. The airline was a certificated airline that linked New England cities and

New York, but it shut down on October 31, 1981, citing the Patco strike, adverse economic conditions, and the loss of federal subsidies because of deregulation. However, most airline analysts see the company's failure as another example of management unable to cope with the exigencies of competition.

John V. Coleman, director of the Bureau of Domestic Aviation, claims that Air New England's "biggest error" was its application for a certificate from the CAB to use larger planes. The airline was given the certificate in the middle seventies, in the midst of an oil crisis and slackening demand. In addition, certificated airlines are subject to more costly regulatory obligations, and higher maintenance and fuel costs.

"It was bad judgment that exhibited a lack of foresight," says Coleman. He adds that the change in subsidies had little to do with the company's difficulties, pointing out that it was given $6.1 million in grants in 1981, compared with $1.5 million in grants in 1975.

Charles Butler, former president of Air New England, contends otherwise. "That's hogwash," he says in response to government assertions that the shift in subsidies didn't appreciably hurt the airline. He points out that although the airline received subsidies right up to the very end, most of it was eaten up by inflation and the added costs of being certificated.

"Our operating efficiencies were as good as any other carrier," Butler says to charges that Air New England was mismanaged. However, he did say that "it's quite possible" that getting certificated was a mistake.

The fates of Golden Gate, Swift Aire, and Air New England demonstrate that deregulation favors commuter carriers that keep a lid on operating costs and debt, allowing them to offer lower rates and more flights in a market sector that depends on frequency. They also demonstrate that deregulation has created a Darwinian environment in which airline executives are highly accountable for their decisions. As Sally Scanlon, managing editor of *Aviation Monthly,* puts it, "Management isn't isolated from the mistakes it makes now."

—CURTIS HARTMAN
BROOKE TALIAFERRO
JOHN F. PERSINOS

TAILSPIN

ooking through the window of his brother's office, Peter Van Arsdale could see the reporters across the old airport road, milling about in the harsh Florida sun—CBS and ABC, minicams and instant eyes, a whole pack of them, swarming at the scent of disaster. That noon, Saturday, November 10, 1984, Federal Aviation Administration officials had delivered an "emergency order of revocation" to the Naples headquarters of Provincetown-Boston Airline Inc. (PBA), America's largest commuter carrier, and already the reporters were out in force. Peter could hear them outside, shouting their questions through the closed door, baying for blood.

And blood there was. Peter's older brother John, chairman and chief executive officer of the company their father had founded thirty-five years before, was disgraced, stripped of his pilot's certificate, and accused by the FAA of "reckless" flying that "endangered the lives" of passengers and crew. Vice-president of operations John Zate, a twenty-four-year PBA veteran and member of the board, was gone, too. Zate was accused of certifying a pilot on PBA's DC-3 without giving her a flight test, and of multiple "fraudulent or intentionally false statements" on official flight-test records. The chief pilot, the assistant chief pilot, and the three pilots with management rank had all lost flight status, likewise accused of faking flight-test records. The FAA also cited the airline for more than 160 violations of training regulations, including 136 specific cases of flight attendants serving as crew members when their requirements for "recurrent training" had not been met. In addition, the FAA listed no fewer than six violations relating to aircraft inspection and maintenance, including "exceeding [the] time limit for required inspection" and "use of unauthorized personnel to perform maintenance."

An emergency order of revocation is the most severe action the agency can take. Four thousand passengers traveling on PBA's more than 600 daily flights were stranded, 103 planes grounded, dozens of cities left partly or wholly without air service. And 1,500 PBA employees were suddenly out of work. Peter's first thought, sitting there in the beleaguered corporate headquarters, was that the airline would go broke. Air Illinois, faced with a similar crisis eleven months earlier,

153

had dissolved. Air Vermont lost its certificate in January 1984 and had lurched along under the protection of the federal bankruptcy courts for months. PBA, Peter knew, paid out $5 million to $6 million each month in bills and debt service. Without a certificate, it was technically no longer even an airline, and thus was already in default on its loans.

Even before the latest disaster, 1984 had been a turbulent year for the Van Arsdales. In July, after more than thirty years of safe flying, PBA had suffered its first crash: A Cessna pilot flying an unscheduled trip from Provincetown, Massachusetts, to Boston undershot his approach, plunging into the harbor and killing his wife, the sole passenger. In September, another Cessna pilot lost power just off the Naples runway and crashed into the nearby woods, killing one passenger. The National Transportation Safety Board (NTSB) would later report that a ground-crew member had accidentally filled the Cessna with the wrong fuel.

Still, neither tragedy—nor the growing numbers of complaints about schedule delays, rude personnel, and lost luggage—seemed to slow PBA down. The airline had been on a fast track ever since the brothers took over from their father in 1980, and 1984 was a financial record breaker. By the end of the first three quarters, PBA had recorded $58.4 million in revenues, up 41 percent from the $41.4 million registered the entire previous year. Profits climbed as well, up to $3.3 million over nine months, 43 percent more than all of 1983's. "Johno," forty, ran the company like a fiefdom, dazzling both competitors and Wall Street with his aggressive style. In October, he bought Marco Island Airways, another Florida commuter, and added the Bahamas to his swelling list of stations. He had $20 million worth of new planes on order and a $15-million private placement in the works. For the whole year the Van Arsdales were expecting to board close to 1.5 million passengers, a record for a commuter airline. In 1985, John predicted, the figure would approach 2 million.

With November's decertification, however, John's plans lay in ruin. The issue became survival.

Peter and the board, or what was left of it, met that afternoon in John's old office, behind closed doors, to consider their grim alternatives. File for Chapter 11? That would protect them from their creditors, but it could mean turning control over to a court-appointed trustee and trying to run the airline COD. Appeal? That would take sixty to ninety days. "Besides," Peter asked, "what the hell is there to appeal?" Sell? Liquidate? John had wanted to play the political card, hoping that such influential regular passengers as Senator Edward M. Kennedy or Massachusetts Congressman Gerry Studds could sway the federal government. But Peter thought that was unrealistic: "No politician is going to oppose safety in the air."

Instead, the board agreed, there was only one course for survival: win a new certificate, and with it the right to fly again. Before competitors took their market share. Before the money ran out. They would have to replace their discredited executives, submit a new management team to the FAA, then rebuild the airline from scratch, winning agency approval for each step. All their manuals would have to be rewritten, each plane reinspected, each crew member retrained and retested. By the book.

It might have been better, Peter reflected, if he had been the one forced out. The airline had been John's life, a twenty-four-hour-a-day, seven-day-a-week obsession; he would have reveled in the challenge. Peter had had other plans. He had just gotten married again, and had bought a new boat, *Slick,* a forty-two-foot racer. So far he had only been able to sail it once.

"There were times, during the meeting, when I wondered if I hadn't gotten the short end of the stick," Peter remembered. "I've always sort of worked in John's shadow. I was temperamentally suited for it. There are times you reflect how nice it would be to get home in daylight hours and see the kids, and I knew I wouldn't be able to do that for a while."

In the office, the joke had always been that PBA stood for "Peter's Brother's Airline." Now Peter's brother was gone.

There was no mistaking John Van Arsdale if you worked for PBA. He would show up at a station, crisp in his black and white pilot's uniform, rattling off questions and barking commands, every inch a former Marine. It was as a working pilot—the Flying CEO—that he built PBA into a commuter giant, and it was as a working pilot that he brought it down. "The key to good management is to set an example that starts at the top," John preached. "At PBA everybody gets their hands dirty."

PBA had been an unusual commuter long before the two brothers bought it from "Old Man Van," however. Its strategic core was a mixed fleet, a variety of plane sizes; PBA guaranteed passengers a seat, then rolled out the right size plane to match capacity to demand and keep load factors high. Operating in two resort markets, Massachusetts in the summer and Florida in the winter, PBA shuttled most of its assets—planes and staff alike—back and forth seasonally. With their Florida markets protected by the Florida Public Service Commission, the Van Arsdales' airline had never seen a year without a profit.

The deregulation of the airline industry in 1978 changed the rules of the game, and the airline had to adapt. It was two years before John could convince his father to step aside, but once at the helm he changed course with a vengeance. His mixed fleet became a competitive weapon, allowing him to schedule frequent service, slash his prices, and still show an operating profit thanks to his high load factors. A master strategist quick to react to the market, John loaded on debt, took the company public, and pushed for growth. Since 1979, PBA moved from six markets to thirty-six, from 300,000 passengers a year to nearly 1.5 million. Revenues increased at a compound annual growth rate of 46 percent, profits at 17 percent. He added sixty-six new planes, including the company's first turbo-prop, the nineteen-passenger, Brazilian-made Bandeirante. Starting with a staff of 230, he built his payroll to 500 in two years and 1,500 in four.

On paper, the rise of John Van Arsdale ended with a single flight. On November 29, 1983, according to the FAA, he had been flying a Martin 404 from Hyannis, Massachusetts, to Naples when he lost all the hydraulic fluid just after takeoff. Rather than landing the plane at once, as required by the FAA, he had flown on to Jacksonville, Florida, where PBA has a maintenance base. In Jacksonville, he moved the passengers onto a Nihon YS-11, and flew down to Naples. Since he had never won an FAA rating on a YS-11, he was flying illegally. Then, when the trip was completed, he forged another pilot's signature on the flight log.

"Blame it on fatigue," John said; the brothers agreed at the time that it was dumb. "But I didn't worry too much about it," Peter said. "I didn't think he'd get caught."

It was, said one PBA executive, a characteristic act. "Johno was a typical entrepreneur. And what does an entrepreneur do to build a company? He takes risks."

In fact, John had a long history with the FAA. The sign over his office door read, "The Lord Giveth, and the Government Taketh Away," and he was outspoken in his criticism of the agency's restrictions on his plans. But well before that November flight, PBA's fast growth had brought major stress. Policies and practices that had worked with 230 employees were outmoded with 1,500. A manager who had been able to oversee the work at six stations could never keep up with thirty-six.

"There was always a crunch; never enough people or enough time," one manager remembered. "So we shortcut proper procedures."

"John tried to run everything himself," another said. "He was a workaholic. But he got so immersed in the details that he couldn't set policy. The only policy was to get the job done at any cost."

That policy, one former pilot charged, led to widespread violations of safety rules. Dominic Carlo Giammette, who was fired in December 1982, testified to the FAA about bacteria that had grown in the fuel tank of the Bandeirante. PBA, he said, refused to put in an anti-icing, antibacterial additive, contrary to both the manufacturer's requirements and the FAA's rules. Giammette charged that his colleagues were allowed to fly more hours than the FAA's maximum and that they were instructed to log times that were in compliance with FAA regulations, that baggage handlers overloaded cargo areas, and that station managers listed adults as children to get loaded planes under federal weight restrictions.

Giammette had had a brief but stormy career with the Van Arsdales. Hired early in 1980, he was fired three years later in a dispute over his refusal to land a plane in heavy fog. PBA management labeled him a hothead and later tried to deny him unemployment compensation, charging that he was fired for "violation of company rules," but the Florida labor board ruled that his dismissal had nothing to do with his performance as a pilot. Giammette had gone once to the FAA in 1983 with no result. Then, in September 1984, after the Florida crash, he went to the FAA again.

The FAA had already inspected PBA twice that year. In February, it investigated 183 charges based on allegations forwarded by the president of the Aviation Safety Institute, but turned up only "five minor items." In February, when Secretary of Transportation Elizabeth Dole ordered scrutiny of the nation's entire commuter fleet, PBA was inspected again, and again found clean. This time, though, Giammette not only brought charges to the FAA, he delivered copies of the company's falsified records as well.

In November, when the FAA set up a motor home outside the PBA office to begin its third investigation of the year, John went into his crisis mode, seeking to minimize the possible damage with equal measures of conciliation, stridency, and bluster. On November 7, when he announced his record third-quarter revenues, he also announced the resignation of his vice-president of operations. PBA, he said, was "cooperating fully" with an FAA investigation into "alleged deficiencies." But in correspondence with the agency, he took a harsher line, accusing its officials of "a witch-hunt," conducted "to make the company an example of the power that the FAA is capable of exerting." He told employees that Giammette was on a "vendetta."

Saturday morning, before he saw the actual revocation order, John escalated his attack on "this massive abuse of federal power." He sent a telex to other stations urging the staff to protest directly to Washington. His pilots were quick to the barricades. John had hired most of them, and they liked his style. "It's time we stood up—this isn't the Soviet Union," one shouted to the raucous crowd meeting in the Naples airport lounge. "If it takes marching on Ronald Reagan, let's do it."

"Why the hell should Johno have to give up this company?" another asked. "Without Johno, it's nothing."

But once the agency letter came, John had no choice; with his license revoked, he would probably never again be allowed to work in a position of responsibility in the industry. By the time he met a reporter from an ABC affiliate for a last interview, John had finally given up. He looked neat, freshly shaven and in a clean shirt. But his red eyes were rimmed with exhaustion and he couldn't help rambling on camera, fighting the quaver in his voice.

"The FAA is determined to put PBA out of business. They've blown everything out of proportion," he told the reporter.

"Do you have any hope of getting the company started up again?"

"No."

"Could Peter start it up again?"

"No," John said. "It's six months to a year before you can get your certificate back. By then you have no passengers and no image. You've lost all of your ticket-counter space. You've had all of your airplanes repossessed. You don't have any qualified employees."

It was, on advice of counsel, his final interview. By the end of its meeting that Saturday, the board had voted to accept John's resignation as chairman and CEO of the airline he had built in his own image.

Ever the hands-on entrepreneur, John Van Arsdale wrote the press release himself.

Like his brother, Peter had been part of his father's airline since he was a boy: first as a station hand; then as a pilot; then, after a sabbatical of sorts, as a company executive. But while John had joined the Marines for his two years away from PBA, Peter had gone to California. Like John, Peter came to work in a pilot's black and whites, and he was deferred to as a Van Arsdale. But he had never had to act the boss. "Coop," he had been called, for Gary Cooper. A tousled blond with a tan, he had never been much of a talker. "Yup," he'd say. Or "nope."

Privately, Peter had been relieved when the ax had finally fallen; the seven days leading up to the decertification had been the worst week of his life. He hadn't even known the airline was being investigated until the Sunday before, when he had checked in at the office after his first overnight on the new yacht and had seen the FAA motor home parked outside. As the week progressed he took over for the disgraced head of operations, found the faked records for himself, and wondered if the agency would discover John's illegal flight. Then, finally, he watched while his brother went down in televised agony.

Like John, Peter was convinced that PBA was safe. Except for John's flight, Peter insisted, all the FAA had were the training flights, now corrected, and some "irrelevant" infractions. "We had unsafe paper, but we didn't have unsafe planes or unsafe people," he complained. "Unsafe . . . give me a break."

It just seemed so unfair to him; he thought PBA had started to turn a corner. He and his brother had wrestled for hours over the strains of growth, figuring out how to build a management structure that would keep PBA sound. Finally, John had agreed there would have to be some changes. They had hired one consulting group to streamline their maintenance procedures and another to develop their training—although neither one, admittedly, had been able to make much headway yet. "Everybody says, 'You guys are on a fast growth track,' and yes, we are, but we've been on it for five years," Peter said. "Less was slipping through the cracks when we got shut down than in any time in the past five years."

The Monday after the FAA's revocation order, the news was grim. PBA stock, at 7¾ before the crisis, fell to 4 afterward; analysts pronounced themselves "shocked" and "perplexed" by PBA's collapse. Peter's competitors were already announcing plans to invade his markets. The president of Southern Express Airways Inc. told the *Naples Daily News* that PBA would never come back. He planned to expand his fleet, he said, if that is what it would take to serve the state.

Peter believed the news would get better. The stock would come back; his competitors would overreach; the media would move on to the next disaster. But it all depended on how fast he could get flying. The sooner he was in the air, the more absurd the agency's action would look, the easier it would be to convince his employees that PBA still deserved their loyalty, and the faster Wall Street would forget its doubts. Most important, the sooner he was serving the public again, the faster his passengers would forget the crisis within what one Boston television station that Sunday called "the most unsafe airline in America."

"It's full speed ahead, and we'll just see what it takes to get recertified," Peter told his staff. "I don't see that much changing."

John had left him with real strengths. PBA had always kept vendor accounts current, and had just paid the month's bills. All the loans were secured to 180 percent, so the banks would be patient. And cash wasn't the crisis Peter had feared; by shutting him down the FAA had shut down most of his expenses as well. It would take only $50,000 a week to keep going while getting recertified, he estimated, and he had nearly $3 million in cash and receivables.

The board was a help, too. The brothers had picked its members carefully when they had taken the company public one year before; most were family friends, with strong ties to the communities PBA served. Edwin J. Putzell, Jr., seventy-two was not only former general counsel for Monsanto Company, he was also chairman of the City of Naples Airport Authority. On John's resignation, he agreed to serve as temporary chairman of the PBA board. Sixty-two-year-old Mike Fenello, a friend of board member C. Bill Gregg, was lured out of his second retirement to oversee operations. A no-nonsense former Navy flier, Fenello had served both as vice-president of operations and safety at Eastern Air Lines Inc. and as an FAA deputy administrator. He knew safety regulations, and he knew how strictly the agency could read them. Board member Philip L. Thomas, a New York City public relations expert and a former vice-president of Esmark Inc., helped Peter with the airline's all-important media strategy. PBA officers would no longer be available to the press, Thomas suggested; henceforth all statements would come by release, signed by the chairman, so no one would be misquoted or have statements taken out of context.

The mixed fleet, traditionally the source of PBA's strength, was a mixed blessing as Peter tried to get back in the air. Each plane type had to win certification separately, so the process would take five times as long. Still, PBA could bootstrap its way back, bringing the line up in stages, one plane type at a time. In most of its markets, PBA had a 90 percent share before the shutdown. With just his small planes in the air, Peter would be running a much lower cost operation; he could make money with only 25 percent of the market.

The FAA was cooperative. On Tuesday, three days after the shutdown, the agency agreed to let Peter serve as CEO, since he hadn't been personally involved in the violations. And it accepted his stage-by-stage start-up plan. That same day, the agency sent down the first of dozens of staffers; tables were set up in the auxiliary offices; and a group started assembling the manuals, creating new directives page by detailed page. Maintenance inspections began. The pilots were sequestered at a resort in the Everglades, half an hour away, and ordered to stand by for ground school.

On Wednesday, the day after the FAA gave PBA the green light, chairman Putzell issued his release, announcing "high hopes" to have the airline flying "by next month," a couple of weeks away. Peter, however, had an earlier deadline in mind. He sent a telex to his staff announcing that first flight would come the following Tuesday, just ten days after the shutdown. They would be open for reservations by the weekend and flying before Thanksgiving.

For the next few days Peter worked day and night, fueled by hot coffee and Diet Coke. He was everywhere, helping write manuals or soothing a tearful secretary; late at night he worked the phones, listening patiently to irate former customers, arranging a rebate for one golden-ager left stranded by the shutdown. He would have worked straight through if he could have.

But it would not be enough. Sunday night, Peter discovered they would miss his self-imposed deadline. He had assumed he could use sections from his old manuals for the start-up, but the FAA was insisting that everything be done anew. That meant a two- or three-day delay.

He sat in his office, frustration and fatigue simmering out together. "Damn. It cost us money, and it cost us credibility." John would have howled loud and long. Should Peter have tried to push the agency harder? His staff would think so. "And I can't even say anything to the press, because the FAA is so sensitive."

It took the chairman of the board to snap him out of his funk. There would have to be some changes, the board agreed. No more public predictions. And no more looking back. Right or wrong, just or unjust, the FAA was his boss, "and you don't get in a pissing contest with your boss."

"And get some rest," the chairman added. "You're no good to anyone if you're exhausted."

It was the best advice Peter had gotten all week. The next morning, Monday, the bags under his eyes were gone and his smile was back. The chairman's advice had struck a chord: Peter resolved that his second week as CEO would be different. He and John had been talking about making changes for years; now Peter could act on them. The shutdown had made PBA a small business again, and in place of 1,500 employees and million-dollar revenue flows he was working with a skeleton crew and $50,000 a week. The company had hired consultants; now was the time to give them their head. The organization chart was ten years out of date; now was the time to revise it. It wasn't his job, he realized, to add to the clutter of coffee cups around the manuals or to try to keep an eye on every fire. That had been one of John's mistakes.

"The only thing I can't do is panic. You get so damn busy running around you can't find time to sit and think. John and I had problems deciding my role; it had never been clearly defined. Now I've got to sit down and decide what I should be doing."

Peter's next crisis—the resignation that morning of Fred Valentine, vice-president of maintenance, a member of the board, and a nine-year PBA veteran—convinced him that he was on the right track.

Val was typical of the old PBA. He knew maintenance as well as anyone, better than most, but he was as autocratic as John and as much a hands-on manager. He couldn't delegate and wouldn't change. Since the autumn he had been fighting a new tracking system the consultants had proposed, a system that promised to increase productivity by 50 percent and save the company $1 million annually.

Now that PBA was shut down, Peter had told him, he would have a perfect opportunity to put the new system in place. But Val had refused, even after his new CEO insisted the issue was not open to debate.

Peter merely shrugged when a secretary delivered his old friend Val's resignation two hours later. "Frankly, it was something I would have had to deal with down the road anyway," he mused. "If something wasn't Val's idea, it wasn't a good one. I've got lots of talent in maintenance, and it's always been stifled."

He knew how it would look to the outside—one more PBA executive gone, and a challenge to the credibility of his maintenance department, which had been largely untarnished by the investigation. So he simply issued no release. He made his promotion that afternoon but kept the news inside the company. Then Peter spent the rest of the afternoon loading his papers into grocery bags and carrying them to his brother's old office.

"The chairman of the board convinced me to change offices," he explained sheepishly. "The captain of the ship used to be here. I have to move so it's clear we've still got a captain."

John's Siberian tiger poster came off the wall, replaced by pictures of spinnakers billowing in the wind. Framed snapshots of Peter's two children and second wife replaced the aircraft portraits John had kept on the credenza.

Actually, he liked his old office better. Before he had looked out the front, at the road. Now he looked out the back, at a pile of dirt. Not that he had much time to stare out the window.

By Wednesday afternoon, Peter felt nothing but optimism. Someone had delivered a cake with "PBA Forever" to the office; "Good Luck PBA" flowers sat at the deserted Naples ticket counter. The crisis had brought everyone together: the operations secretary who worked twenty hours, glued to her word processor, took a six-hour nap, then came back for another twenty; the Miami baggage handler who had come in on his own time and repainted all the carts so the Van Arsdale airline would look spiffy when Peter got it back in the air.

More and more, however, Peter was thinking beyond simply getting back in the air. If he could put the new systems and controls in place now, while PBA was small, and keep them in place as he brought each stage up, the payoff would come in dollars. Reducing expenses by 3¢ per available seat mile, he estimated, could bring $12 million to the bottom line. He would never have a better chance. All of the old managers who would have fought the changes were gone, disgraced or resigned. Most of the men who met in his office for his first managers' meeting that Wednesday afternoon were new to their positions.

The mood at the meeting was ebullient. All systems were go, and the manuals would be finished any hour. The pilots were standing by to start testing. Mike Fenello reported that the FAA is "completely at our disposal."

PBA would be flying by Sunday, four days away.

Peter had given a lot of thought to running a managers' meeting, even before he became CEO. He had always thought John was too critical, too much like their father. His meetings were hour after hour of finger pointing, with no agenda and no objective. So Peter sat quietly, drumming his fingers on his desk as his managers had their say one by one. Having the CEO's ear was a new experience for most of them, and they took it—at length. What should have been a half-hour meeting stretched on to two hours, because every decision was deferred to Peter. We need 200 copies of the manuals—what printer should we use? The pilots would be testing at the airport—what motel should they stay in?

In time, Peter hoped, he would be able to avoid so much detail. But for now his managers needed all the support they could get. "I've got a lot of guys in there who are really trying to watch the dollars, and I've got guys in there who have never had to make decisions." He knew how they felt.

"This is the rough part now," he assured them. "But I have to warn you. You guys are going to be filling out a lot of forms. Our guys are going to get the message. Fill in all the boxes. I want to come out of this squeaky clean. And I want to stay squeaky clean."

He carried much the same message when he went out to give his talk to the pilots at Thanksgiving dinner.

The pilots had taken decertification hard, and they had been under the gun ever since. Rather than marching on Washington, they had been put through flight training, shipped off to some developer's folly in the Everglades, away from their families, for day after day of classes. Testing had started Thanksgiving morning, two hours of flying maneuvers with the FAA inspector watching every move. Most of the PBA executives, with their wives, had driven down to the resort in the Everglades in a show of support.

Peter got to his feet slowly when he finished his pumpkin pie, pushing back his chair and buttoning his unfamiliar sport coat. Public speaking had always been John's job; standing in front of an audience still made Peter's palms wet.

It began as a low-key pep talk. "Think of decertification as a learning experience," he told them. Better training and planning would make everyone's life easier, he promised, and "PBA will be even more awesome than it was before."

Then he tried to explain about the sport coat. The black and whites had always been a symbol of the flying Van Arsdale boys; last Thanksgiving Peter himself had flown five round-trips between New York and Hyannis. But he had decided the uniform had to go. It gave him too much exposure to the regulations: If John hadn't been flying he would still have been CEO. "So I'm probably going to be fifteen minutes later to work, trying to figure out what to wear," he joked. "But I'm not going to be any different inside."

Finally, he began to warm up. "I don't worry too much about those guys," he said of his competitors. "They don't have the balance sheet to go out and get new planes. And rather than keeping things smoth, they're just getting greedy. They're on a self-destruct program."

He scanned the room for effect. Southern Express's planned expansion into PBA's turf was foundering, but the bluster of their president had stung many of the pilots, and the room had fallen silent.

"There are a lot of guys out there licking their chops . . . and I can't wait to take it to 'em!"

Privately, Peter thought his competitors would take it to themselves. Southern Express had been overbooking heavily, leaving reserved passengers stranded all over Florida. But Peter was trying to act a new part. He had always been laid back; now he had to show them he could be aggressive, no longer the kid brother but the boss, willing to go toe-to-toe in the competitive battle. "Take it to 'em," was more John's style—although when Peter thought about it, he liked the way it sounded.

John himself came to the office only once that week.

Time had stopped for John with decertification. He looked tan and relaxed, but the threat of a legal battle dragged on, and his sixty-three-year-old mother worried about what he would do with himself. His plans were vague. Write a book? Move to France? Run for office? In the meantime, he had a house filled with long-deferred projects to keep him occupied, and lunches with his son at McDonald's. He had come by the office to pick up a few personal effects, and to see if he could borrow his brother's boat.

"Sure," Peter agreed. "I could only use it between midnight and six in the morning anyway."

Then he stood with John in his new office, looking at seat fabric for the new planes until his brother was ready to go.

"Anything I can do to help?" John asked.

"Nope," Peter said.

To Peter Van Arsdale, standing by himself on the tarmac that early Sunday morning, it was the sweetest sound in the world. The first PBA Cessna was taking off, with four paying passengers aboard.

He had done it, against the predictions. And he had done it fast. Just two weeks after the shutdown, he had won a new certificate, "the most inspected airline in America," according to the FAA. Across the state, and up north as well, PBA was flying again, but Peter's way— tighter, leaner, and in better control than ever before.

He hadn't expected to see the press at 6 A.M. Journalists, he thought, slept late; to accommodate them Peter had scheduled a "first flights" media event that afternoon. But five reporters had come anyway, more than one for each passenger. For a change, Peter was glad to see them. For two weeks, the pictures on the news had all been grim—grounded airplanes and a deserted airport. But now the story was upbeat, and he wanted it told. Certainly his staff looked slick: uniforms pressed, smiles in place. Each one wore a button, "PBA . . . We're Flying!" And there were cards on the check-in counters with the same message. The baggage handler walked out to each passenger's car, thanked each person for flying and took each bag from curbside; then he weighed each item, down to the pocketbooks, so passengers would know that PBA was squeaky clean.

That afternoon, the turnout stunned even Peter. It seemed half of Naples was there, kissing his cheek or shaking his hand: the regular passengers and friends of the family, chamber of commerce types and his laid-off staff, along with a horde or reporters, feeding at the buffet and standing in line for a glass of New York State champagne. It was more like a party than a press conference, with Peter both the host and the honored guest. Bemused but beaming, he wandered through the crowd, accepting the congratulations.

The coverage was better than he had expected, too. There were pictures of Peter handing the passengers carnations as they got on board, then of the new CEO as he cut a bouquet of balloons and watched them sail off into the blue sky, symbolizing the takeoff of the new PBA. His consultant had written a speech for him to give so he could avoid having to answer reporters' questions, but he knew it sounded wooden, so when the speech was over he decided to ad-lib, just to be himself and tell his story. He had won them over, he could tell; the press was charmed.

For the next three days, Peter was on the go, visiting all of PBA's operating stations, to spread the word: management-by-flying-around, his consultant called it. "There's no letting up now," Peter told his staff. "We're just getting started." So far, PBA had brought up only the Cessnas; it would still have to win FAA approval for four more plane types. Besides, only 60 percent of the routes were open, and more than 1,000 people were still out of work.

But Peter had complete confidence in the future. He thought that a 25 percent to 35 percent growth in revenues in 1985 was still a realistic target, much as John had planned, but with stronger earnings if his new systems and new managers could perform. He planned to open his first new station, in Fort Pierce, Florida, within the month, then move PBA into the Bahamas after the first of the year. The new planes were still on order, and he had even put the private placement back in the works.

PBA was flying again, better than ever, and he knew he couldn't have done it without the shutdown.

"The FAA gave us a great opportunity. Our pace has been quickened by three years. We were aware of what we had to do. But you can't just snap your fingers and get it done. That's what the FAA did—they snapped their fingers.

"My initial reaction was, boy, have we gotten screwed. But I realize now we brought this down on ourselves. I know that I can't be innocent. I'm like Ronald Reagan with the Marines in Beirut—I should have known what was going on.

"You know what I've decided through this whole thing?" Peter asked. "Working is better than not working. I've had to make more decisions in the past week than I've had to make in my career. And I think I'm doing fine. If I can get through this, I can get through anything."

It looked, for the next three weeks, as if PBA would have clear skies. When its second plane type, the nineteen-passenger Bandeirante, went up on schedule it was able to return to full service. In two weeks PBA was carrying 2,400 passengers a day, and even Peter was astonished. "That means I'm the third or fourth largest commuter in the country," he said, "already."

There was no time to go sailing yet, but he allowed himself a few days off. As a regular $10,000-contributor to the Republican National committee, "a Republican Eagle," he and his wife, Karen, were invited to the White House for a State Dinner—"and how many times in my life am I going to be invited to the White House?" Peter had never seen anything like it: the elegance, the Marine Band, a glittering guest list that included Joan Collins and Dino De Laurentiis. Karen sat next to the President himself. It was a night Peter would never forget. And it was a symbol of the triumph he had fought so hard to win.

Two days later, Peter was at his desk, planning schedules, when he got the phone call. At 6:15 P.M., PBA flight 1039, a Bandeirante making its fourth commuter trip of the day between Jacksonville and Tampa, had gone down just after takeoff with eleven passengers and two crew members on board. There were no survivors.

Early details were sketchy. It was a clear night, with visibility for seven miles. The plane had climbed for two minutes off runway 31, rising to about 500 feet, before it suddenly went out of control, plunging into the swampy woods.

Why? One by one, Peter discarded each grim explanation. The plane had been FAA inspected; the pilot had been FAA tested; on paper, everything was clean. Could the plane have been misfueled, like the Cessna that crashed in September? But a Bandit will run on any kind of fuel. Pilot in trouble? But there had been no radio call to the tower, and there was a copilot aboard. Could the pilot have lost an engine? But the Bandit is a twin-engine plane, and the pilot had just demonstrated a one-engine takeoff during recertification.

Every airline has written disaster procedures; PBA had gone through theirs twice in the past six months. Assemble a crisis team, make up a list of victims, choose someone to go to the site, call the FAA, the NTSB, and the insurance company. Peter's job was to contact the next of kin. The victims' bodies lay sprawled in the twisted rubble, burned beyond recognition; identification would require dental records. What could he say? "There was an accident. We think your husband was on board. There were no survivors."

Peter had gone through crash procedures before, but he had never had to make those calls himself, all thirteen of them, one after the other. Once again he could hear the press outside, see them at the door and through the window, but until he had put together a list of victims there was nothing he could say to them. Once again, the press was shut out; all information would be by written release.

The next day's papers were lurid, and all three networks showed pictures of investigators picking through the smoldering rubble. The stock dropped to 5, and reservations fell by 75 percent. Peter canceled all his advertising and pulled the buttons and the counter cards. "I have asked myself over and over what has PBA done to deserve this," he wired his staff. "There is no answer and never will be." Then he started to write a letter to each next of kin. No words had ever come harder.

Friday morning, the NTSB issued preliminary findings. The investigation showed that the horizontal stabilizer had broken off the plane's tail. Metal stress? Metal fatigue? An act of God? Although there was no evidence that either PBA or the FAA were to blame, the questions and criticisms were just beginning. Did the FAA let PBA back in the air too quickly? If the airline was so unsafe a few weeks ago, why let it back in the air at all? Congressman Dan Glickman of Kansas, chairman of the Subcommittee on Transportation, Aviation, and Materials, called for an investigation. Secretary of Transportation Dole's office announced it would begin an investigation into "possible conflicts of interest" on the part of Mike Fenello. "What about that dinner at the White House?" a *Washington Post* reporter asked Peter. Or those $10,000 contributions to the Republican National Committee?

Once again, the issue for PBA was survival. Peter grounded all his Bandeirantes, days before the FAA ordered all carriers to do so, and took each tail section apart, far more than the FAA required, searching for a clue. But he found nothing.

"If you sat down in one of those think tanks and asked what is absolutely the worst thing that could happen to the airline, this is it," Peter said later. "I feel like the guy who made Tylenol, or the head of Union Carbide.

"The sad thing is, the next time a commuter plane crashes, they'll bring it up again. Ten years from now, PBA will still be the airline that had three fatal crashes in 1984."

For a while, Peter clung stubbornly to his belief that he could bring the airline back. The Bandeirantes were still down, and traffic was falling daily. Cash flow was becoming a critical problem—and the banks, which had been so eager to lend him money in the past, were now playing hardball. "But what am I supposed to do? Roll over and play dead?" He racked his brains for ways to raise the money to see the airline through. In time, he still hoped, the passengers would return. The media glare would move on. His work would not be in vain: PBA could grow again.

On December 12, a Southern Express plane crashed, injuring two. Every news story mentioned PBA's crash as well.

On December 27, PBA grounded two pilots who had taken off with the gust lock on their DC-3's tail still in place. They would later face disciplinary action by the FAA.

On January 15, Peter was forced to guarantee PBA's payroll with his personal stock holdings. Four days later the banks ordered PBA to close ten stations.

On January 23, a former PBA employee, his voice disguised and his name not revealed, turned up on a CBS news program alleging widespread drug abuse and alcoholism among the pilots.

On February 1, facing bankruptcy, John and Peter Van Arsdale sold their controlling interest in Provincetown-Boston Airline to Tampa attorney Hugh F. Culverhouse, owner of the Tampa Bay Buccaneers, in exchange for $1 million in loan guarantees.

Peter was ousted as CEO of the airline his family had built. On February 3, he began moving out of the office that had been John's. He had been in it less than three months.

—CURTIS HARTMAN

THE ONCE AND FUTURE KING

When Frank Sands graduated from Harvard Business School in 1963, it was hard for him not to feel an overwhelming sense of opportunity. The business world was in the throes of an expansion and merger spree that saw companies, both large and small, devouring competitors and noncompetitors alike. The unquestioned assumption of the day was that growth would not just solve problems, it would also ensure success.

Yet in Frank Sands' case, his academic orientation, and the business atmosphere that fostered it, were to prove nearly fatal for Sands, Taylor & Wood. The family-owned, Boston-based company had sold the same type of unbleached, unbromated, high-protein wheat flour throughout New England since 1790, the year of George Washington's inauguration. In 1963, when Sands joined his father at Sands, Taylor & Wood, the company was a profitable, $3-million operation that relied exclusively on the uniqueness and solid reputation of its sole product, King Arthur Flour. Within five years, Sands had embarked on what turned out to be a decade-long round of acquisitions that would see sales shoot up to $45 million and the number of employees climb from 20 to 160.

Today, fifteen years later, Sands, Taylor & Wood is once again a small operation, with sales of $3.5 million, and it produces its long-standing product, King Arthur Flour. The company narrowly escaped going under. Warehouse space that had once been full of baking ovens and 10,000-gallon corn syrup tanks is now empty, and Frank Sands is a much wiser man.

Sands' long, cyclical odyssey from success to near failure and back began in 1968, when his father retired from Sands, Taylor & Wood and Frank became company president. That same year, there were 4,500 mergers in the United States, a 50 percent increase over the previous year, but still far less than the 6,100 that would be registered one year later. Sands himself wasted no time. Within months of taking over the company, he had paid $300,000 in cash for Allied Bakers Supply Company's assets, a marginally profitable bakery-ingredients supply distributor in Cambridge, Massachusetts.

Sands justified his acquisition in two ways. His company distributed King Arthur in both family- and larger-size bakeries, but family flour consumption was declining. At the turn of the century, over 90 percent of all flour usage in the United States was family flour, that is, smaller bag sizes bought by consumers in stores; by the end of World War II, that figure had dropped to 40 percent, and by 1968 it had dropped even further, to 8 percent, where it has since plateaued. Sands was convinced he should pursue a wider share of the bakery market and sell not just flour but other bakery ingredients as well.

Sands also took note of Allied's faithful customer base. He figured he could penetrate the bakery market faster and easier by absorbing a supplier that had existing relationships with retailers. "By picking up those customers, we telescoped a penetration that would normally have taken five years into sixty days," summarizes Sands. "Making it work meant turning over sugar faster." He began turning it over so fast, in fact, that he recouped his initial investment in sixty days. By the end of the year, sales had doubled to $6 million, and fifteen new employees were added.

The company now had two operations, and the would-be flour mogul immersed himself in the business, working fourteen hours a day, seven days a week. By the early 1970s, Sands concluded that he could run a more efficient organization and save considerable money by manufacturing some of the goods he was distributing, instead of buying from a middleman. In 1973, he purchased Joseph Middleby Jr. Company, a hundred-year-old manufacturer of fillings and toppings for pastries and other baked goods, located in South Boston. Joseph Middleby had a reputation for quality, but its three manufacturing plants hadn't been upgraded since the early 1900s, and the company was losing money. Sands laid out about $300,000, most of it cash, for the company's assets, which included beneficial tax losses. Company sales leapt to $12 million.

Then, in 1975, Sands bought H. A. Johnson Company, another bakery supply manufacturing business, whose primary asset was a block-long, two-story, 140,000-square-foot manufacturing plant and warehouse in the Boston neighborhood of Brighton. On the surface, it looked as if he had struck a sweetheart deal. Johnson was a money loser, and its owner, Aerojet-General Corporation, a giant California aerospace company, had neither the qualified managers nor the inclination to save it. Sands obtained a $2-million bank loan to pay for a company that Aerojet had originally bought for $4.5 million. Johnson produced fourteen different product lines, including toppings, fillings, glazes, and extracts; with its addition, Sands, Taylor & Wood boosted sales from $12 million to $25 million within two years.

Sands quickly consolidated the sales, production, trucks, and customers of the two companies into a new, wholly owned subsidiary renamed Johnson-Middleby Company. The parent company's profit margin soared. Sands says the company's meteoric growth did not trouble him at the time, and, indeed, its performance during the first two years after forging Johnson-Middleby was remarkably strong. In 1976, it earned more than $400,000 after taxes, which was a record. And 1977, while less spectacular, showed an after-tax profit of about $250,000.

Sands, Taylor & Wood now offered a comprehensive line of products and ingredients to such customers as bakeries, candy and ice cream stores, hotels, restaurants, prisons, hospitals, schools, and other institutional food industries. In addition to King Arthur Flour, the company sold every other edible ingredient a bakery uses, including sugars, syrups, toppings, flavors, icings, breads, cakes, doughnuts, muffin mixes, and a wide variety of fruits, extracts, and pastry fillings. Sands was going strong.

Those years were significant for Sands in personal ways as well. Divorced from his first wife, he married his old college sweetheart, Brinna Baird, herself divorced with three children. Together, they decided to distance themselves from a business that was taking up the majority of Frank's time. Sands made serious plans to give up day-to-day operation of the company and move to an eighty-five-acre farm in Norwich, Vermont, near Dartmouth College, his alma mater. He recruited an outsider, William O'Connor, as general manager, with the intention of retiring as president and having O'Connor succeed him.

O'Connor, fifty, a native Australian, had been vice-president of food service at The Gorton Group, a fish-processing company in Gloucester, Massachusetts. He was brought aboard a conglomerate that was highly leveraged, fast growing, and in the hands of a president preparing for semiretirement in the backwoods. Sands wanted to adopt the role of chairman of the board and check in on his growing conglomerate every month or so. In the meantime, the Johnson-Middleby operations, antiquated and long neglected, needed infusions of capital for major renovations. In fact, the entire company required more capital for increased operational expenses. O'Connor arranged a $3.5-million working-capital loan at 1.5 percent over the prime rate, which then hovered at 8 percent.

For Sands, it still looked like clear sailing. Commodities needed for the company's operations, such as sugar, cocoa, wheat, and soybeans, remained cheap. Interest rates were stable. Profits appeared certain. At the time, in late 1976, when asked about new markets, Sands was quoted in a regional business magazine as saying, "We are nowhere near saturation, even in the baking industry."

But in 1977, Sands made a move that plunged the company into quicksand. He submitted a bid and won a two-year distribution contract with a buying group for nearly 200 Dunkin' Donuts Inc. stores in New England. The bid was about 80¢ per unit, but Sands reasoned that although profits would be marginal (they turned out to be nil), he would still improve cash flow, double his volume, and consequently strengthen his bargaining position with his suppliers.

To handle the added volume of goods, the company bought a lease on a warehouse in Andover, Massachusetts, and transferred its corporate headquarters there. The warehouse had to be refitted, a fleet of trucks had to be rented, the Dunkin' Donuts distribution system had to be mastered. But the company had reached almost $45 million in sales, and Sands never lost his optimism. He made yet another acquisition in 1978, paying less than $100,000 for Goodhue Products Inc., a $300,000 maker of frozen bread dough. He even toyed with the idea of putting out frozen dough under the King Arthur name. The scheme never materialized, though, because shortly after the Goodhue purchase, things started to unravel.

In the late seventies, the company was clobbered by three concurrent developments in the national economy. First, commodities prices, which had been depressed, began to turn around, and such essential ingredients as sugar doubled in cost. Second, the energy crisis hit. "When we bid on the Dunkin' Donuts contract [in 1977], gas was sixty cents a gallon," says Sands, noting that one of the major expenses for a distributor is gasoline. "Two years later, it was one dollar and twenty cents." Finally, interest rates began an upward trend that almost brought the company down. In 1981, Sands, Taylor & Wood exhausted its line of credit, prompting the banks to raise interest on the $3.5-million capital loan from 1.5 percent over prime to 2 percent over prime. The company found itself paying 22 percent interest on a loan it had first obtained at 8 percent; payments had risen from $200,000 a year to $750,000.

Meanwhile, the company was pumping about $2 million a year of its increasingly scarce capital into the distributorship just to keep it running. Operational costs had mushroomed, and it took $450,000 a week merely to fund receivables. The company was losing around $150,000 a year on the deal.

According to Peter Linneman, professor of finance at the Wharton School, overreaching is a common mistake made by entrepreneurs who seek diversification. "Too many small businessmen overestimate their expertise," he says. "Their company experiences rapid growth, and suddenly they think they can do anything. Just because you know flour doesn't necessarily mean you know dough, and just because you know dough doesn't mean you know doughnuts."

In 1978, in the midst of this turmoil, Sands took off for Vermont. The company lost $130,000 that year, the first substantial loss in its history.

Sands remains defensive and unrepentant over his decision to move. "My family came first," he says. "And it still does. Maybe if I had stayed everything would have worked out. But sometimes, you just have to say the hell with it and summon the courage to do what you want."

Nevertheless, the loss shattered Sands' sky-is-the-limit ethos, and he finally realized that the company was out of focus. Cost-cutting measures became imperative. Sands, Taylor & Wood immediately closed Goodhue's inefficient and aging manufacturing plant, saving $60,000 a year in upkeep. An outside manufacturer was contracted to produce the same goods under specification, and the products were then passed to Goodhue for marketing and distribution. He also tightened control of inventory management by trimming down the distributorship's inventories. And, he retired a large part of the company's crushing bank debt by selling off the Andover building and moving back to the old building in Brighton.

Still, it was obvious that the crisis called for harsher measures, so Sands hired outside managers and solicited advice from students working under the direction of his former mentor at the Harvard Graduate School of Business Administration, Ray Goldberg. The first thing they told him was to get rid of the Dunkin' Donuts distribution side of the business and concentrate on manufacturing. In 1979, to no one's dismay, the Dunkin' Donuts distributorship was dropped.

Of Sands, Goldberg says, "Frank was an apt pupil, and what he did made sense on paper. He wanted to minimize cost by adding more products to a distribution line and minimize risks by diversifying those products. In reality, the savings made by adding products were offset by being burdened with new items that weren't unique.

"The company's biggest strength is the uniqueness of its flour, the way it appeals to the naturalness that more and more consumers are searching for. But Frank diluted his genuine advantages by expanding. I have to give him credit for being wise enough to see his mistakes and rectify them. Now he's going back to basics, and the market is going back there with him."

While laboring to keep the company going, Bill O'Connor went hunting for a financial expert who could help find more cost savings. He found William Walsh, a comptroller at International Minerals & Chemical Corporation. Walsh jumped into the fray with both feet.

"It was a nightmare," Walsh remembers. "Most commodity vendors demand prompt payment, with no ifs, ands, or buts. I spent seventy percent of my time on the phone with vendors, trying to get extended terms. Most assumed I was lying and would never pay them. There was one guy, a fruit supplier, to whom we owed eight hundred thousand dollars. He called on me one day to say he was going to try to put us into bankruptcy. We eventually worked things out, but, I tell you, this company was almost over the brink. We didn't fear bankruptcy every day—we feared it every hour."

The company managed to show a small profit in 1979 of less than $10,000. But the cash squeeze remained relentless. In 1980, Sands, Taylor & Wood posted a loss of $170,000. As Sands puts it, the company was still "discombobulated."

Surveying the wreckage from his bucolic retreat, Sands could see that the rest of his acquisitions had to go. "That was the value of living up in Vermont," he says. "You could see it from afar. And I just said, 'This is ridiculous. I'm gonna sell everything.'"

Sands continued to distill Sands, Taylor & Wood to its core. He liquidated the remainder of the wholesale bakery supply and distribution end, which did roughly $12 million in sales, and in 1980 sold it to Nutmeg Bakers Supply Company, in Beacon Falls, Connecticut. The sale freed up cash the company had invested in inventory and receivables, and wiped clean a $200,000 loss. With all modes of bakery distribution gone, the company focused on its 200-year-old cash cow, family flour. Sands kept his home in Vermont but took over again as full-time company president and commutes to Brighton at least once a week.

In 1981, O'Connor and Sands sold the Johnson-Middleby division to L. Karp & Sons Inc., a Chicago-based manufacturer and distributor of bakery ingredients. All of the division's inventory and assets were liquidated and sold to Karp for the same amount they had originally cost. According to O'Connor, that divestiture was one of the hardest decisions of his life.

"Karp moved the plant to Chicago and laid off close to eighty out of the one hundred people employed there," he says. "Frank and I knew that was going to happen, and it was very agonizing for us both. Some of these people had been with the company for over forty years. I still feel very sorry about the dislocation we caused in their lives." Even sacrifices like these, though, did not prevent the company from losing close to $1 million that year.

Undaunted, Sands sloughed off his one remaining acquisition, Goodhue Products, in the spring of 1983, selling it to Bill O'Connor for about $125,000. The long roller-coaster ride from diversification to divestiture had finally ground to a halt.

"We're now reaffirming the qualities that distinguish us from the others," says Sands, "the qualities we've had since the beginning." The company has launched an aggressive advertising campaign to spread its all-natural gospel, spending about $150,000 a year on radio and magazine commercials. Sands' wife, Brinna, has taken charge of consumer relations, and New Englanders frequently can hear her on the radio, espousing the wholesomeness of King Arthur Flour. By flaunting the intrinsic merits of its product, the company has rediscovered its identity and reversed its decline. For the latter part of 1982 and all through 1983, the ledger numbers were back in the black.

King Arthur currently accounts for 25 percent of the New England market, compared to 6 percent in 1963, placing it third behind General Mills' Gold Medal and Pillsbury's Best brands. In the ten- to twenty-five-pound bags, King Arthur outsells Gold Medal and Best combined two-to-one. Although national consumption of family flour has leveled off, the industry continues to be a scrappy one. Private labels, which make up about 10 percent of the market, are constantly introducing natural brands in attempts to cut into King Arthur's turf. But Sands is less of a worrier these days. "We have tradition, and we've gained trust," he proclaims. "No one can touch us."

The natural-foods industry is growing at about 15 percent a year, and Sands, Taylor & Wood, having prefigured that boom, is positioning itself to ride the wave. Sands may have learned the limits to growth, but his competitive instinct remains strong. Last year, the company introduced a stone-ground whole-wheat flour that has already captured 50 percent of the market, an impressive blitzkrieg into potentially rich territory. In addition, the company recently hired a new food broker, Morris Alper & Sons Inc. in Framingham, Massachusetts, which has increased distribution of King Arthur Flour in its current market area and is helping it move onto grocery shelves in metropolitan New York and surrounding New Jersey areas. "Right now those states amount to only a very small percentage of our sales, but we have a foot in the door," he says. "Laying the groundwork will have to go slowly, and it will be a year or so before we make any serious inroads. But it will pay off in a big way. That market is twice the size of New England."

Despite Sands' close brush with disaster in the late seventies, he hasn't lost his enthusiasm for both new markets and new products. "I've gotten that preoccupation with growth pretty much out of my system," he says, "but I get itchy from time to time. I still have ambitions for my company."

—JOHN F. PERSINOS

PLANNING FOR "THE NEXT ECONOMY"

Part IV of this *Best of* Inc. *Guide to Business Strategy* looks at how an approach to doing business that incorporates a world view and considers economic changes can improve product and service quality, help solve production problems, and explore new business opportunities.

Paul Hawken is the quintessential representative of this new breed of entrepreneur. A one-time carpenter-student and global wanderer, Hawken formed a unique mail order business based on his observations of the world economic order. In "Planning for 'The Next Economy,'" *Inc.* looks at what Hawken has learned from his years of experience as a corporate consultant, author of three books, and founder of two successful businesses.

The core of Hawken's philosophy is the notion that the world economy has shifted from an emphasis on mass resources and production to specialized information, technology, design, utility, and services. He believes—and has demonstrated in his work—that success in the future depends on how well information, creativity, and innovation are integrated with existing mass-production capabilities.

"Made in Japan"—or Taiwan, Hong Kong, Haiti—has been stamped on or sewn into everything from off-the-rack clothing to silicon chips and household bric-a-brac. For years, offshore manufacturing was the most economical way to produce American goods, and everybody knew it. But the economy and technology have changed so rapidly over the past decade that offshore manufacturing is no longer such a bargain. Why? The people who do the manufacturing are becoming production experts—and that expertise is an increasingly valuable resource.

Jim Toreson's solution to this glut of technological simplification in the mass-production arena is to set up shop on the Nevada prairie, where people and land come cheaper than they do in Silicon Valley.

"Made in USA" takes a hard look at the issue of on- and offshore manufacturing and how Xebec and other companies are finding solutions to their manufacturing problems.

David Birch, expert on economic and new business growth, describes the phenomenon of America "breaking into pieces." "The Atomization of America" describes economic changes that are creating opportunities for small companies to provide exactly the services Paul Hawken anticipates—at a job creation rate of 36 million since 1966.

Inc. writer Karl Frieden's interviews with professors Michael J. Piore and Charles F. Sabel, coauthors of *The Second Industrial Divide: Possibilities for Prosperity,* explore the shift away from mass production and towards "flexible specialization" and services. In "The Second Industrial Revolution" a three-way conversation stimulates remarks on what to expect and how to prepare for anticipated changes.

Our final article, "Tow-Away Zone," looks at America's auto industry in light of ongoing economic change—a diversifying economy that presents challenges to Chrysler, Ford, and General Motors that may in turn threaten smaller companies.

The future success of American business relies on, as it always has, the ingenuity of the entrepreneur. But as natural resources and production materials become finite, the nature of the challenge changes—increasingly, the wit and skill of the entrepreneur will be called on to uncover new uses for old or forgotten resources. We present these stories with the hope that they will stimulate and encourage thought, debate, and experimentation.

PLANNING FOR "THE NEXT ECONOMY"

A t the age of sixteen, after he had already left home and high school
to begin his true education on the streets of California's Bay Area,
Paul Hawken apprenticed himself to a building contractor, a West
Indian named Leonard Gordon. Gordon taught Hawken how to swing
a hammer and string electrical wire and master an array of craft
skills. He also taught him how to read the signs and live by his wits.

"We were tearing down an old building once," Hawken recalls
twenty-two years later. Hawken was inside whacking away at the walls
of one of the upper floors. Suddenly, Gordon bellowed to Hawken that
the building was about to collapse and that he should make a run for
it. Hawken bounded a few strides to the open window and vaulted the
sill to alight on the scaffolding just outside. The trouble was, the
horizontal plank was missing. Hawken plunged twenty feet to the
sandy ground.

As he shook off a daze and blinked away the stars, Hawken
realized he had just been tricked by one of his mentor's object lessons.
"Aha, Mister Hawken," cackled Gordon in his West Indies lilt. *"Pay
attention!"*

Hawken has taken Gordon's deceptively simple advice. He has
paid attention, close attention, ever since. In fact, he owes his entrepreneurial success to his facility for observing the world and its economic
shifts with a special clarity and then applying those observations to
the mundane, day-to-day decisions of business.

Hawken's guileless face and lanky frame don't suggest the rib-
crunching vigor of his building-trade days, but seeing the thirty-eight-
year-old entrepreneur in action in his catalog marketing company,
Smith & Hawken Ltd. of Mill Valley, California, gives a sense of the
subtler, agile sort of toughness in him. Clad for the Marin County
spring in jeans and a knit shirt, Hawken plays his position in the busy
office as if he were a free-wheeling shortstop. Up on his feet, with his
knees loose and his hands up, with his jaw working and his amused
eyes sweeping a 300-degree range, Hawken rocks on the soles of his
running shoes. He seems ready to move in any direction to field the
tasks as they arise: an employee's question, a balky computer terminal, a ringing telephone, a customer in the retail store a few steps

away. The strength in Hawken isn't brute; it is tensile, tempered to bend, but to snap back with surprising speed and force.

"Don't let the gentle manner fool you," cautions a friend, writer David Harris, a graduate of Stanford University and the La Tuna Federal Correctional Institution in Texas. Harris did time for draft resistance, and he passed some of it by competing at penitentiary handball. A few years ago, he taught the game to Hawken. Says Harris, "On the court, he's an absolutely ferocious son-of-a-bitch."

But Hawken is willing to credit and follow a spiritual and even mystical dimension in life and to use it in business, even if he can't record it in a business plan. Thus, as he pays attention and reads the signs around him, he is open to heeding evidence as concrete as the earth we walk on or as abstract as the music of the spheres. This unusual cast of mind and diverse body of learning is what accounts for the three sides of his remarkable success:

• He is cofounder of a highly successful company, Smith & Hawken, an importer and direct marketer of high-quality garden tools. Its success lies in its novel approach to marketing. As Hawken puts it, "Our marketing strategy is really an educational strategy." Through a meticulously detailed catalog and an unusually well-informed group of employees handling customer service, the company provides its actual and prospective customers with a body of information on methods and schools of thought in gardening and on the tools themselves—where they come from, how they are made, how they can be used, why they are good. "Then we just sit back and let our customers decide," Hawken says. Enough of them have made the Smith & Hawken decision in its four years to bring its annual revenues from $40,000 to a projected $4 million.

• He is creating the means for bringing a strategic outlook to small businesses. To Hawken, strategic thinking isn't and shouldn't be the sole preserve of the large corporation. Individuals and small businesses should and do think and plan in strategic terms. Through his writings and his speeches, and through his own consultations to scores of smaller companies, Hawken has shaped and tested a simple but distinctive set of strategic principles. These can be found in his current book, *The Next Economy,* which sold around 40,000 copies in hardcover and has just been issued in paperback ($3.50; Ballantine Books; New York). The book argues that smaller companies are particularly well suited to capitalize on the reshaped world economy that is emerging, and it shows small companies how to make use of that advantage. Hawken's book also caught the eye of the corporate world, garnering favorable reviews in the *Wall Street Journal,* among other publications.

• Finally, he is a philosopher in the formal sense of the word. Entrepreneurs cite many factors for their success: a brilliant idea, elbow grease, stamina, good timing, the right location, patient creditors, dedicated employees. A few will also cite such intangibles as faith in God or in themselves. Rarely, however, will an entrepreneur say, "What has worked for me is my philosophy." Hawken says precisely this. And this is where his story should begin.

At nineteen, Hawken returned to the Bay Area after a trip abroad and a tour as a civil rights worker in the South to enroll for the 1965–66 academic year at San Francisco State University's experimental college. Plagued from birth by a chronic health problem, Hawken that year became interested in natural foods as a possible cure.

Although loath to become a food faddist, Hawken says, he began to study how America had altered its food supply. As we industrialized our farming practices in the late nineteenth and early twentieth centuries, Hawken found, we had also industrialized the food supply itself. "We weren't cultivating the soil, we were *mining* it," argues Hawken. Before the nutrients got to our table, moreover, we were adulterating them with artificial additives, he concluded.

This research provoked Hawken's epiphany. He was reading a standard textbook on the soil sciences when suddenly an idea hit him: "I realized the soil is *alive!*" It isn't just dead and inert matter like sand or powdered rock, but is teeming with millions of minute organisms with their own organic systems. With that flash, Hawken scuttled his old metaphysics and took up a new sense of what the world is.

Hawken's old view cast the earth as something cold and sterile, a big, blue marble with vinyl land masses and plate-glass oceans. The earth and its soil were dumb in both senses of the word: stupid and inarticulate. Hawken's new view casts the earth as a living entity, an organism. The earth and its soil are articulate, if only we would pay attention to them; and intelligent, if only we would credit them.

Hawken's new philosophy soon served as the basis for his first major commercial venture, Erewhon Trading Company, a leader in the development of America's natural-foods business. He moved to Boston in 1966 and realized he had outrun his natural-foods supply lines. So he fell in with what was known in those days as a food conspiracy. This one was a small group of people who pooled their time and money, made a weekly station-wagon run into the countryside to find and buy organically grown food, and then returned to a small basement to divvy up some of it and store the rest. Hawken thought they would have an easier time supplying themselves if they opened a store to sell a larger volume of food to a broader public. He volunteered to take the lead: "Remember, none of these folks wanted to be a *merchant!*" He filed incorporation papers for Erewhon, the group turned the basement into retail space, and Hawken ran the store. Initial capital: $500.

At first he bought the food through conventional suppliers, until the day a woman asked him how he knew a bag of grain was organically grown. "Why, it says so right on the bag," he remembers saying. Then he caught himself and figured it was time to pay a little attention. He checked the origins of the grain and the rest of the store's wares with his own eyes and ears.

"Just about everything we sold was fraudulent," Hawken discovered. "It wasn't grown organically. You could get the same stuff at other stores for cheaper prices."

Hawken's solution was to integrate the business vertically. He hit the road to recruit his own network of fifty-five farmers on 40,000 acres in thirty-seven states. He signed up his own trucks and rail cars. He set up manufacturing facilities in Los Angeles and Boston. He leased his own warehouses. Soon, Erewhon was growing and making and selling several hundred different products: wheat, rice, nuts, fruit, bread, cereals, pasta, peanut butter, jams, beverages, cosmetics, and more. It supplied retail stores and institutions and opened its own string of stores on both coasts. Its gross revenues rose in its first six years to about $10 million, while its workforce grew to 150 employees.

Erewhon enjoyed the advantages of being a pioneer in a new field, but Hawken didn't learn much about business while he was building and running the company, he concedes. "I mainly learned what *not* to do. How *not* to treat workers, how *not* to plan—although it later proved to be a good experience to reflect on."

But, as he had been taught so compellingly, Hawken paid attention to what he saw and heard in the field and in his business. His shrewd sense of which information to credit and how to use it shaped Erewhon's ingenious marketing strategy. Simply put, Hawken persuaded people to pay high prices for what were literally commodities. He did this by making the case, exhaustively and imaginatively, for the distinctive origins, good taste, and high nutritional value of his merchandise.

"We could give every carrot a pedigree," says Hawken. Thus, bags of food on Erewhon's shelves carried in loving detail the story of the produce's origins: the name of the farmer who grew it, the farmer's methods, the location of the farm, the nature of its soil, the wind and weather conditions, and the source of the water.

"We wanted customers to know *why* our food had better taste and better nutrition," Hawken explains. "And we also wanted to make our food interesting." The typical Erewhon store, with its rows of products bearing detailed stories of their provenance, was like a living catalog.

As the company grew, however, Hawken lost his close ties to farmers and customers. He found himself a prisoner atop the Erewhon hierarchy. In 1973, after seven years at Erewhon, he decided he had to escape. He went off to Europe, where he worked on his first book, *The Magic of Findhorn,* a study of a Scottish coastal village known for the abundance of its gardens.

During this time, Hawken's marriage ended. He lost his ties to and equity in Erewhon in the divorce settlement. At the end of 1974, he hightailed it back to the West Coast. Erewhon's ownership changed hands over the years and—despite the dramatic growth in the natural-foods business—wound up in receivership in 1981.

For the next five years, Hawken earned his living as a writer and consultant while he shaped and tested his strategic principles for small business. He successfully took on three corporate turnarounds for companies in the fuel, adhesives, and jewelry businesses, occasionally sifting through the ashes of his Erewhon years to find lessons. He also served on the board of a number of not-for-profit agencies, such as the Farallones Institute, Ecology Action, and The Point Foundation. They had begun to look for ways to become self-sustaining, and Hawken tutored them on how to set strategies for entering the marketplace and build cost controls into their philanthropic work. "The challenge was to sharpen their business sense without weakening their spirit of service," he says.

He also met David Smith, now forty-one, his future partner in Smith & Hawken. Smith was managing a cooperative store, Briarpatch Market, and Hawken was a member. They began to spend a morning a week at a diner called Late for the Train, where they would counsel small-business owners who came to them with problems of all sorts.

Through social ties, meanwhile, Hawken began to kibitz with a circle of futurists at SRI International, the vast think tank in Menlo Park. Eventually, Hawken worked with them to think through and write up a series of strategic studies of the future. This circle was working on SRI contracts for such clients as Ford Motor Company and Royal Dutch/Shell Group.

As Hawken and others immersed themselves in huge pools of information and analysis for SRI's large corporate and government clients, they decided they should find a way to put that sort of knowledge into the hands of ordinary people and smaller organizations. Hawken quietly disputed one of the vital but unspoken premises in the work they were doing: namely, that you had to be big and official in order to be strategic in your view of the future. "We were serving the institutional market for the future but we knew there was also, of course, an *individual* market for the future"—and for ways to get a strategic handle on it, Hawken says. Further, he believed that individuals and small businesses, especially existing or likely start-ups, were more likely than large institutions actually to *act* on such strategies.

Consequently, Hawken and two SRI staffers, James Ogilvy and Peter Schwartz, decided to write a popular paperback to equip ordinary citizens to do their own strategic thinking. Although Hawken estimates that it has sold 40,000 copies, *Seven Tomorrows* isn't truly a popular work, since some of its concepts and passages are difficult for the lay reader to follow. However, in setting the stage for *The Next Economy,* it does argue for an appreciation of how economic change occurs chiefly from the bottom up through small organizations, rather than from the top down through large organizations.

"There comes a point of diminishing returns beyond which the economic and political advantages that accrue to larger organizations are offset by organizational inefficiencies resulting from sheer size," say the authors.

The Next Economy, a solo performance by Hawken, begins to answer this call. It credits the vitality of bottom-up change through smaller businesses, breaks older molds of economic thinking, and roots much of its analysis in realities of ecology and the energy supply. More to the point, it sets forth Hawken's own strategic principles for small business to apply in addressing a changing economy. His thinking can be broken down into five broad and simple propositions:

- *Pay attention.* Be open to all the evidence. Search for it as widely and deeply as you can. After Erewhon began, Hawken realized years later, he saw and credited information that he would have missed in a traditional business setting. "Because Erewhon was without precedent, there were no rules to guide us," he says, "and this meant there were no blinders on us, no reason to ignore some things or trivialize them reflexively."
- *Be direct.* Middlemen waste time and money and block the flow of vital evidence into the eyes and ears of the entrepreneur, argues Hawken. Try to collapse as many functions as possible into your business. Do this to get closer to your suppliers, closer to your customers. "It's important for small businesses to grow not so much in sheer size as in sophistication," says Hawken. "They should strive to become more highly differentiated organisms by broadening their scope to embrace more functions."
- *Understand the basic shift in the economy, from mass to information.* As his book explains, every product or service is made up of two elements, mass and information. The mass is the physical stuff, usually matter and energy. Hawken defines the information as the design, utility, durability, and knowledge that are added to the mass. For the user of Hawken's principle, the key is the relationship of the two elements.

Since the oil crises of the 1970s, mass's costs have jumped as the costs of energy and energy-related materials have jumped. This puts a premium on the other element, the information. Success in the emerging economy, argues Hawken, depends on the ability to use far less mass and far more information. The market already displays a behavioral grasp of this change, contends Hawken: "Consumers wanting to preserve their standard of living are choosing those products that conform to this adaptation while shunning those that ignore it."

The sheer dollar leverage of the big company doesn't help here, Hawken goes on: "One of the reasons U.S. business is slow to grasp the kind of changes necessary to make the shift . . . is that no one can buy what is needed to make the transition. . . . To make a company more intelligent, to bring a workforce together, to create and design better products, to eliminate waste, and to solicit innovative techniques and ideas from employees—these are elements that cannot be purchased like new plants, machines, or licenses. These changes are not forbidden to big business, but they are more difficult to achieve in a large company that does not already strive for these qualities than in a smaller and newer company."

- *Craft still makes a difference.* The premium on information and intelligence, says Hawken, shouldn't lead reflexively to an increased use of the new information technologies. To be sure, these devices can imbue goods and services with more intelligence. This is a major reason why their use is spreading so rapidly, but this doesn't mean tomorrow's economy will be a hardware jungle of computers and robots. As Hawken emphasizes, the older virtues of craftsmanship and personal service can work just as well or even better to inform economic life. "As a matter of fact," says Hawken, "they probably give you a distinct edge. The changing economy doesn't exclude anybody." Hawken's own businesses, although they aren't strangers to the new technologies, have stressed the classical virtues.

• *Trust your own experience.* "Don't try to figure out the market—be it," urges Hawken. "The market is as fickle as fog in a swamp. It is constantly changing, and there is not any agreement yet as to how to measure it. How else can you explain the fact that the largest companies, the ones with the most money to spend on marketing, launch some several thousand new food products every year for supermarket shelves, and only a tiny fraction make it?"

To organize one's experience, Hawken suggests using his mass-to-information principles. He likens it to a pair of spectacles and says it will help to see patterns that were unnoticed before. Look at our cars, he says. They have shed up to 2,000 pounds of metal. But they have built microprocessors into the engine and dash: mass to information. Look at our homes. They are shrinking in size, and thus mass, but are bursting with information as personal computers and home media centers become commonplace.

"Manufacturers are shifting from duplication to simulation," he notes. "Time was, the only way you could test a car in a wind tunnel was to build a car and build a wind tunnel and put the car into the wind tunnel. Now, you can use a Cray supercomputer to simulate a car in a wind tunnel. This is virtually pure information."

But for Hawken, this sort of analysis is not idle philosophizing. He puts it into practice. For instance, Hawken was hired as a consultant by Lazzari Fuel Company of San Francisco to develop new markets for its mesquite charcoal. The company was selling the hardwood charcoal to some Bay Area restaurants but was barely breaking even on the business, and it couldn't add new accounts because conventional charcoal briquets were cheaper. "We ran into lots of price resistance," recalls Kay Rawlings, one of the owners at the time. "But Paul took a very wise approach to solving our problem."

He paid attention to mesquite charcoal's qualities, such as its ability to enhance the flavor of meat and fish and to sear them quickly enough to lock in their juices. Hawken told the company it was selling its charcoal short by selling it as a commodity. "The way he put it was, 'This isn't a fuel, it's an *ingredient*,'" says Rawlings. Consequently, the company began to urge restaurants to see the mesquite charcoal as an element in their recipes for fine food. To advance this view of it,

Hawken recommended a price increase and designed a new package to explain the charcoal's culinary value. The approach is classic Hawken: Through the new positioning and the fresh package, he added information to the charcoal's mass. The company's charcoal accounts increased dramatically.

But the concepts are broad enough to apply to companies regardless of size. One of Hawken's *Seven Tomorrows* collaborators, Peter Schwartz, is now the head of Business Environment for Royal Dutch/Shell, the world's second-largest company. He and others in the London office of the petroleum giant are now drawing on Hawken's mass-to-information principle in shaping corporate strategy. "You can grasp how critical this principle is for an energy company," says Schwartz. "Oil has been the fuel of this century. But the fuel of the twenty-first century will be gas. The key to its use is information: How do we move it economically from the well head to its end uses?"

At the same time, Schwartz appreciates Hawken's resolve to use his strategic principles on a smaller scale. "Strategy is simply understanding the proper connections of means and ends. Paul has the best intuitive sense of this I've ever seen. He just happens to apply it to small business." And, as he adds, Hawken's principles are powerful enough to lend themselves to exceedingly flexible use. Thus, he doesn't see Hawken following the lead of large strategic consulting firms by offering a standardized approach. "For Paul, businesses are like gardens or snowflakes or fingerprints," says Schwartz. "They're all different, unique. You can't impose S-curves on them. You've got to let them speak to you."

If Paul Hawken were a novelist or a painter, then we would call Smith & Hawken a mature work, because it fuses his business experience and his economic philosophy into a single, successful application: the direct marketing of imported gardening tools.

The company fills up both floors of a recycled post office opposite the Mill Valley firehouse. Downstairs, a third of the twenty-two employees sit in chest-high acoustic cubicles and handle orders and inquiries by mail and telephone. Sometimes they post data into a computer terminal; other times they counsel a caller at length until the problem is solved. On slow days, the first floor is virtually silent. On busier days, just after a half-million-catalog mail drop, for example, the noise and bustle match the trading floor of a grain exchange. Upstairs, the imported garden tools of a dozen nations and a score of manufacturers fill supply shelves, awaiting order pickers and mailers. To the untutored eye, then, Smith & Hawken is simplicity itself: It takes the orders downstairs, it fills them upstairs. In fact, its strategy is subtler than this suggests.

For one thing, Hawken has paid attention to market conditions. He noticed how Americans hated their garden tools but the British loved theirs, how American companies made throwaway tools but the British and other overseas companies kept alive a centuries-old craft of toolmaking, and how American companies treated gardening as a chore to get through quickly while the overseas toolmakers saw it as a craft and possibly an art.

"People enjoy it," argues Hawken. "They express themselves in the garden. They want the moment to last. They want to get as deeply involved as they can."

Clearly, the Smith & Hawken approach is also direct. By eliminating middlemen, the company can sell its tools at much lower prices than a conventional distributor or retailer could. It also puts the company closer to its customers and lets it do more to shape the way they interpret the tools and Smith & Hawken itself.

It obviously puts a strong premium on information. The company's major information vehicle, of course, is its quarterly catalog. Hawken writes the copy himself, takes the photographs, designs the book. His text carefully explains the history, the nature, and the uses of the tools. "We want our tools to mean as much to gardeners as their gardens do," explains Hawken. The catalog is used to create this sense of meaning.

The company also cultivates the information base of its employees. It hires people with an interest in its ethos of quality and service, pays them about $10 an hour—well above the normal rate for catalog order clerks—offers them incentive stock option plans after two years, and expects them to learn the products and business itself, largely through job rotation and the sharing of such tasks as data entry and grabbing the ringing phones. "Everyone here can talk tools," says Hawken. And task sharing and job rotation create more than just knowledge, argues Laura Burgess, the office manager. "It creates a sense of mutual sympathy. We all know what our colleagues are doing; we understand how it connects to the whole, and it gives us a sense of almost organic unity."

The craft lies in the tools, the sense of service lies in the staff, and Smith & Hawken's people trust in their own experience of their own products. "We love the tools," says thirty-nine-year-old Lou Wheeler, who does his own gardening on the weekends. "We know we're going to make our customers feel good by getting the tools and letting us help them to use them."

Although there is a sympathy at the center of Smith & Hawken, its corporate culture also looks outward to its customer base. For this reason, and because the company doesn't get locked into rigid ways of doing things—"What makes it fun here is that we make it up as we go, and come into the office every morning wondering what we'll think to try next," says Laura Burgess—it might be evolving into a new and interesting form. Once a tool hooks a gardener and turns the person into a customer, the company is committed to serving the customer's gardening interests in the fullest sense. "We'll frequently help customers to find and get things we don't sell," says Wheeler.

Smith & Hawken has joined Brookstone Company, a unit of the Quaker Oats Company, and Gardener's Eden Inc., an offshoot of the highly successful catalog marketer Williams-Sonoma Inc., in the arena of high-quality garden tools, but Smith & Hawken's sense of personal commitment and involvement with customers can give the company an edge against even those foes. As the customer base grows, and as customer-driven services become diverse, Smith & Hawken is likely to become virtually a membership organization—a vast garden club, tied together by the mail and the phone, and tutored and staffed at the center by the Mill Valley professionals.

This freedom to grow by following the wind and the slant of the ground is what pulled Hawken into business eighteen years ago and what keeps him there today. He stepped onto the bottom line in the middle 1960s, a time when members of his generation were taking to the streets to protest the involvement of American corporations in Vietnam. Characteristically, Hawken paid close attention to what was happening then and drew a distinctive conclusion: "If a corporation has the freedom to create such evils as napalm and Agent Orange, then think of the freedom corporations have to do *good*." Hawken pauses for a pulse beat and then concludes: "Of course, this freedom would mean a lot more if a lot more of us would get into business and *use* it."

—RALPH WHITEHEAD, JR.

MADE IN THE U.S.A.:
The Case for Onshore Manufacturing

It got to be something of a regular event. In the early months of 1982, Xebec chairman and chief executive officer Jim Toreson would stretch out in his Sunnyvale, California, office and listen as the visitors from Southeast Asia made their pitches. Hailing from such low-wage havens as Taiwan and Korea, they would lay out elaborate offshore manufacturing schemes that, they promised, would turn Toreson's eight-year-old disk-drive controller company into the next high-growth superstar of Silicon Valley.

On the surface, the argument seemed so simple. Given Xebec's well-developed engineering and marketing capabilities, Toreson could use offshore manufacturing to ramp up his production, taking full advantage of both low-wage labor and a grab bag of tax holidays, low-interest loans, and other government largesse. Most of his competitors seemed to be doing it—the faster he followed suit, the better off Xebec would be.

"The temptations were tremendous," recalls the forty-two-year-old entrepreneur, who has steered Xebec from $14.7 million in sales in 1981 to $158 million in the fiscal year ending in September 1984. "But as an engineer and an American, the whole thing made me sick. It implies we can't *make* anything in this country anymore. It just created a sense of challenge in me to prove everything they were saying was bullshit."

Wounded national pride aside, Toreson was thinking strategically as well. For too long, he believes, American entrepreneurial companies have relied on continued technological breakthroughs to fuel their long-term growth. Yet "the distinction between being a commodity producer and high tech doesn't exist in our world anymore," Toreson says. "You have to be both or you can be neither. The question is, How do you maintain your edge? It's not enough to be brilliant marketers or designers. You have to combine good product technology with the best manufacturing technology. You need the one-two punch or you'll end up, in the long run, as consultants to the Japanese."

Determined to avoid that fate, Toreson decided to bet Xebec's future on a radical new idea: staying home. Although profits have declined due to the current shakeout in the microcomputer market-place, Xebec is now spending some $30 million to implement an onshore manufacturing strategy. Toreson directs a far-flung operation that includes two highly automated factories in Nevada, another in Pennsylvania's Lehigh Valley, a major computer-aided design center in Reno, Nevada, and $20 million worth of the latest generation of IBM robots. His long-term goal: to turn Xebec into a billion-dollar company by the end of the decade.

"At some point," he says emphatically, "Americans have to take up the Japanese challenge in mass production and with high quality. We have to stop this tendency to say, 'Screw it, let the dumb Japanese or dumb somebody elses do the manufacturing.' The problem is, they usually turn out not to be so dumb."

The Fast Track to Nowhere

As a disk-drive controller company, Xebec competes in one of the most volatile sectors of the turbulent high-technology marketplace, and as a result, the company's production problems might seem something less than typical. But if you examine Toreson's reasoning care-fully—and in particular, his ideas on how to manufacture successfully at home—the broad implications of his decision become clear. The future of *all* American manufacturing, and, perhaps, of the American economy itself, may hang on the kind of choices Jim Toreson had to make.

This is not to suggest that Toreson is part of any back-to-the-U.S.A. mass movement. While a handful of other leading entrepreneurial companies (such as Micron Technology, Tecstor, and Apple Computer) are pursuing strategies similar to Xebec's, there is little evidence that the decades-long trend toward offshore manufacturing is slowing down. In fact, most small American high-tech businesses seem increasingly resigned to a future in which they will serve, in the words of one Hong Kong engineering manager, as "prototype shops" for more efficient offshore producers.

"You do what you do best and let us do what we do best," suggests George Koo, the Chinese-born president of Microelectronic Business International Inc., an equity investment firm in Mountain View, California, that actively solicits American companies for Taiwanese high-tech manufacturing ventures. "Americans are great at inventing and marketing products, but we are the ones who know how to manufacture well and cheaply. The people in the Far East are better. They have more of a work ethic and work longer and harder than you do."

Koo's arguments echo the widely accepted belief that America's decline in manufacturing is really no cause for concern—that it is simply a proper and natural outgrowth of our evolution toward an "information economy" dominated by service industries. *Megatrends* author John Naisbitt, a leading proponent of the offshore-is-beautiful scenario, reassures us that while Japan may be number one in manufacturing, that is like being a "new champion in a declining sport." The events of the past three decades, however, can be seen in a much less reassuring light.

Granted, some export-oriented American companies, such as IBM Corporation and Hewlett-Packard Company, have used their foreign manufacturing operations as an adjunct to continued domestic production, and as a means of effectively penetrating foreign markets. But other companies' moves offshore reflect a very different, and dangerous, strategic focus. Faced with mounting competition from Asian producers, these companies have simply closed up shop at home and moved their factories overseas, sometimes even contracting to have their products built for them by natural competitors in such countries as Japan.

Such strategies are often justified in terms of immediate cost savings, but the long-term costs may be staggering. U.S. companies that eschew domestic manufacturing for offshore production may end up losing both their market share and their technological edge.

"The thing that makes offshore production so dangerous is that it puts you in the mentality of letting the other guy do the hard stuff," says Harvard Business School professor Robert Hayes, a leading expert on manufacturing strategy. "When the other guy enters the market, he's worked with the process on a daily basis, has a sense of the wider potential of the technology, of possible applications that you wouldn't have been thinking about. He's got all the advantages. Eventually, he who can do nothing but sell is at a great disadvantage."

Perhaps nothing more starkly reveals the risks of this fast-track offshore strategy than the American debacle in consumer electronics. Virtually the uncontested world leaders in this field during the 1960s, American companies started shifting production to low-wage countries like Taiwan in the late 1960s and 1970s as a means of countering the assault of efficient Japanese manufacturers. The American companies were committed to using low wages as their "process innovation," according to New York City attorney James Millstein, who follows the consumer electronics industry closely. And this tactic made them reluctant to implement the kind of new, automated manufacturing techniques being used in Japan, or to bother applying such U.S.-invented technologies as solid-state circuitry and video recording.

In part due to such shortsightedness (and despite protectionist measures covering such items as television sets), by 1982 the United States was importing nearly half of all consumer electronics products sold here—some $4.5 billion worth. Nor is the situation getting better. As William Relyea, an electronics industry analyst with F. Eberstadt & Company, states flatly, "Leadership in consumer electronics has passed to Japan, and it isn't coming back."

This loss of manufacturing leadership—repeated in other fields, such as automobiles and steel—has become so serious that American merchandise trade deficits reached $61.1 billion in 1983 and topped $100 billion in 1984. Prowess at the "declining sport" of manufacturing in such nations as Japan and Korea has generated economic growth rates that are more than twice as great as this country's over the past two decades. And these same countries are now launching a powerful assault on the information industries that even Naisbitt sees as crucial to America's long-term economic future.

Nevertheless, entrepreneurs in these emerging industries seem hell-bent on following the consumer electronics companies' lead. Instead of solving their manufacturing problems at home, many of high tech's most prominent young companies (including such now troubled businesses as TeleVideo Systems Inc. and Atari Corporation) have chosen to shift their production overseas—all in search of an illusory panacea to the fundamental manufacturing challenge posed by the Japanese.

Nowhere has this trend been more pronounced than in the disk-drive industry. Even as Toreson gears up for onshore production of his new Owl disk drive, nearly all the established industry leaders— among them prime Xebec competitors Tandon Corporation and Seagate Technology—have committed themselves fully to offshore production.

Many analysts, looking at the short-run costs, encouraged these manufacturers to go offshore, and their early success made this advice look good. Yet today, these same companies suffer from some unantici- pated problems that followed the offshore decision (see "Winning the Battle, Losing the War?" below). Tandon has developed a reputation for uncertain quality, and its inventories have risen to unhealthy levels. Seagate also shows signs of trouble, attributable in part to poor coordination among the marketing, engineering, and manufacturing divisions that resulted from the company's move to Singapore.

"It's becoming clear that for Tandon and Seagate, offshore wasn't the salvation they thought it would be," says Blake Downing, a partner and computer-industry analyst at the San Francisco–based investment bank of Robertson, Colman & Stephens. "Maybe we're at a stage of economic development where we're simply not very good at manufac- turing. It sure seems that way."

Home-Court Advantage

But what if it is true that we are "not very good at manufactur- ing?" Does it really matter? When you can head off to a faraway production heaven with deferred taxes, cheap credit, low-cost, highly motivated labor, and even state-of-the-art equipment, who needs homegrown assembly-line skills?

"Every week it seems I get two or three propositions telling me why I have to move my operations to Hong Kong or Jamaica," claims Leonard Bleininger, president of Tecstor Corporation, a four-year-old manufacturer of high-density disk drives in Huntington Beach, Cali- fornia. "No one is going around trying to convince you to build your plant in this country. Nobody seems to think that there may be advantages to manufacturing at home."

Yet Bleininger, like Jim Toreson and a number of other American entrepreneurs, believes that there are compelling advantages to staying onshore. In the short run, they argue, these include such benefits as better quality control, ability to adapt quickly to changing markets, better communication with customers, and in some cases—surprisingly—lower costs. Even more important, they say, are the long-term gains. For companies to survive in an increasingly automated future, they will need to *control* manufacturing automation, developing the human resources to take full advantage of the tremendous investment it represents. This is no less true for an aluminum foundry in Missouri, where manufacturing offshore was never in the cards (see "Lessons for the Rust Belt," page 59), than it is for a go-go high-tech start-up like Xebec, which could put a plant in Taiwan in a matter of months if it wanted to.

Let's look first at the immediate benefits that, according to onshore proponents, a home-court strategy has to offer.

• *The customers get to kick the tires.*

Leonard Bleininger's company sells a line of sophisticated disk drives. In many cases, these drives, which cost from $6,000 to $50,000 apiece, have to be altered to fit the specifications of individual customers. In an average month, for instance, Tecstor may have to turn out as many as fifteen versions of its basic drive.

To meet the exacting needs of these customers, Bleininger believes, there must be close personal contact between Tecstor's engineering and production staff and representatives of a purchasing company, something all but impossible to achieve over 10,000 miles and with severe language and cultural barriers.

"Maybe you can save a few dollars by building parts in Singapore," says Bleininger, whose company will have sales of around $10 million for the fiscal year ending this month, double last year's. "But when you're dealing with hundred-thousand-dollar machines, you have to meet the specifications of the systems house—and to do that from offshore would be ruinously expensive. We have to be very close to what the customer wants or we're sunk."

Priam Corporation, a manufacturer of a broad range of disk drives, rejected offshore production in favor of a highly automated, $10-million factory in San Jose, in part to maintain closer links with present and potential customers. "One advantage we have found is that our customers can come here and kick the tires," says Joe Smith, vice-president of operations. "They feel good about it. They can see the process we use, the product being made. They're a lot less likely to do that in Singapore."

With computer product life cycles narrowing, explains Priam president William J. Schroeder, working shoulder-to-shoulder with customers on the specifications of the next generation is increasingly imperative. And "seventy-five percent of our potential customers are in the United States," he says. Last November, Priam projected a $3-million to $4-million loss in the fourth quarter of calendar year 1984 after making $3.2 million on sales of $44 million in the first half of the year. But Schroeder doesn't blame his current problems on his onshore location. After all, he points out, one of his keenest competitors— Fujitsu Ltd., a $5.4-billion Japanese computer and electronics company—announced plans last September to set up its new disk-drive operation near Portland, Oregon.

• Quality can come first.

Of course, a huge company like Fujitsu can fall back on manufacturing expertise developed back in Japan. But young American companies don't have such an option. If they want to match the high standards of their Japanese competitors, Tecstor's Bleininger believes, they first must perfect their manufacturing techniques under their own roofs.

In building long-run relationships with customers, Bleininger says, quality and serviceability are simply more important than any slight price advantage. "There are costs to being offshore—such as poor quality and being out of touch—that people just don't figure on," he explains. "When Tandon went offshore, he became dependent on offshore for his quality."

The same kind of offshore quality problems have surfaced in the semiconductor industry. For much of his career, Fritz Beyerlein built offshore semiconductor-assembly plants for such companies as Signetics, Rockwell International, and RCA. Now vice-president in charge of manufacturing for Cypress Semiconductor in San Jose, Beyerlein finds that onshore assembly produces quality improvement simply through management synergies. With his highly automated assembly operation next door to Cypress's engineering section, for instance, Beyerlein can provide assembly-related input in the early stages of Cypress's product designs—something offshore assembly managers can rarely do.

• It's easier to fill orders fast—and change when the market changes.

Beyerlein sees speed of delivery as another strong argument for onshore assembly operations. Products assembled offshore can take up to six weeks from shipment to return to the U.S. market. At Cypress, on the other hand, turnaround time can be as short as three days. This time differential can make a critical difference to a start-up that needs to show it can fill customers' shifting needs quickly and efficiently.

"In a start-up in this business, you can't fool around with long lead times," says Cypress president T. J. Rodgers. "If a customer wants our design, he wants it because we have it first. He doesn't want to wait six weeks for it to come back from Penang."

Nor is the speed advantage confined to high-technology industries. Quick turnaround, for example, can be crucial in the garment industry, which, like electronics, has been hard hit by foreign competition. (Between 1976 and 1981, apparel imports more than doubled, to better than $6.7 billion; they now account for more than half of the total market.)

The garment industry moves at a pace that would make even a semiconductor engineer's head spin. In women's apparel, for example, a manufacturer needs a new product line every six months. For domestic manufacturers, such as R.J.M.J. Inc., of New York City, responding quickly to the constant changes in fashion can help compensate for the cost advantages usually associated with offshore production.

Early last year, for instance, R.J.M.J., which manufactures women's slacks and shorts, ordered a small amount of a fabric called French canvas. So did most of its offshore competitors. But by the height of the season, the fabric was selling so fast that the retailers were screaming for more. Companies that rely on offshore manufacturers, which have to order their fabric and garments six to eight months ahead, could not respond to this unexpected demand. But R.J.M.J. president Robert Shipman could simply order the fabric overnight and have it processed at his wholly owned factory in Westminster, South Carolina, as well as through two trusted subcontractors in Florida and Georgia.

"You need a crystal ball in this business," says Shipman. "But once I knew it was hot I could move right away. I was able to call up for one hundred thousand yards of French canvas here in New York and start turning it around in three weeks. The importer can't do that."

So what started off as 50,000 yards of French canvas ended up as 300,000 yards, and R.J.M.J.'s sales of slacks made out of the material soon reached $3 million, up from around $60,000 the year before. Particularly gratifying for Shipman have been the thirty-five new accounts—some of which used to rely almost totally on offshore lines—generated by his French canvas coup.

"We killed the offshore guys with our flexibility in manufacturing," says Shipman, who expects to earn a 15 percent before-tax profit on sales of $20 million for the fiscal year ending this month. "Now we get calls from guys who never talked to us before."

• *You actually can save money.*

There are even ways in which onshore manufacturing operations can be flat-out cheaper than going offshore, at least according to Fritz Beyerlein. This new development relates to the decreasing percentage of assembly cost taken up by labor.

As recently as the mid-1970s, Beyerlein notes, integrated circuit assembly was highly labor intensive. With U.S. operators making at least $3 an hour while their Filipino counterparts made as little as 15¢, the differential more than made up the expense of flying fabricated circuits to the Philippines for assembly and re-export to the United States. But today, wage rates in the Philippines have jumped to about one-tenth, instead of one-twentieth, of U.S. rates, while new automated wire-bonding equipment—which increases each worker's productivity from 125 units an hour to as many as 5,000 units an hour—has reduced drastically the labor content in the assembly process. Given these changes, Beyerlein believes that the direct cost of onshore assembly at Cypress is less than it would be overseas. "Labor just isn't the key factor anymore," he concludes.

Equally important, onshore manufacturing allows for a more efficient use of capital. Because Cypress makes relatively expensive circuits (they average around $8 each), time-consuming offshore production would have tied up the company's capital in a very expensive way. Even though offshore assembly would save about 3.2¢ per chip in labor costs, that would be more than offset by combined shipping and customs costs of 2.5¢, and an additional 16¢ in opportunity costs, which are calculated as the capital cost involved in holding inventory.

"I've been looking at this situation for years, and now—with automation—the numbers really add up," says Cypress chairman L. J. Sevin, who is also the company's lead venture capitalist. "Some people just look at the labor rates, but it's inventory cost that matters. It's simply cheaper to sell a part in one week than in five or six. You have to figure what you could have done with the inventory, or the money you could have made simply by pulling the interest on the dollars you have tied up in the part."

"It's the People Who Do It for You"

Yet to hear Jim Toreson tell it, all these benefits are less important than the long-term strategic advantage he expects to gain by controlling the means of his own production. This is where Toreson really parts company with the postindustrial theorists—and Xebec's fascinating, risky gamble in Nevada can be seen as an alternative model of the American economic future. It is a model with two basic premises: first, that automation is the key to modern manufacturing; and second, that for a company to automate successfully, its people—particularly those on the factory floor—must play a central role.

As Toreson and his team planned to expand Xebec from a small-scale producer of controllers into a large-volume disk-drive maker, they rejected the offshore examples of Tandon and Seagate, seeking inspiration instead from Japanese competitors whose successes have long depended on their manufacturing muscle. Most important, however, was Xebec's analysis of the new strategic focus at IBM, the company that accounts for nearly half of Xebec's current sales. IBM has committed more than $11 billion over the past five years to land, buildings, and equipment, in large part to boost its manufacturing capacity and productivity. A company spokesperson confirms that while it continues to buy components overseas, IBM has committed itself to manufacturing onshore virtually all products sold in the United States.

"We took a hard look at what IBM was doing," explains Marcia Glow, Xebec's executive vice-president of operations. "They seemed to be taking a long-range strategy when, for example, they put three hundred and fifty million dollars into automating their typewriter plant. They realized they had to get control of their destiny by improving their manufacturing technology."

To control *its* destiny, Xebec had to solve two enormous problems at once. When Toreson took Xebec public two years ago, the company was making a disk-drive controller that dominated a narrow market niche. But the staff knew the time was coming when controllers, then a separate element from the disk drive, would simply be folded into a chip. Thus the first challenge was to develop a drive with an embedded, rather than a freestanding, controller before anyone else did. The second was to acquire the kind of mass manufacturing capacity needed to survive in a viciously competitive field.

Rejecting offshore solutions to this second problem, Toreson still had to find an environment more suitable than Silicon Valley for low-cost mass production. So in 1983, he moved the bulk of Xebec's controller manufacturing operation to a plant in Gardnerville, Nevada, a small town in the high desert country about an hour's drive south of Reno. To guard against possible communications problems with the new plant, he also moved Xebec's corporate headquarters to a suite of offices just outside the San Jose airport, and purchased a twin-engine Cheyenne.

Gardnerville is no Singapore, but it does have substantial cost advantages over Xebec's old production facilities in Sunnyvale. For one thing, Nevada, unlike California, has no corporate income tax. And wages run 10 percent to 15 percent below those in the Valley.

But perhaps more important, the new plant gives Xebec an almost perfect laboratory in which to apply the latest thinking about automated production. "This plant is sort of an experiment," explains Gardnerville manager Michael Rainey. "We are developing a new kind of manufacturing intelligence here."

Using some of the $20 million worth of robots Xebec is buying from IBM, Rainey and his team oversee a facility that is already heavily automated. An IBM Series 1 computer monitors the production lines and the position of each assembled board and collects all relevant data. Robots and other automated equipment perform numerous tedious tasks, such as component insertion, wave soldering, and even some test functions.

The automation process, which continues at a gradual pace, has already improved Xebec's product quality while cutting "substantially" the per-board cost, according to Volker von Detten, Xebec's manager of advanced manufacturing, engineering, and automation. By late spring, Von Detten predicts, the plant will increase its capacity by 33 percent, from 150,000 to 200,000 controllers a month—without adding a single employee.

A far greater payoff, however, may come from the knowledge Xebec is developing about the automation process itself. Lessons learned at Gardnerville can be applied to the far more complex task of automating the company's recently opened disk-drive plant in nearby Carson City. And with successfully automated production, Xebec's new Owl drive can be offered with a quality level and at a price to match those of potential competitors from Japan or anywhere else. "You want to learn as much as you can about your manufacturing process before you go into producing your next technology," explains Von Detten. "Here's where we're trying to learn about how to make a new product that might not be reaching its potential for two years. That's how you develop the confidence to compete."

The key to that confidence may lie with a new buzz word—*upskilling*. It implies a radically different view of how workers and new machines should interact. "Automation isn't like managing a sweatshop," Toreson says. "To succeed, we need to move assembly workers up into being knowledge workers." And he has made this belief a central part of Xebec's corporate strategy.

To best develop the automation process, explains Marcia Glow, Xebec must maintain high employee productivity and loyalty. A no-layoffs policy at Gardnerville, for instance, allays fears that robots will take people's jobs, and training programs teach workers new functions—such as computer operation and robot maintenance—that they will need in the automated environment.

During the past three years, Glow notes, Xebec has continually improved its sales-per-employee ratio, reaching a high of $240,000 (compared with an American industry average of $90,000 and a Japanese average of $130,000). With automation and upskilling, she believes, the company can achieve its ultimate goal: "a billion dollars in sales with only a thousand employees."

In return for its pledge to turn assembly line personnel into knowledge workers, Xebec expects employees to commit themselves to the company. That is one reason it put its production facilities in Nevada and Pennsylvania. As Rainey puts it, "We wanted an atmosphere where our people could learn the very basics of roboticization. We wanted people who would stay with us as we learned, who wouldn't go next door for another ten percent."

It is far too early to proclaim Xebec's experiment a success. The company's Nevada operations—and its automation strategy—remain largely untested, and even if they work out, they won't immunize Xebec from the maladies now plaguing most microcomputer-related businesses. In September 1983, for instance, the company had to write off $2.7 million owed by the bankrupt Victor Technologies Inc. And according to company insiders, Xebec exacerbated its problems by purchasing expensive computer chips from brokers—chips that have now dipped drastically in value. As a result of these and other problems, Xebec, despite a nearly threefold jump in sales last year, has been saddled with just-above break-even earnings for the year.

But the same policies seem already to be proven at Micron Technology Inc., a semiconductor manufacturer in Boise, Idaho. Like Xebec in Nevada, Micron is located in an area short of experienced semiconductor manufacturing workers. And with some manufacturing talent, such as experienced operators of assembly equipment, in short supply even in Silicon Valley, training workers for the automated factory has become a major priority for Micron's management.

"Automation is usually associated with a misleading concept that people lose their jobs. All it has meant here is that people increase their skills," explains Juan A. Benitez, Micron's vice-president of engineering. At Micron, automation is carried out piecemeal. Benitez has increased the proportion of automation by 30 percent over the past two years, but he always consults with workers on the assembly line and says, "We don't automate until the operators are ready and see the need."

Due in part to this policy, Benitez claims, workers at Micron—most of whom also own company stock—have approached the automation process with both enthusiasm and a sense of responsibility. To upgrade skills, the company makes generous use of videotapes, quality circles, and on-the-job training. Each employee is encouraged to reach for more and more responsibility. And with the company's sales growing rapidly (in the quarter ending November 30, 1984, sales were at $37.2 million, up from $8.3 million a year earlier), there is likely to be plenty of room for upward mobility even with the use of labor-saving equipment.

To ease the way for upgrading, Micron has a strict policy of not hiring managers from outside the company. Rather, management has promoted assemblers to numerous key positions, including manager of assembly and manager of fabrication production. "No matter how much equipment you have," Benitez insists, "it's the people who do it for you. The whole process is people-intensive. It keeps morale up to know they can go up as we grow and automate. We're looking for commitment—and in exchange we give a career, not just a job. After all, we expect those same people to be running Micron in twenty years."

Beyond the Disposable Company

What Benitez, Toreson, and the other made-in-U.S.A. strategists are saying is this: If American companies hope to play a significant part in the industrial future, they must make a serious commitment to a long-range manufacturing strategy. The great industrial companies of the American past—from the steel empire of Andrew Carnegie right up to IBM—were based on something more profound than any single technological opportunity. They were built on a vision of the future, on a commitment to be a leader not just for the next year, but for the decades to come.

Even if Toreson hasn't yet built a great American industrial company, at least he has the audacity to dream that dream—and that may be his greatest contribution. His approach marks a break with the trend toward the sort of "disposable companies" that have become increasingly commonplace in recent years. Often started by brilliant and innovative entrepreneurs, these companies rush through a market window, use cheap offshore labor to boost production, and then, shortly after enriching their owners, fall victim to their lack of planning and foresight.

"It's hard to fight it this way instead of being a fast-growth darling of Wall Street," says Tecstor's Bleininger, "but in the long run, it's better to be on a little slower track and control what you're doing. That's why, when a lot of those offshore companies are gone, we'll still be here. You can't worry about the herd."

Perhaps as important, such entrepreneurs as Bleininger don't waste their most valuable resource—people—by laying them off in search of short-run profits. That approach almost always shatters the bond between the CEO and employees that seems to separate great companies from those that shine briefly and die.

"It really affected morale when they started laying off the production people," recalls one Seagate engineer. "We weren't affected directly in the engineering group, but we know a lot of loyal employees got it, people who were working twelve hours a day for the company. . . . It makes everyone wonder, 'What's going to happen next?' and produces a lot of distrust. There just doesn't seem to be any sense of long-term planning. I guess nobody really expects they are going to retire at Seagate."

The marketplace itself is not likely to get easier for those who rush offshore to solve their manufacturing problems. Donald F. Taylor, a former Tandon vice-president in charge of marketing and product development, predicts that the tightening of product cycles—sometimes to as short as six to nine months—will wreak havoc on companies that plan to profit solely by being first through a market window.

"When you shorten the product cycle so quickly, from two years to a few months, there won't be time to make those quick, early profits anymore," says Taylor, who is now a private consultant. "The time will come when the cycle is so short that nobody will be able to make money before the Japanese come in. Then the whole house of cards will fall apart."

But nothing will prevent this collapse unless there are dramatic changes in the way the financial community approaches the problem. For the past few years, most analysts, venture capitalists, and investment bankers seem to have accepted the idea that entrepreneurial American companies are somehow intrinsically incapable of competing here at home against Japanese and other foreign companies. While a few venture capitalists have committed themselves to domestic production, many of the companies with a strong long-term commitment to domestic manufacturing, such as Xebec, have been built without conventional venture capital and against the prevailing wisdom of Wall Street.

Indeed, this "wisdom" may not change until someone—perhaps Toreson—proves that it can be done. "You know, when we went out to raise our money, everyone expected we'd be driven out, that Tandon would roll over us. They told us we couldn't deliver the product at the right price," Toreson recalls, breaking into a slight grin. "Well, they didn't understand, and they still don't. You can't fight the Japanese by running from them. You have to match them by being better the way they are better. You don't build a sand castle—you build a house of stone."

Lessons for the Rust Belt

Can Jim Toreson's automation-and-people-centered manufacturing strategy be applied outside the high-technology field? Glenn Stahl, an aluminum foundryman, thinks it can. He has been using the same approach for years.

With his slight Southern accent and his down-home manner, Stahl seems the antithesis of a Silicon Valley entrepreneur. And as the president of an aluminum foundry in the nation's heartland, the seventy-two-year-old Stahl isn't exactly the sort to be courted by offshore manufacturing promoters from the Far East. Yet he, like Toreson, has learned that the best way to compete with offshore manufacturers—which now control an estimated one-quarter of the U.S. casting market—is to perfect the art of production at home.

"Too many foundries have stayed still. People get killed by imports that way," Stahl says. "The only way to do it is to invest in the latest machinery and have a higher level of technology than they do. That gives you a flexibility and ability to diversify they can't compete with."

At a time when capital spending at most U.S. foundries has been falling, Stahl Specialty Company has continued to buy from $2 million to $4 million worth of new equipment every year. Today the company's facilities in Kingsville, Missouri, a hamlet of 365 people an hour's drive from Kansas City, boast more than a dozen of the most modern numerically controlled machine tools, an IBM System 38 computer for payroll, and a $400,000 McDonnell Douglas CAD/CAM system.

This huge capital expenditure reflects Stahl's strong personal commitment to his company. Over nearly four decades, Stahl, who owns 57 percent of the company, has refused to take anything more than his salary out of the business. His net worth on paper is probably in the millions, but he still lives in a modest $40,000 one-story house, and continues to work—"taking it easy," he says—some forty hours a week. "I don't have the slightest inclination to drive a Cadillac or stay in Palm Springs," he explains. "I just enjoy seeing the company grow and challenging the employees."

If growth and challenge are the ticket for Glenn Stahl, he must be a happy man indeed. Shipments of U.S. aluminum castings declined 35 percent from 1979 to 1983, but Stahl Specialty has enjoyed consistent profits recently, with sales jumping from $24 million in 1980 to more than $41 million in 1984, and has boosted its workforce from 310 to 520 since 1981.

This remarkable performance would not have been possible, Stahl believes, without his massive investment in new equipment. The new machines—along with dozens of sophisticated foundry processing tools that the company makes itself—have allowed Stahl to expand his production capability dramatically. A decade ago, for instance, the vast majority of the company's sales consisted of such relatively unsophisticated items as lawn mowers and barbecue grills. But today Stahl Specialty's products range from the castings for IBM 3380 storage devices to engine parts and brake cylinders for Deere, Caterpillar Tractor, Bendix, Ford, and Delco Products.

"Quite honestly, if we had stuck with the lawn mower and barbecue business, we'd be out of business," says company controller Dan Davis. "You can't afford not to modernize and diversify. Now we can do the sophisticated stuff they can't do in Taiwan. IBM doesn't want to fool around with a casting that has to be accurate to one one-thousandth of an inch. In that, the machines make all the difference."

Beyond the simple investment in machinery, however, Stahl Specialty—like Xebec and Micron Technology Inc.—has given the "upskilling" of employees a central role in the company's rapid modernization. Training gets a high priority: From the moment workers are hired, for instance, they are shown extensive videotapes on a whole range of foundry skills. Stahl also draws heavily on resources from nearby Central Missouri State University. Professors are brought in to lecture on the latest technical developments. Students receive extensive internships at Stahl Specialty, which has recruited many key managers and technical personnel from the school.

Yet despite the university tie, Stahl, like Micron vice-president of engineering Juan Benitez, insists that new production employees work their way up through the ranks. "We want to work with them as raw material and teach them the whole trade," Stahl says. "Often kids come out of school with no practical knowledge and tend to have too much concern about how things were done in the past. They sometimes don't respect the fact that sometimes people on the floor know how to do it better. We can't afford to have people around here who look down their noses at people who produce things."

Winning the Battle, Losing the War?

Nowhere has the offshore-onshore debate been more clearly joined than in the disk-drive industry. At first, the offshore side—represented by such fast-growing superstars as Tandon Corporation and Seagate Technology—appeared to be winning big. Venture capitalists, analysts, and investment bankers backed their Far Eastern manufacturing strategies, and most of these backers have yet to change their minds. E. F. Hutton vice-president Bob Grandhi, for example, hails Seagate founder Alan Shugart and Tandon founder Sirjang Lal Tandon as "fathers of this industry," who correctly realized that they couldn't compete effectively at home. "They believed that they had to knock the price down and pass on that price advantage to the customers," says Grandhi. "The only way to accomplish that was offshore."

But while offshore manufacturing helped these companies win the early battles, it may be setting them up to lose the war.

Until very recently, the belief in offshore production seemed to be borne out by the results. Aided by the low cost of labor at its facilities in India and Singapore, Tandon was able to ramp up large-scale production long before most of its competitors and enjoyed spectacular growth, with sales skyrocketing from $6.6 million in 1979 to more than $400 million last year. Seagate enjoyed a similar takeoff, with sales rising from $9.8 million in 1981 to $343.9 million in fiscal 1984. Last fall, yet another disk-drive producer, the Longmont, Colorado–based MiniScribe Corporation, decided to shift most of its high-volume production overseas.

In announcing its move, MiniScribe cited competitive pressures as a major cause. And it is certainly true that increasing competition at home and abroad, vicious price-cutting, and an unexpected slowing in the growth of the microcomputer market have disrupted an over-crowded marketplace. Yet, had MiniScribe looked more closely at Tandon and Seagate's experience in the Far East, it might not have been so eager to follow their lead. Instead of proving a defense against Japanese competition, as its promoters planned, the offshore strategy may have caused a whole new set of problems for the disk-drive industry.

Both industry analysts and former Tandon executives, for in-stance, blame offshore operations for exacerbating Tandon's reputation for inferior quality. "It's tough to control quality across the nation, but it's more of a problem across an ocean," says Bill Frank, senior vice-president at InfoCorp, a market research firm specializing in the information processing industry. Tandon, he adds, "forgets it's very expensive to make a poor quality product. I have heard that, at times, thirty percent of the Tandon drives intended for IBM have had to be reworked before shipping. . . . If [Tandon] had overcome that quality problem, he'd have been king of the hill—but he couldn't."

Paul Merten, who for two and a half years served as a manufactur-ing engineer at Tandon, elaborates on this theme. "Communications was the biggest problem," says Merten, now a manufacturing executive at Microcomputer Memories, Inc., in Van Nuys, California. "Engineer-ing changes took a long time in the pipeline. It's all facsimiles, telephones, and telexes. Sometimes it could take up to two months to see the changes stateside. Meanwhile ten thousand—or thirty thou-sand—units have been shipped without the proper changes."

This reputation for uneven quality, along with problems relating to the introduction of new product lines, may help explain the spectacular rise in Tandon's inventories, which jumped from $128 million in June 1983 to more than $209 million a year later. David Moy, an analyst at Morgan Stanley & Company, notes that the rate at which inventory is turned over by other companies in the same industry is often twice as fast. Commenting on the inventory problem, John Levinson, who follows the company for Goldman, Sachs & Company—and who strongly supports its offshore strategy—admits that "Tandon has had notorious quality problems for years," and calls offshore production "one of the big factors."

The unhealthy inventory situation may also have been partially responsible for a drop in Tandon's earnings for the fiscal year ending in September 1984. Despite an attractive increase in annual sales and a respectable increase in annual net income, the company suffered a disastrous quarter, with sales down slightly from the comparable period in 1983 and a net loss of $724,000—Tandon's first quarterly loss since its founding.

At the end of the quarter ending September 1984, Seagate—the other big offshore disk-drive maker—saw its quarterly sales volumes cut nearly in half from the previous quarter's $100-million level. Analysts and company insiders alike blame the decline on delays caused by poor coordination among the marketing, engineering, and manufacturing divisions, created in part by the company's move last year to Singapore. Explains one top Seagate engineer, "Engineering is so removed from manufacturing because the product is being made overseas. We don't even see the problems that crop up for weeks. It's not like you can go and check it out yourself on the line."

Nor did offshore production do much, in the long run, for the disk-drive company founded by Seagate's Shugart in 1973. Shugart Associates was purchased in 1977 by Xerox Corporation; in January, Xerox reported that it took an $85-million writeoff and operating loss for 1984, announcing plans to close its operations and eliminate more than 1,650 jobs. At the same time, Xerox also announced its intention to sell the Shugart line of 5¼-inch disk drives to Shugart's prime offshore contractor, Matsushita Communication Industrial Corporation.

Ironically, the dreaded Japanese—the oft-cited excuse for the offshore shift—seem undeterred by their cost-cutting American rivals. Despite wage rates three or more times higher than those in such countries as Korea and Taiwan, highly automated Japanese producers seem poised to dominate such key, mass commodity areas as 5¼-inch floppy disk drives (sales of which are expected to double by 1985 from last year's levels). Japanese companies have increased their world market share of these drives from 28 percent in 1983 to an estimated 50 percent for 1984, with 1985 projections showing them likely to capture a mammoth 60 percent of total sales, more than double U.S. production.

—JOEL KOTKIN

THE BOOMING HIDDEN MARKET

Are you finding it tougher and tougher to maintain growth and market share? Do your competitors seem to have some edge that you lack? Do you ever get the feeling that new business development is playing a more important role in your company's fate? I'm not surprised, and you are not alone. Either you're caught in a downdraft in our increasingly turbulent economy, or you're doing business with a company that is.

The downdrafts are part of an economy that I have previously compared with a huge thundercloud—peaceful and generally unchanging when viewed from the outside (in the aggregate), but chaotic on the inside. The cloud is dominated by hundreds of thousands of rapidly rising companies (mostly smaller in size) offsetting the declines of hundreds of thousands of rapidly sinking ones (mostly larger). For any business selling goods or services to other businesses, these updrafts and downdrafts mean trouble or opportunity—or both. Understanding the activity in the cloud will help you understand the companies you're selling to now, and the ones you might want to be selling to instead.

Historically, many businesses have focused their marketing and selling efforts on larger companies because these are the easiest to identify and the most efficiently reached. Unfortunately, larger companies have been particularly prone to finding themselves in a downdraft. During the years 1980 through 1986, *Fortune* 500 companies alone laid off a net 2.8 million workers—the rough equivalent of today's entire labor force in Massachusetts. Large corporations have been the most severely affected by international competition, an overvalued dollar, and a host of other problems.

Yet while so many large businesses have been struggling, nearly 10 million jobs have been *added* to the U.S. economy. Virtually all of that growth on a net basis has come from companies with fewer than a hundred employees. And most of it comes from a relatively few businesses buried in a sea of some 7 million others that are scarcely changing. Figure 1 shows that over the past five years, the top 5 percent of companies, ranked by growth, created 83 percent of the jobs added by all companies that existed at the start of the period. The top 10 percent created 93 percent of all new jobs.

What more is known about these select rapid growers? Usually, they start very small. As Figure 2 shows, a large majority of the past half decade's fastest-growing enterprises began the period with fewer than twenty employees. Also, they are volatile. They grow, but not on a consistently rising line. Of course, the discovery that growth and volatility go hand in hand should come as no surprise. Risk, growth, and uncertainty are all parts of the same equation.

This newly turbulent economy has brought managers an enormous marketing challenge. The old tried-and-true customers who used to buy a lot are struggling. And their places are being taken by a relatively few rapidly growing, unstable companies, most of which emerge quickly out of a morass of 7 million smaller concerns.

These companies—tomorrow's expanding market—are tough to find exactly when you most want to find them: at the point when their growth creates huge needs and when they are forming their first (and perhaps lasting) bonds with suppliers. To capture them as customers, you must switch from doing an excellent job of selling to a few obviously visible companies to doing an excellent job of selling to a few mostly invisible smaller companies. The latter will become the big companies in the near future; today they represent virtually all the growth in the economy. A real change is taking place, and you are going to have to change with it. If you wait for the new crop of companies to "grow up," there is a good chance your competitors will already have nailed them down as customers.

NEW JOB CREATION, 1982–1986

FIGURE 1

	Percent of companies, ranked by growth	Percent of gross new jobs created
	Top 5%	83%
	Top 10%	93%
	Top 15%	98%

Almost every new job in the United States is created by a small group of fastest-growing companies. (The percentages represent "gross" additions, not percentages of "net" new job totals that would result after subtracting job losses by declining companies. The percentages of net new jobs created by rapidly growing companies are well over 100 percent.)

FIGURE 2

Percent of companies, ranked by growth:	Percent of indicated rapidly growing companies that started with employment of:				
	0–19	20–99	100–499	500–4,999	5,000+
First 5%	63.7%	24.3%	8.5%	3.0%	0.4%
Next 10%	79.5%	17.0%	3.1%	0.5%	0.1%

And if you succeed in finding the next crop of rapid growers? Then your marketing task will be complicated by their volatility. Their growing pains and fluctuations of fortune will become your problems. Still, your understanding of their volatility could become a major selling point if you can tailor your product or service (and the terms under which you offer it) to your customers' ups and downs.

The struggle to meet these challenges will likely be worthwhile. It is hard to imagine that companies that locate and successfully cater to the rapid growers will not be richly rewarded.

However, a few cautionary observations are in order. While trying to capture the major source of growth in the economy, you can't afford to ignore several other groups of companies. The first are the growing businesses that happen to be large. In many cases, these are rapidly growing, small companies that simply outgrew the "small" category. Their founders may be still directly or indirectly involved. Wal-Mart Stores, Compaq Computer, K Mart, Digital Equipment, Federal Express, and Mrs. Fields Cookies come immediately to mind. Such companies are obviously not to be ignored, but the competition to win their business is very intense.

Large, declining companies also may be perfectly acceptable targets for particular products or services: consulting services, for example, or real estate management (to deal with the consolidations taking place), and, of course, outplacement assistance, whose entire purpose is to help declining companies in the process of finding jobs for the workers they no longer need.

Last, but certainly not least, is the vast pool of steady-state companies—a pool that includes the majority of companies in our economy. These businesses don't change much (nor do their needs), but their number is large. They all need to replace the supplies they use, the people who leave, and the equipment that wears out or becomes obsolete. And they all need to manage their money, their travel, their retirement plans, and their insurance. The problem is that they are much less likely to make a decision in the next twelve months or to switch suppliers at all—because their world is, almost by definition, in balance. And, most important, they are extremely unlikely to become the Wal-Marts and Apple Computers of the future. Selling to them is expensive, and the long-term payoff is no greater than the payoff you receive today.

Discussion of other company groups aside, it remains true that a small group of rapidly growing companies accounts for most of the action in today's turbulent economy. Important as that may be, more critical is understanding what kinds of companies you are dealing with in "economic thundercloud" terms. If you want to focus your efforts consciously on large, declining businesses, that's fine so long as you know: first, that that is what you're doing; and second, that in the slightly longer term, your market will be rapidly shrinking. If you want to focus on the *Fortune* 1,000 and *Fortune*'s Service 500, that's fine, too, so long as you're aware that the competition will be very tough and the net growth very small—if there is any. If you want to market to the large pool of stable companies, that's fine so long as you do so knowing that you are missing most of the next wave of economic growth in the United States. And if you want to identify and sell to this next wave, you should remember that it is a volatile, difficult group of companies to identify and hang on to.

In short, whatever you're doing, you ought to make sure you realize *what it is* you're doing, and design your products, terms of sale, and marketing strategy to fit the dynamics of the companies you are trying to reach.

—DAVID L. BIRCH

THE SECOND INDUSTRIAL REVOLUTION

Infrequently in human history, a series of developments arrive that are so startling, so contradictory to our understanding of the world we live in, that they alter forever the landscapes of work and home life. Such was the case with the Industrial Revolution in the late eighteenth and early nineteenth centuries. Now, according to Massachusetts Institute of Technology professors Michael J. Piore and Charles F. Sabel, coauthors of *The Second Industrial Divide: Possibilities for Prosperity* (Basic Books Inc., 1984), we may have reached another such historical juncture.

The first industrial divide ushered in the reign of mass production, with rigidly defined divisions of labor, standardized products, and large-scale corporations. The new developments portend a shift toward an economy of "flexible specialization," with less hierarchical organizations, more (and more customized) consumer goods, and increased market share for smaller-scale companies.

Piore and Sabel's prognosis is both disturbing and hopeful. The bad news is that the economic turbulence of the past decade is neither temporary nor an aberration. Mass-production society is under siege from forces that are so powerful that the halcyon days of the postwar period have been banished forever. The good news is that out of this constant turmoil may emerge a less rigidified economy: efficient, yet on a human scale, and flexible enough to avoid the extremes of the business cycle. Piore and Sabel caution that nothing is for certain, as the mass-producers have yet to mount their final defenses, and small and medium-size companies still need to adapt quickly to the flexible technologies as they become available.

Piore and Sabel's provocative thesis was born, of all places, in a Paris café. The two had known of each other's work through mutual friends, but it was at this meeting in 1975 that Piore the economist and Sabel the political scientist began their decade-long collaboration. It led them to Italy, France, Germany, and the United States, where they searched for clues to the industrial transformation in interviews with business people, labor leaders, government officials, and academics.

Their efforts were recognized when both men were awarded the prestigious MacArthur Fellowship, which is given annually to outstanding individuals. And *The Harvard Business Review* recently reviewed their book, *The Second Industrial Divide,* describing it as "quite simply, a tour de force. . . . It is a book that could become a landmark."

Piore, forty-four, and Sabel, thirty-seven, fit the image of serious scholars: spectacled, bearded, alternately thoughtful and animated, steeped in Industrial Age history, and yet deeply curious about the world around them. In Piore's MIT office—lined with books, piled high with papers, with the requisite degree of clutter, a typewriter tucked into one corner and nary a personal computer in sight—Piore and Sabel were interviewed for *Inc.* by Karl Frieden.

INC.: You have an idea, we gather, that the whole course of economic history may be changing?

SABEL: Well, we believe that the industrial world has entered a crucial period. Mass production, with its hard-and-fast divisions of labor and standardized products, may be giving way to craft production, with its flatter organizational structures and greater variety of consumer goods.

INC.: But mass production has been the dominant mode of production in the twentieth century. Washing machines, televisions, automobiles—much of what we associate with affluence is provided by mass-producers. You're saying that this process is reversible?

PIORE: We dispute the notion that mass production is the one and only path of technical progress. Mass production, with its lower costs per unit of production, supplanted craft production during the first industrial divide in the nineteenth century. But the historical circumstances have changed. On the one hand, new technologies, like the computer, have developed, which have lowered the cost and increased the innovative capabilities of craft production. So you're getting a more dynamic craft system—what we call flexible specialization.

At the same time, the costs of mass production have increased. A combination of the saturation of demand for mass-produced goods in the wealthier nations and more intensified competition for markets from newly emerged Third World mass-producers has made the system more unwieldy and increased the cost of stabilizing demand within it.

INC.: So you believe that the mass-production economy as we know it—with large companies turning out standardized products—will follow the craft-production economy to the dustbin of history?

PIORE: Actually, mass production never completely displaced craft production. What happened was that craft production was subordinated and limited to certain subsidiary roles. It lost its technological dynamism and was no longer the engine of economic growth. This could happen to mass production. You would still have it, but it wouldn't be the lead element in the economy.

INC.: How is all of this going to play itself out? How will we know when we have crossed the industrial divide?

SABEL: Well, it won't be a specific event. It's sort of like war. A war is seldom decided by one battle: There are a lot of battles, and then finally, there can be a kind of cataclysmic event, the outcome of which is very uncertain until maybe the last hour. The same is true of an industrial divide. There are a whole series of little things that are shaping a new possible course, and eventually they coalesce. The notion of a divide is not that there's a kind of clock ticking and that you get this sort of change every hundred years or so.

INC.: Could you be more specific about how the application of technology differs in mass production and craft production?

SABEL: Mass production is characterized by rigidity. It involves the production of standardized commodities, like toothpaste or refrigerators, using single-purpose machines that are built to make that commodity and only that commodity. The guiding principle of mass production is the breakdown of every task into simple steps, each of which can be performed faster and more accurately by special-purpose machines and semiskilled labor.

Craft production is the reverse. In craft production, skilled workers use general-purpose machinery to turn out a wide and constantly changing assortment of goods for large but constantly shifting markets. It is based on the idea that machines and processes can augment the craftsperson's skill, allowing the worker to embody his or her knowledge in ever more varied products. In its more advanced form, craft production is a strategy of permanent innovation, an accommodation to ceaseless change, rather than an effort to control it.

INC.: So machines in craft production can make more than just one product?

SABEL: That's right. You can think of it almost like a musical instrument. That is, if you have a musical instrument, then you can have a thousand different people play anything, anytime at all, on it. Whereas in mass production, it's much more like a record; you can just play it. One is a way of expressing skill, the other is just a way of reproducing someone else's skill that has been literally grooved into the record.

INC.: So you think we're approaching the point where a rigidly structured mass-production economy will fade as a symbol of industrial efficiency? What will this do to the image of small businesses? Not too long ago, the popular perception of small businesses was that they were marginal enterprises that made money, not through innovation but through hard work, long hours, and self-exploitation.

SABEL: I think small-business people will continue to work long hours and exploit themselves. It's in the nature of these companies to do that, because they get enthusiastic about their work and they have to struggle to survive. But they will also be innovative, have a completely different image of themselves, and be perceived differently in American society.

The opportunities are much greater today for small, dynamic companies. Things are opening up for them. Just as mass production, with its large economies of scale, favored big companies, so flexible specialization, with its batch production, creates new possibilities for smaller companies. Technology will be used in a whole new way by these companies, and their relations with government and labor are probably going to change as well. I think they're facing a series of very big changes, and some of them are already emerging.

INC.: For example?

SABEL: One region we looked at closely was in central and north-western Italy. In response to upheaval and strikes in the mass-production sector during the 1960s, a network of flexible small and medium-size companies developed, using more and more computer-controlled machines to adapt to rapidly shifting markets.

There was a whole range of new companies set up by middle-level managers or skilled workers from the larger companies. The small companies then began to look for a way to avoid dependency on the big companies they were often supplying, and that way was to develop independent products so that they could go to market themselves. They did this under conditions in which the world market was changing and new technologies were becoming available.

INC.: Did this occur primarily in the high-technology sector?

PIORE: Not at all. The small businesses operated in textiles, specialty steel, precision machine tools, luxury shoes, motorbikes, ceramic building materials, furniture, and industrial instrumentation. They weren't initially in high tech at all, they were in everything else.

SABEL: And now what's happened is that they have exploded into high tech, and there's a great fusion now going on between high tech and these very flexible companies in the traditional industries.

A world-famous example is the textile company Benetton. The way Benetton works is that they have key stores located in all the fashion centers. As soon as they see what's selling, they've got the technology set up so that they adapt quickly to changing market conditions. For example, they can dye stuff that doesn't have to be dyed until after it's woven; so if they see that a color is taking off, they smash everything into that vat of dye, and two weeks later, it's in the stores.

INC.: Has the growth rate been faster in those regions of Italy where the new entrepreneurial activity is concentrated?

SABEL: Oh, yes, it's very clear. They call this area the Third Italy. It has flourished amid high inflation, labor unrest, and a national government stalemate. It's not just the statistics. When you visit this area you can physically see the boom in the economy.

INC.: In your view, the limits of a mass production–based economy have been reached. The world is perched on the precipice of a vast industrial transformation. What makes you think your crystal ball works better than the others?

PIORE: We don't think the limits have been reached in terms of the technological possibilities of mass production. We think the limits have been reached in terms of the institutional supports that you need for mass-production systems.

SABEL: The industrialized world is saturated with the classic goods of mass production. For example, by 1970, 99 percent of American households had television sets, refrigerators, radios, and electric irons, and more than 90 percent had washing machines, toasters, and vacuum cleaners. Because of this saturation, it has become more and more difficult to increase economies of mass production through the expansion of domestic markets alone. This has brought the major industrial economies into direct competition for one another's markets and for those of the developing world. This situation has been exacerbated by the transfer of mass-production technology to Third World nations, which now compete for mass-goods markets in the industrialized world.

Thus, in order to maintain growth, you have to include new areas of the world into the mass-production system. To do that would involve opening up Third World markets to mass production, redistributing income through the international monetary system to create the purchasing power there, and changing very complicated power relations between the developed and the developing world. That's one way of extending the mass-production system. Theoretically, you could extend it the same way the postwar system was built up, and some of that is going on, but there are a lot of political obstacles in the way.

INC.: You mentioned earlier the role that new technological developments were playing in reinvigorating craft production and making smaller-batch production more cost-competitive. Could you expand on that?

PIORE: The development of more flexible technologies, such as microcomputers and computer-controlled machinery, has lowered the cost of batch production as compared with either one-of-a-kind customization or mass production. The new kind of numerically controlled machinery is easily reprogrammable for an enormous variety of tasks.

INC.: What are some other examples of flexible machinery?

SABEL: One good example are these flexible steel minimills. There's a perfect case of people, from Big Steel actually, jumping off big steel and deciding that this is the wrong way to do it. This is an interesting case, because the electric-arc furnace technology that these minimills use is actually an old technology, developed for alloys. The technology was available, and they took it off the shelf and began to improve it and adapt it to new uses.

INC.: What about the impact of flexible production on labor relations?

SABEL: The United States had a system of labor relations that was very good for mass production. But once you begin to need constant reorganization, narrowly defined job categories and restrictive work rules get very cumbersome.

INC.: And this is because a more flexible technology requires a more flexible, less hierarchial work environment than mass production does?

PIORE: Yes, and you're moving that way all over the American economy.

SABEL: Flexible technology requires skilled workers. The whole point is that if you have flexible machines, then they can do a lot of things. Skill is the ability to make the machines do a particular thing. It's no good having a general-purpose machine if you have workers who don't know how to do a lot of things with it. Workers have to have the skills to use the new flexibility in the machines, and they've got to have the ability to communicate quickly with the people who are doing the designing. It won't work otherwise. Rigid shop-floor relations inhibit the necessary degree of communication and participation. It isn't a question of being nice or not nice. It's a question of a different style of work dictated by changed circumstances.

The alternative dream, which no one really believes, is that you have a designer with a computer, and he designs the product. Then he touches a button, and the computer translates the thing to a set of specifications for numerically controlled machine tools. Then the machine builds the product. This sort of thing doesn't exist. And as long as it doesn't exist, to get this flexibility you need a less rigid work environment.

INC.: Has the consumer played any role in these changes? There's a theory, isn't there, that as consumers get more affluent, their tastes splinter, creating demand for more differentiated products.

PIORE: Well, in the 1950s, which was perceived as a great period of affluence in American society, there was an enormous amount of consumerism that was based on having the mass product, whatever it was, and everybody wanting the same thing. And now people want to be unique or different. For me, the turning point was the 1960s. When I was an adolescent, everybody wanted to wear the same thing, but in the sixties everybody wanted to look different. Now, maybe the range over which they wanted to look different was narrow, but it seems to me that's really a question of style rather than something that emerges with affluence.

INC.: You don't think that greater disposable income in the hands of consumers is causing a mushrooming of the demand for less-standardized products?

PIORE: Listen, there's no question that tastes are changing; that seems indisputable to me. The question is, Why are tastes changing, and what's the relationship of that to production? And I guess what I think is that if mass production were still enormously more efficient than batch production and there was this shift toward changing taste, people would have to pay a very high price in order to indulge in their changing tastes. What has happened is that the cost of indulging individuality has fallen enormously.

INC.: Is it possible that new mass products will emerge, as the automobile or the television did, to capture a new generation of consumers for the mass-production economy?

SABEL: There is a paradox here, because the new sort of mass-production items, like the personal computer or the videocassette recorder, are very easily customized to suit individual taste. These are mass-produced items, but what's happening is that the actual hardware cost is going toward zero. It's getting cheaper and cheaper. All the money is being spent on adding things to it and making it into just the thing you want.

The whole success of products like the VCR is their adaptability. Just compare the VCR to the RCA Videodisc Player. The RCA Videodisc was a hard sell. All you could do was play it; you couldn't record on it. RCA understood it as an extension of television. People turned it on, and they got entertainment. The VCR is such a success story because the whole point is that you can customize the time you want to use it, and all those other things.

INC.: It sounds like the very strengths of mass production are now becoming liabilities.

SABEL: Yes, all the standardization of products, the specialization of machinery, the centralization of resources, the rigidity of work roles, and the clear subordination between the parent company and the smaller supplier companies, they are all becoming an albatross on the mass-production system.

INC.: Can we get to some specific numbers? What evidence have you uncovered of a shift away from the mass-production economy? For example, has the small-business share of economic output increased in recent years?

PIORE: The share in the United States, at least, has not been changing dramatically. There has been a small increase in the number of small companies in relation to large companies. But I think what is involved is a change in the *role* of small and medium-size companies rather than a change in market share. We're moving away from a situation where the small company was typically subordinated to the large company and operated largely at its direction, and we're moving toward a situation where the small company is the dynamic leading edge of the economy. Smaller-scale companies are becoming less dependent on large companies; they are engaging in more cooperative and interactive relationships with larger companies.

INC.: Is it possible that the market share of small and medium-size companies will increase, perhaps dramatically, over the next couple of decades?

SABEL: It's conceivable. There are two things to bear in mind. One is that there is evidence in several countries of a turnaround, an increase in small-business share. This is true in Germany. There has also been a dramatic increase in Japan, not just of small-business market share, but also of the productivity of small business in relation to large companies. So there is some evidence, but you have to be cautious because of problems with data collection and definitions. The other factor is that there's a lot of internal decentralization taking place in large companies. That is, there is the move toward intrapreneurship.

INC.: Is that how large corporations will adapt to flexible specialization?

SABEL: It's a real possibility. There are a lot of ways to retain this flexibility within large companies without necessarily enlarging the share of small business. For this to happen, however, big companies will have to adjust, and they are aware of this. If they persist in maintaining their old culture, people will go off to form their own companies, and the small-business share will go up. But it could well be that the large companies will try to adjust by giving more space to their employees through profit sharing, greater autonomy, and the like. Many companies are already taking steps in this direction.

Nonetheless, as larger companies make their units more autonomous, the boundaries of the company get blurred. And some of these units will go off and become independent companies.

INC.: You are saying, aren't you, that entrepreneurship both inside and outside of large companies is bound to increase.

SABEL: Put it this way: The economic space in which entrepreneurs operate will have to be enlarged. What we now perceive as a sharp choice between the culture of a large company and going into business for oneself will become less obvious. So there will be a lot of mixed forms, and the idea of small business itself will lose the kind of clarity that it had when it meant subordination. Anyway you look at it, this transformation means that entrepreneurship is going to grow.

INC.: You seem to focus primarily on the technological changes occurring in the manufacturing sector. Will flexible specialization be limited to industry?

PIORE: Oh, no, it's the same all the way through the economy. We've studied the changes as they occur in the manufacturing sector, but the same thing is happening in retailing, finance, and other service sectors.

INC.: Everyone seems to have an opinion these days on what's wrong with corporations or what part of corporate structure needs to be modified. In what ways do your ideas differ from those of other prominent critics, such as Peters and Waterman in their book *In Search of Excellence?*

PIORE: We agree a lot with the other critics. I think we have diverged on distinct points that I would like to stress. We don't agree with the implicit idea in these books that American corporations have become old and are sclerotic. What we think is that the world has changed. It's not that there is a unique corporate form that is perfect for all circumstances; it's that the world of the moment is not the world that American corporations were designed to operate in. Without an analysis of the limits of mass production, these analyses are incomplete.

Second, while we don't doubt that large corporations can adapt to the new environment in ways that other critics are suggesting, we think there is another possible scenario, which involves the emergence of a more independent and innovative small-business sector.

INC.: What sort of advice do you offer companies that want to join the ranks of flexible craft producers?

SABEL: There is a threshold that smaller companies have to cross in order to move from their old methods to flexible specialization. The latter is, by definition, technologically dynamic: You're using the new technologies for controlling inventory, doing your accounts receivable, and producing. Meeting that threshold, taking advantage of the flexibility of the market, is the big challenge now for these companies.

One set of problems that emerges, characteristically, is with companies that were already pretty autonomous but trapped in their minutiae. Then there is a second set of problems with companies that are more clearly linked into mass production, like the parts suppliers.

PIORE: Many companies think their goal is to find a product that can be mass-produced. Their notion is that they will discover such a product, start mass-producing it, and then sell out to a large corporation.

INC.: Or become big themselves?

PIORE: Yes, or become big. But generally, the expectation is that they're going to sell out. So they're engaging in all this creative activity, but they see it all as temporary. It's not their real business; it's just what they're doing until they've discovered this mass-production type of product. Part of what's involved in the transition to flexible specialization is the recognition that this is real life, that the chances of finding a product that you can mass-produce are becoming smaller and smaller. What the large companies are increasingly looking for in their mergers is the dynamic part of the small businesses.

INC.: What about the small companies that are suppliers to large mass-producers? How do they keep their independence and keep innovating?

PIORE: The Italian experiment is relevant here. Small-batch production developed in Italy through companies that were satellites to large companies. They were looking for niches in larger markets that would give them some freedom from their mother company. That was a kind of safe strategy in the sense that they held on to their relationship with the larger company and the mass-production end of their business. At the same time, they looked for little niches and developed within the space where craft production could actually grow.

INC.: Yes, but how do small companies go about getting ideas for new products or for changes in their use of technology?

PIORE: One important thing is to get outside your company. You get dynamism, you find market niches, and you get ideas by traveling—that is, looking at other companies, moving around, going to trade fairs, looking at new equipment. You can almost judge the difference between a dynamic and a nondynamic company by how much the management in these small companies gets outside their own company.

Flexible craft production involves thinking about the productive process in a different way from mass production—it is really a different way of looking at the world. Mass production gets its charge by breaking down the production process further and by developing ever more specialized equipment. By contrast, the dynamic of flexible craft production is to think of new products that can be made that weren't made before—that is, to enlarge the repertoire of products and enlarge the generality of machines, to determine how a bundle of resources might be pushed in a direction where it can do something it didn't do before.

INC.: So flexible specialization involves not just a different form of production, but also a different way of looking at consumer demand?

SABEL: That describes it exactly. You need to reeducate consumers as well as yourself. Once you begin to tell the consumer that things are going to change all the time, you have to be able to gear up so that you can produce on short demand. That means a change in the manufacturing process. Companies are responding to blockages in the mass-production system, and they're responding by trying to break up the market and find a way of appealing to the consumer with more quality or more particularizing of products. They're using the new technologies in this flexible way to do that.

INC.: One would think that all this would have a great impact on competition.

PIORE: Yes, but not in the traditional sense. What is involved is a shift away from the notion that the market is extremely limited to the notion that the market has all sorts of possibilities, if you can find them and exploit them. The notion of creating new products is that if you're just creative enough, you can't find a market. In a sense, supply creates its own demand.

INC.: So mass production—huge quantities of standardized goods—limits the imagination as well as the marketplace?

PIORE: Right. For example, we asked one entrepreneur whether he was affected by business cycles. He responded, "No, because I produce one hundred fifty new products a year, and some of them are bound to fly." He was very competitive in a technical sense, but I don't know that you would say he had a sense of competition. He had the sense that his business was based on creativity, and he had to constantly come up with new ideas. If he came up with enough new ideas, the thing would work. That's the sense in which successful small businesses compete; they won't be driven so much by this notion that the world is tight and confining and you have to crawl your way to success.

INC.: It seems as if you don't think all forms of competition are equally beneficial to the economy.

SABEL: There is still obviously going to be a huge amount of competition, and what you want to do is two things. You want to encourage people to take risks for new products, but you want to discourage them from trying to get an edge by competing the old way, by cutting corners. In other words, at any one moment, a company could be tempted to say, "Well, I haven't invented a new product. What I'm going to do is try to take something that's selling well and produce that more cheaply by cutting wages." And, of course, if too many people do that, then the system loses its dynamism. So you want to encourage risk-taking, but you also want to discourage competition through squeezing employee wages.

One of the ways you can do that is through community norms—you just don't treat workers in a certain way. You don't make them bear the cost like that. The reason is not just humanitarian. It comes from a recognition that the character of the whole system of flexible production depends on putting obstacles in the way of this other form of competition.

Unions can also play a big role in this by standardizing wages. Of course, small-business people hate unions in the United States, because they associate them with the unions in mass production, where they impose rigid job rules. But there are lots of constructive ways in which unions can operate, and have operated, even in the United States. The basic idea is to set limits to competition without destroying internal flexibility, and that's the kind of thing you have to bargain out with whoever is representing labor.

INC.: Are you suggesting that complete flexibility for entrepreneurs is counterproductive?

PIORE: Yes, although the basic point is that flexibility is not anarchy. It has a certain structure to it. The emphasis on flexibility can go awry. People will say, "Let's tear this down because it's not flexible; let's tear that down because it's not flexible." But you've also got to devise the structure in which that flexibility is going to occur—to determine what the limits of flexibility will be.

SABEL: We can build a system that is efficient at producing an ever-changing variety of goods as opposed to producing one thing at the lowest possible price. And it turns out that such a system doesn't mean the absence of constraint. Flexibility is perfect freedom in the sense of the total absence of constraint. But paradoxically, what we're arguing is that in order to be flexible, you've got to create a community in which some things are constrained. Creating that community involves the redefinition of a lot of the existing institutions. That's our message: You've got to be flexible, because that's where the world is going.

INC.: Does this explain your ambivalent feelings toward the term *entrepreneur*? While you've used the word freely in this interview, it hardly appears at all in your book.

PIORE: The reason is that the term *entrepreneur* has come to be associated with the image of the Lone Ranger. Our image of successful small-business people is that they are creative and independent individuals. They have many of the characteristics typically associated with the term *entrepreneur*. But they are also very dependent on the community structure they operate in, on a network of relationships with other people who are like them, on their employees, and so on. This facet of small business has little to do with the image of the Lone Ranger. They do not ride in from nowhere on a horse into a community.

INC.: So it's really a tempered sense of individualism that you're advocating?

SABEL: That's right. In fact, the Lone Ranger story is kind of fascinating. Don't forget that the Lone Ranger himself had a sidekick, Tonto, and it's interesting to see what they called each other. *Tonto* means "fool" in Spanish, so the Lone Ranger called his Indian assistant a fool. But Tonto's name for the Lone Ranger was Kemo sabe, which can be interpreted as meaning "he who doesn't know." And in a sense, we think this relationship correlates with our concept of an entrepreneur. Even the Lone Ranger couldn't get by alone, and in fact, had to rely on help from someone with whom he was so deeply connected that they could insult each other in this sort of amicable way. That's our idea of how this works, but it's hard in American culture to get this idea of interdependence, of community. Americans hate to think of themselves as dependent on others. Perhaps they are afraid it will be used against them.

INC.: What specific role do you foresee for government in all this?

PIORE: For one thing, I think there will be a switch from an emphasis on Washington as the central governmental element in the economy to the state and local governments. One way of looking at it is to go down the list of things that businesses need to get an operation going. They need physical infrastructure; they need certain kinds of roads and sewers; they need an educational system that provides a certain type of trained manpower; they need a zoning system that provides locations that are properly situated in relationship to each other. Well, these are the functions of state and local government.

INC.: Are you optimistic about these institutional changes?

SABEL: I think that the need for the changes will become widely recognized at a certain point. They will be seen as the way to solve problems, get over the hump, and take advantage of the possibility of new markets. People will recognize the need to eliminate the wrong kinds of competition and increase the possibilty of taking the right kinds of risks. And because it is very likely that the changes will happen, society is much more open. I mean that the institutions like the government—especially at the state and local levels—and the trade unions are much more open to recasting the relationship between independence and community, if only because of the way they've been battered around by the failures of the old system. It is a real moment of openness, and small business doesn't have to be afraid.

TOW-AWAY ZONE

Otto Deemuth has reason to worry that General Motors Corporation will move into the electrical motor industry and threaten his business. "They can afford to do anything they want to do," says Deemuth, plant manager at Motronics Corporation, a $5-million company. "I just hope that they don't start building motor plants."

Magnet makers probably had the same fears just before GM rolled into their industry last year. Their worst visions came true. The automaker, which posted sales of nearly $84 billion in 1984, is building a factory to produce a new magnet—called Magnequench—that can be used for all kinds of motors. "If GM chose to, it could put us all out of business," says Sherman Smith, president of Thomas & Skinner Inc., one of many small magnet companies. "I don't think GM will do that, but I could be wrong."

Until recently, General Motors probably wouldn't have made Magnequench itself. But GM, Ford Motor, and Chrysler have all seen the future, and it is not parked in the garage. During the next decade, the Big Three are sure to continue losing market share to imports. "The auto industry is going to be a bloody business," says Gregory Macosko, a principal of Easton Consultants Inc., in Stamford, Connecticut.

The Big Three plan to refuel through diversification and vertical integration, moves that will be unsettling for small companies both inside and outside the car business. The automakers have one of the deepest supplier pools of any industry, comprising about 8,000 companies with sales of roughly $70 billion. Suppliers also face demands by the Big Three that they meet stringent cost and quality standards. The cumulative effect of these pressures could knock out as much as half of the supplier network over the next decade.

The carmakers have aggressive diversification plans. "They've all decided that diversification is the smart way to go," notes Arthur Davis, an analyst with Prescott, Ball & Turben Inc. "They're all moving fast." By the year 2000, GM wants nonauto sales to be 20 percent of its business, compared with about 4 percent, or $3.5 billion, in 1984. At the same time, Ford is planning to speed up its nonautomotive businesses from 7 percent to at least 10 percent. "We don't want to become a conglomerate," says a Ford spokesman, "but we should have some strengths in other areas, for better balance." Chrysler, which lags in resources, plans "to do a lot of diversification," according to Davis.

Last year's buying spree was the most public display of the automakers' new strategy. They wrote checks for almost $7 billion for acquisitions in financial services, farm equipment, and aerospace, all areas in which foreign competition is weak. Like hood ornaments, the cash outlays are very visible—but there is more happening underneath. "We have seen only the tip of the diversification iceberg," warns Thomas Nastas, president of Innovative Ventures Inc., a consulting firm in Lansing, Michigan. "It is going to produce dislocations in many industries, and a lot of suppliers are going to be awfully shocked."

The initial shock waves have already hit. "Big mergers always cause some consolidation in the existing outside supplier base," says Nastas. When GM acquired Electronic Data Systems Corporation in 1984, one observer notes, "some suppliers that were providing data-processing services [to GM] found that EDS had taken over those responsibilities."

Once diversification has begun, it gathers momentum as the new partners get into other businesses. For example, GM and EDS—along with Hughes Aircraft Company, a satellite maker and defense contractor that GM acquired last year—could together develop a telecommunications system that would signal trouble for that industry's suppliers.

The fallout from vertical integration can devastate a supplier network even faster. Magnet makers are worried. Last year, about forty small domestic manufacturers sold $300 million worth of magnets. GM's factory should be finished in June—and many magnet makers may be finished soon after, as the industry's biggest customer becomes its fiercest competitor. "When GM decides to go into my business, it scares me," says one industry member. "That company is already bigger than most countries."

Magnequench, which reduces the weight of starter motors by half, will soon appear in cars and perhaps later in robots, disk drives, and home appliances. GM will produce an estimated 180,000 magnets a day, at least half of which will be sold for nonautomotive uses. Once GM is making magnets, the entire electrical motor is a natural next step. "To get the full effect of its advantages, new motor designs will result from Magnequench," says Jeff Day, Magnequench product manager.

The carmakers are also directing many of their subsidiaries to look beyond their parent for business. More of them are selling to other auto companies and to other industries as well. Small companies that haven't had to compete with an auto giant may be shaken when a Big Three division suddenly pushes them onto the shoulder of the road. Chrysler's subsidiary for four-wheel-drive components, for instance, has stepped up business with other carmakers, the military, and off-road vehicle manufacturers. Ford's glass division has seized a window of opportunity by selling architectural glass more aggressively. And a GM division is working on commercializing a metal-stamping process that could hasten a shakeout in that industry, where the average company has 150 employees and sales of $7 million. "It would put a lot of small-company people out of business. There's no doubt about that," says Donald Smith, a product manager of Mills Products Inc., a stamping company.

Survival may require bold new initiatives, as auto suppliers are finding. "For some, this means they will either diversify or go out of business," says Peter Van Hull, a director of automotive consulting practices at Arthur Andersen & Company, the accounting firm. But when they diversify into a "quasi-automotive" industry such as appliances, suppliers—surprise—may run into the automakers again. "A supplier that goes knocking on the appliance industry's door may find a GM division is moving into the same area," notes Nastas, who is helping the automakers map out diversification plans.

Suppliers are also jockeying for favored-status agreements, under which carmakers guarantee them business. For some, this means "breaking even until you can catch up with the technology," says Macosko. Even then, a supplier's future is assured only until its next performance review, which in many cases occurs every six months.

Some suppliers are looking for new markets within the automotive industry. One strategy is to sell replacement parts to wholesalers, garages, and retailers. "You can get a better price, and the profits are better," says Macosko. "But it's getting tougher and tougher." Others are trying to shift from supplying parts to providing whole assemblies. They might supply, for instance, a complete air-conditioning unit rather than components of it.

Ironically, foreign competitors may also provide a way out. Chardon Rubber Company, a small Ohio supplier, recently signed an agreement with Kinugawa Rubber Industrial Company, a Japanese company with sales of about $200 million. The two are now building a plant in Winchester, Tennessee, not far from Nissan Motor Company's factory. "We want to be able to be familiar with the Japanese technology and also learn more about Japanese management," says Jeff Keener, Chardon's president.

Suppliers may also enter into short-term agreements with foreign competitors, hoping to earn enough cash to invest in modern equipment that can improve their chances for long-term survival. "They are disappearing fast," says Eugene Jennings, a professor of management at Michigan State University's Graduate School of Business. "This is a major restructuring. It is not an episode in the life of the auto industry. It is a new life."

—JOSHUA HYATT

INDEX